Enoch and the Gospel of Matthew

Princeton Theological Monograph Series

K. C. Hanson, Charles M. Collier, D. Christopher Spinks,
and Robin Parry, Series Editors

Recent volumes in the series:

Darin H. Land
*The Diffusion of Ecclesiastical Authority: Sociological Dimensions of
Leadership in the Book of Acts*

Michael D. Morrison
*Who Needs a New Covenant?: Rhetorical Function of the Covenant
Motif in the Argument of Hebrews*

Christopher W. Skinner
*John and Thomas—Gospels in Conflict?: Johannine Characterization
and the Thomas Question*

Bart B. Bruehler
*A Public and Political Christ: The Social-Spatial Characterstics of Luke
18:35—19:43 and the Gospels as a Whole in Its Ancient Context*

David Rhoads, David Esterline, and Jae Won Lee, editors
Luke-Acts and Empire: Essays in Honor of Robert L. Brawley

Mitzi J. Smitht
*The Literary Construction of the Other in the Acts of the Apostles:
Charismatics, the Jews, and Women*

Michael A. Salmeier
*Restoring the Kingdom: The Role of God as the "Ordainer of Times and
Seasons" in the Acts of the Apostles*

Enoch and the Gospel of Matthew

AMY E. RICHTER

PICKWICK *Publications* · Eugene, Oregon

ENOCH AND THE GOSPEL OF MATTHEW

Princeton Theological Monograph Series 183

Pickwick Publications
An Imprint of Wipf and Stock Publishers
199 W. 8th Ave., Suite 3
Eugene, OR 97401

www.wipfandstock.com

ISBN 13: 978-1-61097-523-0

Cataloging-in-Publication data

Enoch and the gospel of Matthew / Amy E. Richter.

Princeton Theological Monograph Series 183

viii + 234 p. ; 23 cm. —Includes bibliographical references.

ISBN 13: 978-1-61097-523-0

1. Bible. N.T. Matthew—Criticism, interpretation, etc. 2. Ethiopic book of Enoch—Criticism, interpretation, etc. I. Title. II. Series.

BS1830 E7 R6 2012

Manufactured in the U.S.A.

Contents

Acknowledgments

I WOULD LIKE TO EXPRESS MY GRATITUDE TO THOSE WHO HAVE helped and supported me during my graduate studies and during the writing of this book. I would like to thank my dissertation directors, Dr. Deirdre Dempsey and Dr. Andrei Orlov, for their guidance and encouragement, the members of my dissertation committee, and the members of the faculty of Marquette with whom I was fortunate to study. I would like to thank the people of St. Paul's Episcopal Church in Milwaukee, the bishops and staff of the Episcopal Diocese of Maryland, and the people of St. Anne's Church in Annapolis, Maryland for their encouragement and interest in my studies. I want to thank my family, especially my parents, the Rev. George Richter and Patricia Richter; my parents-in-law, Stephen Pagano and Mary Pagano; June Richter, Andrew Richter, Jennifer Prough, and Joel Richter for their support and encouragement. Finally, I want to express my deepest gratitude to the Rev. Dr. Joseph Pagano, my husband, to whom this book is lovingly dedicated.

Tables

1

Introduction

THIS BOOK SHOWS THAT THE WRITER OF THE GOSPEL according to Matthew[1] was familiar with themes and traditions about the antediluvian patriarch Enoch, including the story of the fall of the watchers, which is recorded in the apocalyptic and pseudepigraphical work known as *1 Enoch*.[2] Matthew was familiar with the Enochic watchers' template and Enoch's role in responding to the watchers' transgression. My use of the word "template" follows John Reeves who uses the phrase "Enochic template" in his research on early Jewish mythologies of evil,

1. For the sake of convenience, I will use the name Matthew to refer to the writer of the Gospel according to Matthew. I will also use it as the title of the Gospel. I will also name Matthew as the "writer" of the Gospel, as opposed to the "redactor" of the Gospel, largely for convenience's sake, even though it will be clear that I agree with the majority scholarly opinion that Matthew made use of various sources in the composition of his Gospel. The redaction history of Matthew is the subject of a rich scholarly discourse and is largely beyond the scope of this dissertation. However, this dissertation will elucidate some aspects of materials used by Matthew in the composition of the Gospel and some of the theological concerns of the evangelist. For more on the authorship, sources, and redaction of Matthew's Gospel, see Abel, "Who Wrote Matthew?"; Beare, *The Gospel According to Matthew*, 5–49; Brooks, *Matthew's Community*; Davies and Allison, *A Critical and Exegetical Commentary*, 1:7–148; Hagner, *Matthew 1–13*, xliii–lxxvii; Harrington, *The Gospel of Matthew*, 1–19; Luz, "Matthew and Q," 39–53; Luz, *Matthew 1–7*, 1–60; Overman, *Church and Community in Crisis*, 1–26; Stanton, "Literary Criticism," 54–84.

2. *1 Enoch* is a collection of traditions, the earliest of which date from about the fourth century BCE. The earliest evidence for the collection as a whole comes from a fifth–sixth century CE Ethiopic translation of a Greek translation of Aramaic texts. Nickelsburg, *1 Enoch 1*, 1. The textual history of *1 Enoch* is beyond the scope of this book. I rely on the text and translation of *1 Enoch* by George W. E. Nickelsburg and James C. VanderKam (*1 Enoch: A New Translation*), and use this translation unless otherwise noted.

I

including the books ascribed to Enoch. The Enochic template is one of three groupings of elements found in early Jewish myths about the advent of evil in the world (the other two templates are the Adamic template and a Transitional template). In summary form, the Enochic template contains these elements:

- Humanity already present on earth
- Women are born among mortals
- Some angels in heaven see them and desire to possess them sexually and beget children
- The angels bind each other with oaths to effect this deed
- Angels descend from heaven
- Angels fulfill their desire: engage in sexual activity and teach magical spells
- Result: bastard race of giants engendered
- These hybrids engage in violence and lawlessness against humanity and each other; blood spilled
- Earth and humanity complain to heaven
- Loyal archangels relay the complaints to God
- God dispatches these archangels to punish the watchers by binding/burial/fire
- Flood purges earth of giants' corruption
- Immortal spirits of dead giants become the origin of demons and continue to plague humankind.[3]

However, not only was Matthew familiar with the elements of the Enochic watchers' template, he also refers to them in his Gospel in such a way as to show that Jesus completes what Enoch does not. That is, Jesus is able to bring about the eschatological repair of the consequences of the fall of the watchers. The use of Enochic themes and material can be seen in Matthew's genealogy and infancy narratives (Matt 1:1—2:23), the focus of this dissertation. However, as the infancy narratives set the

3. This template is part of Reeves's efforts to document and compare "distinct mythological scerarios of the manifestation of evil in the created order." By laying out the elements that make up the Enochic Template, Reeves compares the elements of this typology of the origin of evil with the Adamic and Transitional Templates. His list of features of the three templates includes elements found in various texts, for example, in Genesis, *1 Enoch*, and *Jubilees*. See Reeves, "*Sefer 'Uzza Wa-'Aza(z)el.*"

stage for future developments in the Gospel, the Enochic themes present in the infancy narratives are also developed in stories of the adult life and ministry of Jesus. Matthew does not directly quote material from *1 Enoch*[4] and this fact warns us against claiming any literary dependence of Matthew on a text of *1 Enoch*.[5] However, Matthew does refer to material that may be described as "Enochic," that is, material similar to that found in the pseudepigraphical literature ascribed to the seventh antediluvian patriarch, particularly in *1 Enoch*, the Enochic work which will be explored within this dissertation. Matthew's familiarity with and use of Enochic themes and the Enochic watchers' template, as shown in Matthew's opening two chapters, are the subjects of this dissertation.

In light of the knowledge of the Enochic watchers' template and attendant traditions about Enoch as part of the background to Matthew's Gospel, a number of the aspects unique to Matthew's Gospel are elucidated, including Matthew's inclusion of four women named in the canonical Hebrew Bible in his genealogy, Joseph's suspicions of Mary's pregnancy, the revelatory dreams which drive the narrative action forward, and the magi led by an astral body to worship the child. This dissertation, then, contributes to scholarly understanding of the unique Matthean aspects of the understanding of Jesus' origins and identity. The child Jesus is shown by Matthew to be the fulfiller to the legacy of Enoch, the promised one who will redeem and save his people, establish righteousness on the earth, and ultimately redress the effects of the watchers' transgression. Moreover, by viewing Matthew's genealogy and infancy narratives through the lens of the Enochic watchers' template, one gains a view into how, according to Matthew's Gospel, women play a particular role in the story of Jesus. That is, alongside Joseph, Herod, the magi and some other notable male characters in the narrative, women's participation in Matthew's Gospel is prominent. Women in Matthew's Gospel are more than merely the necessary means by which

4. However, see below on David Sim's argument for literary dependence of Matt 22:13a on *1 En.* 10:4a (Sim, "Matthew 22.13a and 1 Enoch 10.4a," 3–19).

5. I am cautious throughout this dissertation not to make claims that Matthew had access to a text containing the Enochic material. He may have had, but the fact that there is little, if any, evidence of Matthew's quoting material from *1 Enoch* advises against making such a claim. However, I find the volume of material—even in the first two chapters of Matthew's Gospel—that can be explained in light of Enochic material to be evidence that Matthew was aware of many of the same traditions as those that would be gathered as *1 Enoch*.

the generations are born and Jesus comes into being, or people "important not as women but as Gentiles,"[6] or as characters whose role is "finally only to serve as messengers to the (male) disciples."[7] It is often in the examples of women and Jesus' interaction with women in the Gospel of Matthew that Jesus overcomes the watchers' transgression described in *1 Enoch*.

In addition, by seeing the particularly Matthean aspects of the Gospel in light of the Enochic material, this dissertation contributes to our understanding of Matthew's association with apocalyptic literature—the apocalyptic book of *1 Enoch*, in particular. The prominence of apocalyptic eschatology in Matthew's Gospel, and even the understanding of Matthew as an "apocalyptic gospel,"[8] has come to the fore during the last fifty years.[9] However, this dissertation, by linking Enoch and the Enochic watchers' template with Matthew's Gospel, shows more clearly how Matthew's apocalyptic vision is present even within the first two chapters of the Gospel. Further, in focusing on the story of the watchers' transgression, this dissertation shows Matthew's familiarity with *1 Enoch* separate from a discussion of the *Book of Parables*, also known as the *Parables of Enoch* and the *Similitudes of Enoch* (*1 Enoch* 37–71). Although scholarly consensus may be moving in the direction of accepting a date for the *Book of Parables*, or at least of the traditions within the *Book of Parables*, which might pre-date the composition of the canonical gospels,[10] there is a great advantage in establishing the

6. Luz, *Matthew 1–7*, 16 n. 91.

7. Ibid.

8. Donald Hagner, in a 1985 study of Matthew wrote, "From beginning to end, and throughout, the Gospel makes such frequent use of apocalyptic motifs and the apocalyptic viewpoint that it deserves to be called *the apocalyptic Gospel*" [Hagner's emphasis]. Hagner, "Apocalyptic Motifs," 60.

9. In 1960 both Gerhard Barth and Günther Bornkamm remarked on Matthew's use of the apocalyptic themes of judgment and expectation of the end-times, finding them to be of great importance for Matthew's overall Gospel, especially in how the evangelist conceived of the church and discipleship. On judgment, see Barth, "Matthew's Understanding of the Law," 58–164. On the end-times, see Bornkamm, "End Expectation and Church in Matthew," 15–51.

10. For example, Paoli Saachi notes that at the Third Meeting of the Enoch Seminar in Camadoli, Italy, 6–10 June, 2005, a consensus was seen for dating the *Book of the Parables* to around the time of Herod. This view of the dating was seen in papers presented by Michael E. Stone, David W. Suter, Darrell D. Hannah, Daniel C. Olson, Luca Arcari, Sabino Chialà, Adela Yarbro Collins, George W. E. Nickelsburg, Pierluigi

possibility of Matthean knowledge of Enochic traditions while avoiding the pitfalls of arguments concerning the date of the *Book of Parables*. Very few studies have been done, outside of those linking the Son of Man of the *Book of Parables* with the Son of Man in Matthew's Gospel, that show the influence of Enochic material on the Gospel of Matthew. Perhaps those who accept a date for the *Book of Parables* as early enough to provide source material for the writers of the canonical writers see no need to look further afield in *1 Enoch* since the Son of Man material in the *Book of Parables* provides plenty of grist for the mill of finding parallels between *1 Enoch* and Matthew. In any case, this book finds evidence that Matthew was aware of Enochic material outside of the *Book of Parables* that influences his Gospel.

The date of the *Book of Parables* is of particular interest to New Testament scholars because of the prominence in the book of the character called the Son of Man. Determining a date for the *Book of the Parables* is one way to tell if the *Book of Parables* could have influenced the Son of Man traditions in the New Testament or vice versa, or if both traditions developed separately but during the same time period. However, the dating of the *Book of Parables* is notoriously complex and has been hotly debated. Current scholarship proposes dates ranging between 50 BCE to 117 CE.[11] According to Suter, the majority opinion among scholars currently is that "the Romans and their associates" are "the villains of the Parables," possibly narrowing the date to 40 BCE to 70 CE.[12] The fact that the *Book of Parables* is the one section of *1 Enoch* not found at Qumran has provided material for debate about the dating and nature of the text. J. T. Milik, for example, used the absence of the book from Qumran to argue for the latest proposed date of composition, ca. 270 CE, and further identified the *Book of Parables* as a Christian work composed in Greek, a view now widely rejected.[13] Other scholars state that the absence of the book from Qumran is not a legitimate basis on which to propose a date for the text. For example, Michael Stone writes,

Piovanelli, Leslie W. Walck, and Gabriele Boccaccini. See Saachi, "The 2005 Seminar," 510.

11. See Suter, "Enoch in Sheol," 416.

12. Ibid., 425.

13. See Milik, *The Books of Enoch*, 89–98.

"the rule should be that absence from Qumran *proves* nothing."[14] [author's emphasis]. Other scholars posit reasons within the text itself why the *Book of Parables*, even if extant in time for potential inclusion at Qumran, would be rejected by the Qumran community. For example, Jonas Greenfield and Michael Stone point out that in *1 En.* 41:5–8 the sun and moon are given equal roles, a view out of keeping with the beliefs of the Qumran community.[15] Paoli Saachi says that the pertinent question is not why the *Book of Parables* is absent from Qumran, but rather why no Pseudepigrapha written after 100 BCE are found at Qumran. The absence of all post-100 BCE Pseudepigrapha points to a division between the Qumranians, who favored predeterminism to explain human sin from the Enochians, whose later works reveal a diminishment of the concept of impurity and a belief in human responsibility for sin.[16] Crispin Fletcher-Louis argues the fact "that the *Similitudes* has such an explicit priest-king messianic expectation will partly explain why it has not been found in the Qumran caves."[17] Scholars also look to *1 En.* 56:5–8 to provide possible internal evidence for the date of the *Book of Parables*. Greenfield, Stone, and Adela Yarbro Collins see this passage as a reference to the Parthian invasion of Syria and Palestine in 40–38 BCE and set 40 BCE as the earliest possible date for the *Book of Parables*.[18] Gillian Bampfylde proposes 51–50 BCE, the date of Parthia's first invasion of Roman territory in Syria.[19] However, J. Clifford Hindley suggests 113–17 CE, the time of Trajan's campaign against the Parthians, as the relevant referent.[20] Matthew Black thinks that *1 En.* 56:7a, "but the city of my righteous ones will become an obstacle to their horses," is an indication that Jerusalem still stands at the time of the writing of the *Book of Parables*, and favors a pre-70 CE date.[21] James H. Charlesworth dates the *Book of the Parables* to the time of Herod and the Herodians, based on the fact that it was not found at Qumran, the reference to a

14. See Stone, "Enoch's Date in Limbo," 446, emphasis original.

15. See Greenfield and Stone, "The Enochic Pentateuch," 51–65.

16. See Saachi, "Qumran and the Dating of the Parables of Enoch," 390.

17. Fletcher-Louis, "Jesus as the High Priestly Messiah," 166 n. 44.

18. See Greenfield and Stone, "The Enochic Pentateuch," 58–60; Collins, "The 'Son of Man' Tradition," 563–64.

19. Bampfylde, "The Similitudes of Enoch," 10.

20. Hindley, "Toward a Date for the Similitudes of Enoch," 553, 556–65.

21. Black, *The Book of Enoch or 1 Enoch*, 187.

Parthian invasion, and the curse on the landowners (*1 En.* 48:8 and 63:1–12).[22] In this sample, it is evident that there is no clear consensus on the date for the *Book of Parables*. New Testament traditions about the Son of Man may have been influenced by the Enochic *Book of Parables*, but because of the possibility of a date for the *Book of the Parables* later than the composition of the New Testament texts, the cautious scholar can claim only the possibility of a shared tradition or must continue to work to persuade others of an early date for the *Book of Parables*. A significant contribution of this work is that I examine Enochic traditions about which there is scholarly consensus that they pre-date the composition of the canonical gospels, opening up possibilities outside of the *Book of the Parables* and Son of Man references to demonstrate the evangelist's familiarity with Enochic traditions. The material in the *Book of the Watchers*, for example, certainly pre-dates the composition of Matthew's Gospel. While I cannot say for certain that Matthew had a text of the *Book of the Watchers*, it is possible from a chronological point of view that he was familiar with its traditions.

This book, then, through an examination of Matthew's genealogy and infancy narrative, makes the following contributions to our understanding of Matthew's Gospel: it becomes evident that Matthew was familiar with the Enochic watchers' template; the evangelist's familiarity with the story of the transgression of the watchers and Enoch's subsequent role in addressing the consequences of the watchers' fall contributes to Matthew's distinctive telling of the story of Jesus; Matthew shows Jesus to be a divinely appointed figure who completes the work that Enoch is unable to complete according to *1 Enoch*. A number of the unique Matthean aspects of the Gospel are clarified through this examination of Matthew through the lens of the Enochic watchers' template. Also, it becomes apparent that a number of the stories of women in Matthew's Gospel stand out as locations for which the Enochic watchers' template provides an important anti-type. This dissertation contributes to our wider understanding of Matthew's Gospel as apocalyptic literature and gives us a way to see the influence of traditions seen in *1 Enoch* on Matthew's Gospel without having to rely on scholarly con-

22. Charlesworth, "Can We Discern the Composition Date of the Parables of Enoch?" 455.

sensus for a date for the *Book of the Parables* that predates the writing of the Gospel.

A review of previous scholarship on the influence of apocalyptic motifs on Matthew's Gospel is now in order. However, the paucity of materials that address the influence of apocalyptic motifs on Matthew 1–2 or the influence of Enochic literature on Matthew's Gospel speaks to the need for further research in this area.

The Gospel of Matthew and Apocalyptic Literature

There are two trends in scholarship on Matthew and apocalyptic literature: first, a trend that connects apocalyptic themes in the Gospel with passages describing the *eschaton* and final judgment, and second, a trend that looks outside of these two subjects for apocalyptic themes.

Matthew's Use of Apocalyptic Themes Connected with the End-Times and the Final Judgment

A number of scholars have identified the presence of apocalyptic themes in Matthew's Gospel. However, the apocalyptic themes identified were usually those connected with eschatology only. For some, the sum of apocalyptic discourse in Matthew's Gospel equals eschatology.[23] J. C. Fenton, for example, in his 1963 commentary, includes a reference to "apocalyptic" in the index, but it directs the reader only to a discussion of the imminence of the end-time as understood by Matthew and his contemporaries.[24] At the same time as scholars were identifying particular passages in Matthew as containing apocalyptic–usually eschatological—themes, some scholars saw the presence of eschatological themes in Matthew's Gospel as profoundly affecting the Gospel as a whole. The place to start is with some examples of scholars' work that identified the presence of isolated instances of eschatological apocalyptic material within the Gospel.

Several pericopes in Matthew were easily identified as having to do with apocalyptic eschatology. Those mentioning the end-times

---

23. The development of the definitions of "apocalypse," "apocalypticism," and "apocalyptic eschatology" will be addressed below.

24. Fenton, *The Gospel of St Matthew*, 21.

or judgment fall rather straightforwardly into this category and have been identified this way by many scholars. These pericopes include: the preaching and baptism of John the Baptist (3:1–12); the parables in Matthew 13;[25] the Son of Man and the twelve judging the twelve tribes of Israel, 19:27–28; the eschatological discourse in Matthew 24; and the parables in chapters 24 and 25;[26] and the judgment in 25:31–46. In this way of examining Matthew and apocalyptic literature, where "apocalyptic" is nearly synonymous with "eschatological," if in Matthew's Gospel Jesus mentions the end time or final judgment, then the gospel writer is providing his readers with examples of apocalyptic eschatology.

But some scholars looked beyond specific mentions of the end and found the presence of eschatological themes. For example, in 1976 Robert Guelich examined the Matthean beatitudes, and found in them evidence of the "prophetic-apocalyptic" tradition within Matthew, as the "eschatological pronouncement of the presence of the New Age."[27] In Jesus' words, the future kingdom comes in the present to the hearer who responds. The beatitudes, as Matthew presents them, take on an eschatological character and function as "the product of, not the entrance requirements for, the Kingdom."[28] Although the beatitudes do not mention the end-times or judgment, Guelich identifies them as eschatological in character. It is apparent that several individual instances of eschatological motifs were identified in Matthew's Gospel.

Some scholars began to make connections between eschatological themes and their importance for the entire Gospel. In 1960 both Gerhard Barth and Günther Bornkamm remarked on Matthew's use of the apocalyptic themes of judgment and expectation of the end-times,[29] finding them to be of great importance for Matthew's entire Gospel, especially for how the evangelist conceived of the church and disciple-

25. The sower and its explanation, 13:1–9 and 18–23; the wheat and weeds and its explanation, 13:24–30 and 36–43; the mustard seed, 13:31–32; the leaven, 13:33; the hidden treasure, 13:44; the pearl, 13:45–46; the dragnet, 13:47–50; the householder, 13:51–52; and the reason for using parables, 13:10–17 and 34–35.

26. The fig tree, 24:32–33; Noah, 24:37–39; two men in the field and two women at the mill, 24:40–41; the thief and the owner of the house, 24:43; the faithful or unfaithful slave, 24:45–51; ten bridesmaids, 25:1–13; and the talents, 25:14–30.

27. Guelich, "Matthean Beatitudes," 433.

28. Ibid., 429.

29. Bornkamm, Barth, and Held, *Tradition and Interpretation in Matthew*, 15–51 (Bornkamm), and 58–164 (Barth).

ship. Barth saw Matthew's emphasis on judgment as an aspect unique to Matthew: "in Matthew, more firmly than in the other Gospels, the warning of the judgment and the exhortation to the doing of God's will are emphasized."[30] Bornkamm too saw Matthew's eschatological concerns as unique to Matthew and as shaping his entire Gospel, particularly his major concern, ecclesiology. Bornkamm wrote that the evangelist's discourses "show throughout a union of end-expectation and conception of the Church peculiar to him."[31]

This survey of commentaries and articles shows that scholars identified apocalyptic motifs within Matthew's Gospel, but restricted these mainly to motifs they connected with the *eschaton*. The presence of so many instances of eschatological concern in the Gospel led some, notably Barth and Bornkamm, to state that Matthew's eschatology in fact shapes his entire Gospel. But even at this time, there were scholars looking to see what other form evidence for apocalyptic in Matthew's Gospel might take.

The Presence of Apocalyptic Themes Other Than Those Associated with End-Times and Final Judgment within Matthew's Gospel

Some scholars saw more apocalyptic material in Matthew's Gospel than simply in those pericopes dealing with eschatology. Within this trend of scholarship, some also saw the presence of such material as evidence that the evangelist actually wrote from an apocalyptic viewpoint. For example, P. Hadfield's work in 1959 provides an example of an examination beyond the eschatological. Hadfield examined Matthew's use of Mark and Q and found that in parallel passages, Matthew heightened the use of apocalyptic language.[32] Such was the emphasis on apocalyptic themes in Matthew's Gospel that Hadfield stated, "We assume that the final editor of St Matthew's Gospel belonged to the apocalyptic school of thought."[33] In addition to the themes of judgment and the end times, Hadfield identified the belief in angels (especially guardian

30. Ibid., 62.

31. Ibid., 15.

32. Hadfield, "Matthew," 128–32.

33. Ibid., 128.

angels), righteousness, rewards for the righteous and punishment for the wicked, and the description of the good works of the righteous, as apocalyptic in nature and reflecting the influence of material outside of what became canonical scripture. In Hadfield's brief article, he did not specify what he meant by "the apocalyptic school of thought." His set of apocalyptic themes beyond those connected with eschatology contains only angels and righteousness. However, he did move beyond the eschatological in what he was willing to consider as evidence of apocalyptic themes. Further, he saw enough evidence of apocalyptic themes in Matthew to posit that the person behind the final form of the Gospel wrote from an apocalyptic viewpoint and part of a tradition shaped by that viewpoint.

Already, in the identification of two trends in the research into apocalyptic themes in Matthew's Gospel, the confusion and disagreement over what scholars meant by "apocalyptic" is apparent. Were "apocalyptic" and "eschatological" largely interchangeable? Before going further, it is necessary to pause and briefly mention significant attempts to define the words and phrases used in studies of Matthew and apocalyptic motifs. This brief excursus will provide an opportunity to see how evolving definitions of "apocalypse," "apocalypticism," and "apocalyptic eschatology" opened the doors for scholars to add more motifs outside of those related to end-times and final judgment and participate in the second trend, which includes more material within its scope.

Attempts to Define Terms More Accurately

In 1979 the SBL attempted to define "apocalypse" in order to clarify what scholars meant by the term and to allow better access to the meanings of ancient texts. The definition is now well-known, but is worth mentioning here for the sake of clarity. An apocalypse is "a genre of revelatory literature within a narrative framework, in which a revelation is mediated by an otherworldly being to a human recipient, disclosing a transcendent reality which is both temporal, insofar as it envisages eschatological salvation, and spatial insofar as it involves another supernatural world."[34]

34. Collins, ed., *Apocalypse*, 9.

The definition was intended to take into consideration both so-called "historical" apocalypses which involve a review of history and culminate in eschatological crisis and upheaval, and "otherworldly journey" apocalypses in which a visionary, almost always guided by an angel, is given a tour of other realms.[35]

Attempts have also been made to clarify two related terms, "apocalyptic eschatology" and "apocalypticism." Eschatology, from the Greek *eschaton*, "end," refers to beliefs about the end of the world, the culmination or fulfillment of history.[36] Eschatology may or may not be "apocalyptic" in nature. Thus, for example, Bonnard can claim that the Matthean beatitudes are "eschatological," but not "apocalyptic,"[37] and John Dominic Crossan can argue the same of Jesus, "that he was *eschatological but not apocalyptic*"[38] [emphasis is the author's]. Apocalyptic eschatology refers to the religious perspective one finds in apocalypses.[39] In relation to historical apocalypses, then, apocalyptic eschatology usually includes an expectation of divine intervention that will lead to "judgment of the wicked and vindication of the righteous, thereby ushering in a new era of prosperity and peace."[40] Apocalypticism refers to the ideology of movements that "shared the conceptual framework of the genre, endorsing a world view in which supernatural revelation, the heavenly world, and eschatological judgment played essential parts."[41] However, one needs to be aware that "there may be different types of apocalyptic movements, just as there are different types of apocalypses."[42] The lack of any reference to the function of apocalypses in the 1979 definition resulted in this addition in 1986 to the definition of apocalypse given above: apocalypses are "intended to interpret present earthly circumstances in light of the supernatural world and of the

35. See ibid., 6–8 for Collins's "Master-Paradigm" of Apocalypses, which includes variations of manner of revelation, reactions of the human recipient, content of apocalypses emphasizing the temporal axis, and content of apocalypses emphasizing the spatial axis.

36. Miller, ed., *The Apocalyptic Jesus*, 5.

37. Bonnard, *L'Évangile selon Saint Matthieu*, 55.

38. Crossan, in *The Apocalyptic Jesus*, 53.

39. Collins, *Apocalyptic Imagination* (1984), 9.

40. Hanson, "Apocalypses and Apocalypticism," *Anchor Bible Dictionary*, 1.281.

41. Collins, *Apocalyptic Imagination* (1984), 10.

42. Ibid.

future, and to influence both the understanding and the behavior of the audience by means of divine authority."[43]

The success or failure of these definitions is not the focus of this dissertation.[44] However, it is the defining of apocalypse and apocalypticism in ways that include both the temporal and spatial aspects of texts that makes way for examining Matthew's Gospel in light of *1 Enoch.*

Having noted the definitions, and their inclusion of themes beyond those connected only with final judgment and end-times, I now resume the review of specific research that influences views of Matthew's apocalyptic eschatology.

Developments after the 1979 SBL Definition

Adding to, and shaping the debate over precise definitions, two important studies on apocalyptic literature as a whole were written, both of which included sections identifying apocalyptic elements in Matthew's Gospel: Christopher Rowland's 1982 study *The Open Heaven: A Study of Apocalyptic in Judaism and Early Christianity,* and John J. Collins's 1984 book, *The Apocalyptic Imagination: An Introduction to Jewish Apocalyptic Literature.* Neither focused on Matthew's Gospel, but both used an expanded understanding of apocalyptic themes in literature, an understanding that went beyond themes connected with eschatology alone. Both took into account the apocalyptic literature that included otherworldly journeys as well as historical apocalypses.

Rowland, for example, wanted to move away from the eschatological aspect of apocalyptic literature and instead explore the "vertical dimension" of apocalyptic literature, that aspect concerned with an understanding of "things as they now are" as opposed to a concern

43. Collins, "Introduction: Early Christian Apocalypticism," 7.

44. However, these definitions are the subject of much ongoing discussion. See, for example, Greg Carey's attempt to avoid the confusion by providing a broader, more inclusive definition by speaking of "apocalyptic discourse," which he defines as "the constellation of apocalyptic topics as they function in larger early Jewish and Christian literary and social contexts. Thus, apocalyptic discourse should be treated as a flexible set of resources that early Jews and Christians could employ for a variety of persuasive tasks" (Carey, *Ultimate Things,* 5). Carey has received some negative criticism that his use of "apocalyptic discourse" is too broad, and hence, functions in the way that "apocalyptic" once did before it was restricted by the SBL definition from being used as anything other than an adjective. See DiTommaso, review of Greg Carey, *Ultimate Things.*

for future hope.[45] For Rowland, the distinguishing feature of apocalyptic literature is "a belief in direct revelation of the things of God which was mediated through dream, vision, or divine intermediary."[46] Corresponding to this definition, Rowland identified the narratives of Jesus' baptism, temptation, and transfiguration as containing apocalyptic visions, theophanies, and angelophanies.

Collins added the resurrection and ascension to the list of apocalyptic motifs in Matthew, stating that early Christians understood the identity of Jesus as Messiah in light of the "apocalyptic hope of the resurrection"[47] and that the Son of Man as portrayed in Matthew 25 presupposes both the resurrection and ascension.[48] Collins identified the resurrection and ascension as connected with apocalyptic tradition in the epilogue of his 1984 study. When he wrote a second edition, published fourteen years after the 1984 version,[49] Collins included a section on the Gospels within the main body of his book and expanded his references to Matthew to include "the works of the Messiah" in Matt 11:2 as similar to the eschatological works of God in 4Q521 and a more detailed section on the resurrection of Jesus in the persona of the Son of Man as evidence of apocalypticism in Matthew's Gospel.[50] Rowland and Collins, then, participate in the second trend, both seeing evidence of apocalyptic themes in Matthew's Gospel beyond the eschatological.

As noted above in regard to Hadfield's brief study, the presence of so much apocalyptic material led scholars not merely to note individual apocalyptic motifs, but to connect them together to claim an apocalyptic viewpoint behind Matthew's Gospel.

In 1985 Donald Hagner hit the motherlode of what he called "apocalyptic-like" details in the Gospel of Matthew, resulting in this evaluation: "From beginning to end, and throughout, the Gospel makes such frequent use of apocalyptic motifs and the apocalyptic viewpoint that it deserves to be called *the apocalyptic Gospel*" [Hagner's emphasis].[51]

---

45. Rowland, *Open Heaven*, 2.

46. Ibid., 21.

47. Collins, *Apocalyptic Imagination* (1984), 209.

48. Ibid., 210.

49. Collins, *Apocalyptic Imagination* (1998).

50. Ibid., 263.

51. Hagner, "Apocalyptic Motifs," 60.

Although Matthew shares with the other evangelists an "apocalyptic perspective,"[52] it is most prominent in Matthew. Hagner's list of apocalyptic motifs which bear witness to Matthew's apocalyptic viewpoint is impressive and thorough. He makes his point that apocalyptic motifs appear in every part of the Gospel. Broken down according to their respective narratives these motifs are

- in the birth narrative: dream-visions, angelic mediators, astronomical phenomena, "stress on the unusual," and the activity of the Holy Spirit;
- in the baptism of Jesus: the *Bat Qol's* revelation of Jesus' identity;
- in the temptation scene: the confrontation between Jesus and Satan;
- in the transfiguration scene: the high mountain, the glorious appearance of Jesus and his garments, the appearance of Moses and Elijah, the words about Jesus as the Son, and the awe of the disciples;
- in the crucifixion scene: the dream of Pilate's wife, and the darkness over the land; and
- in the resurrection narrative: the angel who announces the resurrection, and the resurrection of the bodies of many saints who appear in the Holy City.[53]

Hagner also identified passages in which apocalyptic motifs appear as they relate to expectations of the future, namely, the preaching of John the Baptist, the commissioning of the disciples, and much of the five discourses, including the final discourse, which describes the woes preceding the messianic age and the *parousia* of the Son of Man. Hagner described Matthew's apocalyptic as an "altered apocalyptic" in which the coming of the Messiah in history makes such impact on the present that "only apocalyptic language is adequate to describe his coming and work."[54] Matthew used apocalyptic language in order to proclaim that blessedness and comfort are possible even now, even in the midst of the present age, not only in the future.[55] Hagner did not

52. Ibid., 53.
53. Ibid., 53–82.
54. Ibid., 69.
55. Ibid., 73.

see Matthew as merely making use of apocalyptic motifs. Based on the number of motifs, their frequency throughout the Gospel, and the purpose they serve within the Gospel, Hagner saw Matthew as writing the apocalyptic gospel, from an apocalyptic perspective.

David Orton also sees Matthew as writing from an apocalyptic viewpoint. In his 1989 book *The Understanding Scribe: Matthew and the Apocalyptic Ideal*,[56] Orton focused not on the frequency of apocalyptic motifs within the Gospel, but rather on the role of the evangelist as scribe as evidence for Matthew's apocalyptic viewpoint. Orton looked at the whole of Matthew's Gospel as the product of a writer who portrays himself as a scribe standing within an apocalyptic tradition, bringing new things as well as old from his store of special revelation (Matt 13:52). Orton showed how Matthew as the ideal apocalyptic scribe demonstrates his scribal interests throughout the Gospel, for example, in the search for, and possession of, the understanding of scriptures, parables, and heavenly scenes; in issues of pastoral care, righteousness, discernment of the times of the ages, the kingdom of God, and judgment; and through use of the method of midrashic exposition of the scriptures.

The same year that Orton's study was published, O. Lamar Cope's article, "The Role of Apocalyptic Thought in Matthew,"[57] offered a follow-up to Bornkamm's article mentioned above. Building on Bornkamm's work, Cope elucidated the importance of apocalyptic judgment for Matthew's entire Gospel. Cope believes that throughout the Gospel, the evangelist "keeps the readers' attention fixed upon the apocalyptic consequences of discipleship."[58] Further, he writes, "the author of the First Gospel not only adopted the apocalyptic viewpoint of some of his source materials, he also formed and framed the Jesus story solidly in the context of an apocalyptic perspective."[59] Cope asserts that the main purpose of Matthew's use of apocalyptic language is to direct the behavior of the disciples, especially by including many warnings about punishment for failure in discipleship.

---

56. Orton, *Understanding Scribe*.

57. Cope, "To the Close of the Age," 113–24.

58. Ibid., 116.

59. Ibid., 117.

David Sim also contributed a broader examination of apocalyptic in Matthew's Gospel in 1996 with his *Apocalyptic Eschatology in the Gospel of Matthew*.[60] Sim's aim was to look at apocalyptic eschatology in order to understand Matthew's concerns and his social setting. Sim holds that apocalyptic eschatology dominates Matthew's Gospel, which is marked by an emphasis on the final judgment within a dualistic and deterministic framework.

Another work which attempted to address Matthew's Gospel more broadly, as opposed to looking for instances of particular motifs, is Robert Branden's *Satanic Conflict and the Plot of Matthew*.[61] While Branden's main concern was to examine the plot of Matthew using narrative criticism and in light of the theme of Satanic conflict, he set his study in the context of Jewish apocalyptic, and his conclusions further illustrate Matthew's apocalyptic viewpoint, especially in terms of the eschatological battle between Jesus' bringing in the kingdom of God and Satan's leading his rival kingdom, as well as the implications of that battle for the life of discipleship in the present.

In this review, it is apparent that, especially since the effort of the SBL to include both temporal and spatial axes in definitions of "apocalypse," "apocalyptic eschatology," and "apocalypticism," scholars of Matthew's Gospel have come to include a wide variety of apocalyptic motifs in their findings. Further, they see an apocalyptic viewpoint at work in the Gospel, as opposed to seeing the evangelist as introducing discreet instances of apocalyptic material. But apocalyptic motifs within the first two chapters of Matthew's Gospel and the presence of apocalyptic themes from *1 Enoch* within Matthew's Gospel have gone largely unnoticed.

Matthew and Enoch

Despite the identification of much of Matthew's Gospel as apocalyptic in nature and the identification of the evangelist as writing from an apocalyptic viewpoint, little has been described as apocalyptic in nature within the first two chapters of Matthew's Gospel, the genealogy and infancy narrative. Also, very little has been noted about the possible

60. Sim, *Apocalyptic Eschatology*.
61. Branden, *Satanic Conflict*.

use of Enochic motifs, which are apocalyptic in nature, by Matthew. Only the research of Hagner and Sim include the first two chapters of Matthew: Hagner's with his identification of dream-visions, angelic mediators, astronomical phenomena, "stress on the unusual," and the activity of the Holy Spirit in the birth narrative;[62] Sim's with his inclusion of angelic mediators[63] and formula quotations as reflecting the dualism and determinism that characterize Jewish apocalyptic.[64] Orton included Enoch as scribe in his description of the scribes of apocalyptic literature in his background to Matthew as scribe,[65] but he did not draw out specific parallels between Matthew and Enoch. Orton, however, did identify the need for "further investigations of relationships . . . between Matthew and apocalyptic literature."[66] This dissertation is part of those investigations.

One exploration of a possible literary dependence of a passage in Matthew on a passage from *1 Enoch* should be noted. David Sim examined the possibility that Matt 22:13a ("Then the king said to the attendants, "Bind him hand and foot, and throw him into the outer darkness") is dependent upon *1 Enoch* 10:4a ("To Raphael he said, 'Go, Raphael, and bind Asael hand and foot, and cast him into the darkness").[67] A possible connection between the two passages was suggested by A. H. McNeile in 1915[68] and by R. H. Gundry in his commentary on Matthew.[69] Sim used the work of R. Rubinkiewicz[70] to look further into this possibility. Sim agreed with Rubinkiewicz's conclusion that the Matthean verse is directly dependent upon the verse from *1 Enoch*.[71] Rubinkiewicz believed that Matt 22:11–13 is pre-Matthean and "can be traced back to Jesus himself."[72] Sim concluded that the pas-

62. Hagner, "Apocalyptic Motifs," 60.

63. Sim, *Apocalyptic Eschatology*, 75.

64. Ibid., 89.

65. For more on Enoch as scribe, see also Orlov, *The Enoch-Metatron Tradition*, 50–59.

66. Orton, *Understanding Scribe*, 175.

67. Sim, "Matthew 22.13a," 3–19.

68. McNeile, *The Gospel according to St. Matthew*, 317.

69. Gundry, *Matthew*, 440.

70. Rubinkiewicz, *Die Eschatologie von Henoch 9–11*, 97–113.

71. Sim, "Matthew 22.13a," 6.

72. Ibid., 7.

sage is a composition of Matthew and that the evangelist used "the C text of *1 En.* 10:4a as his source."[73]

This dissertation makes no claims of direct dependency of the Gospel of Matthew on the text of *1 Enoch*. However, when examining Matthew chapters 1–2 in light of motifs of the Enoch watchers' template, evidence of these motifs as background for the Gospel material is apparent. This evidence appears in the frequency with which Enochic motifs can be identified in connection with material in Matthew's Gospel. The evangelist does not replicate any large sections of *1 Enoch*, nor, as mentioned above, does he quote from *1 Enoch*, with the possible exception of Sim's example. However, again and again in Matthew's genealogy and infancy narrative one finds motifs and allusions to material that one also finds in *1 Enoch*. The number of instances in which Enochic motifs occur, even within the first two chapters of Matthew's Gospel, is too great for Matthew not to have been familiar with the Enochic tradition and for these to appear as background material as the evangelist tells his version of the story of Jesus. That Matthew would make use of Enochic motifs makes sense if the evangelist is familiar with the full range of apocalyptic material extant in his time or writes from an apocalyptic viewpoint broad enough to include Enochic literature in its purview. This dissertation, then, builds on the work of those who have identified apocalyptic motifs in Matthew and identified Matthew as writing from an apocalyptic viewpoint. It goes beyond previous scholarship by examining Matthew's Gospel in light of motifs of *1 Enoch* (importantly, those outside of the *Book of Parables*) and focusing on Matthew 1–2.

The dissertation proceeds as follows. Chapter 2, "Transgression," provides an overview of the Enochic watchers' template in which the watchers transgress their divinely appointed boundaries, have illicit sexual relations with women and teach them forbidden heavenly secrets. Chapter 3, "Transgression Reassessed," examines how the four women of the Hebrew Bible named in Matthew's genealogy (Matt 1:1–17) each foreshadow the repair of the watchers' transgression. Chapter 4, "Transgression Redressed," looks at how events within the narrative of Jesus' infancy show that Jesus is the repairer of the watchers' transgression. Chapter 5, "The Legacy of the Watchers' Transgression Versus the Legacy of 'God with Us,'" shows how the repair set in mo-

73. Ibid., 13.

tion with the birth of Jesus is brought to completion by the adult Jesus. Chapter 6 will summarize the conclusions of this study. This study will show that Matthew was familiar with the Enochic watchers' template; that Matthew's familiarity with the watchers' template contributes to Matthew's distinctive telling of the story of Jesus; and that Matthew shows Jesus to be a divinely appointed figure who completes the work that Enoch is unable to complete according to *1 Enoch*. It will show that often it is through stories of women in Matthew's Gospel that the repair of the watchers' transgression that occurred between angels and women takes place. According to Matthew, the Enochic watchers' transgression and its consequences for humanity are redressed through Jesus.

2

Transgression

The main problem within the Enochic typology for the origin of evil in the world is transgression. Angels called "watchers"[1] transgress the set boundary of their appointed station and enter a realm they were never intended to enter, the earthly realm where mortal humans exist. After transgressing the boundary between realms, they transgress a boundary of interaction by engaging in sexual relations with mortal women and by disclosing heavenly secrets, sharing knowledge humans were not intended to have. The result of the sexual interaction between the angels and women is a race of creatures of a mixed nature, giants, who belong fully neither to the earthly realm nor to the eternal heavenly realm. There are consequences for the watchers' transgression—to the transgressors, to the people with whom they transgressed, and to the rest of us living after the transgression event. Can the transgression be redeemed? Can transgression itself bring redemption?

In this chapter I examine the Enochic typology of the origin of evil in the world. In subsequent chapters I examine the redemption of the Enochic typology of evil as explained by Matthew's Gospel. This examination takes us into the first chapters of Matthew and illuminates the perennial question of why Matthew mentions women in the genealogy with which he begins his Gospel, as well as the Joseph-centered birth narrative of Jesus and Jesus' conception "from the Holy Spirit" (Matt 1:20).

---

1. Although some scholars capitalize the "w" in "watcher," I follow Nickelsburg and VanderKam in using the lowercase "watcher" unless "Watcher" appears in a source I quote. See *1 Enoch: A New Translation*.

In the course of this book I will look at three stages in the onset of evil and its ultimate redemption. These three stages show the pattern of (1) loss of intended state, (2) foreshadowing of restoration, (3) restoration.[2] First, the loss of the intended state of humanity is seen in the Enochic myth in which rebel angels known as watchers descend from their appointed heavenly realm in order to have sexual interaction with women and teach them forbidden skills. Second, the foreshadowing of the reversal of evil is seen in the narratives of the women of the Hebrew Bible named in Matthew's genealogy. By "foreshadowing" I mean the beginning of redemption but not its completed fullness. The stories of the women included in the genealogy show a partial restoration of the intended state. In each of the women's stories, the woman and her actions are vindicated. In the unfolding of the overall salvation history, each character and story plays a role, moving the narrative forward. But none of the stories by itself completes the reversal or redemption of the original transgression. The Hebrew Bible matriarchs show us movement in the direction of redemption, even as they use the illicit arts taught by the watchers and participate in aspects of the Enochic template, specifically through interaction with angels and issues concerning their offspring. The issues about offspring concern either paternity or the unusual or exceptional nature of the children born to them. The third stage, that is, the completed redressing of transgression, is seen in the birth narrative of Jesus. In the birth narrative, Matthew shows the birth of Jesus occurring in a way that reverses the watchers' transgression and evil in the world as it occurs in the Enochic template. Specifically, the birth of Jesus occurs through the union of a woman and a celestial being, but in contrast to the watchers' story, no sexual relations are involved. Further, in Matthew's narrative, the first humans outside of Jesus' immediate family to interact with the child Jesus are the magi who are practitioners of the illicit arts taught by the watchers and use astrological knowledge to find Jesus. In the Enochic template,

---

2. Andrei Orlov shows this same three-fold pattern of (1) loss, (2) foreshadowing of restoration, (3) full restoration in the Adamic typology in which (1) Adam loses his glorious appearance, (2) Moses gains the appearance of glory on his face, (3) Christ in the transfiguration regains the glorious appearance lost by Adam. See "Vested with Adam's Glory: Moses as the Luminous Counterpart of Adam in the Dead Sea Scrolls and the Macarian Homilies," in *From Apocalypticism to Merkabah Mysticism*, 327—43.

the watchers bring idolatry into the world; in Matthew, the magi worship the appropriate object of worship—Jesus.

The three stages may be outlined as follows:

1. Loss: The origin of evil in the world through transgression. Watchers descend to have sexual contact with women and teach illicit arts.

2. Hebrew Bible foreshadowing of the reversal of transgression: Women who are ancestors of Jesus use transgression and it leads to righteous outcomes.

3. Redemption of Transgression: Jesus is born through the mixing of earthly and heavenly realms, but without sexual contact.

This chapter addresses the first of these three stages, giving an overview of the Enochic typology for the origin of evil in the world through the story of the fall of the watchers. In chapter 3, I examine the stories of each of the women from the Hebrew Bible named in Matthew's genealogy, identifying echoes of the Enochic watchers story in each. In chapter 4, I examine Matthew's birth narrative, showing how Matthew uses it to show that the birth of Jesus undoes the grip of evil on the world as it is seen in the Enochic template.

The Enochic Story of the Watchers—Illicit Pedagogy and Willing (?) Women

Genesis 6:1–4 gives a brief account of unfortunate interaction between the "sons of God" and the "daughters of men":

> When people began to multiply on the face of the ground, and daughters were born to them, the sons of God saw that the daughters of humans were fair; and they took wives from them of all that they chose. Then the Lord said, "My spirit shall not abide in mortals forever, for they are flesh; their days shall be

one hundred twenty years. The Nephilim were on the earth in those days, and also afterward, when the sons of God went in to the daughters of humans, and they bore children to them. These were the mighty men [הגברים] of old, men of renown.[3]

Immediately following this account, God sees that human wickedness abounds upon the earth and in every human heart save one: Noah, who alone is righteous (Gen 6:9). Grieving deeply (Gen 6:6), God decides to blot out all living things, with the famous exception of Noah and his passengers aboard the ark. As Genesis tells it, then, sons of God, often interpreted as angels,[4] and women bear offspring, and the next thing we know human wickedness runs amok. God decides there is no recourse but to wipe the slate clean, as it were, by sending the flood. Only righteous Noah and his immediate family and menagerie are spared. The author of Genesis does not explicitly make a connection between the getting of wives by the sons of God and the multiplication of wickedness. In between the account of the sexual interaction between angels and women and the report that "every inclination of the thoughts of [human] hearts was only evil continually" (Gen 6:5), one learns only that God decides to limit the lifespan of humans to one hundred twenty years (Gen 6:3) and that the angelic-human unions resulted in "mighty men of old, warriors of renown" (Gen 6:4). What, if any, were the con-

---

3. My translation. Exploration of this passage falls outside the scope of this dissertation. See Wenham, *Genesis 1–15*, 135–47; Westermann, *Genesis 1–11*, 363–81; Hamilton, *The Book of Genesis*, 261–72; Sarna, *Genesis*, 45–46; Newman, "The Ancient Exegesis of Genesis 6:2, 4," 13–36; Alexander, "The Targumim and Early Exegesis," 60–71; Bartelmus, *Heroentum in Israel*; Cassuto, "The Episode of the Sons of God and the Daughters of Man," 17–28; Clines, "The Significance of the 'Sons of God' Episode," 33–46; Eslinger, "A Contextual Identification," 65–73; Petersen, "Gen 6:1–4," 47–64; van Gemeren, "The Sons of God," 320–48; Hendel, "Of Demigods and the Deluge," 13–26; Marrs, "The Sons of God," 218–24; Wifall, "Gen 6:1–4," 294–301.

4. "Sons of God" is a phrase that describes a category of heavenly beings in Deut 32:8; Ps 29:1; 89:6–7; Job 1:6; 2:1; and 38:7. Psalm 82:6 has a similar expression, "sons of the Most High." According to Annette Yoshiko Reed, the "sons of God" in Gen 6:2 were frequently interpreted as angels by many pre-rabbinic Jews. In the first centuries CE, Christians continued to use an angelic interpretation, although their rabbinic contemporaries did not, using euhemeristic interpretations instead. In the third and fourth centuries CE, Christian interpreters in the Roman Empire also turned away from an angelic interpretation. Reed, *Fallen Angels*, 273. Reed traces the development of the fallen angels motif from Second Temple through medieval Judaism and early Christianity through Byzantine Christianity. See also Hendel, "The Nephilim were on the Earth," 11–34.

nections between angelic-human sexual unions and the complete evil of humanity, save Noah, on the earth? The text itself does not tell.[5] Making these connections would be left to subsequent interpreters.

The tantalizing gaps of the laconic Genesis passage inevitably invited explanation and expansion. The *Book of the Watchers* (the title assigned to *1 Enoch* 1–36, and dated to the third century BCE[6]) contains the earliest extant references to the Genesis report of problematic angelic and human interaction, particularly in *1 Enoch* 6–11.[7] Watchers were angels, meant to dwell in "the highest heaven, the sanctuary of their eternal station" (*1 En.* 12:4; in 15:3, "the high heaven, the eternal sanctuary"). These angels forsook their proper dwelling place in order to have sexual relations with women. Although "watcher" refers to a class of angels whether faithful or fallen,[8] the name watcher seems to have been reserved in Greek translations of *1 Enoch* to indicate rebel angels.[9] The name may come from the root עוּר, "to be awake," or "to be watchful."[10] Nickelsburg identifies the following functions of these

5. However, the text does offer some tantalizing possibilities beyond the proximity of the episode of the sons of God and the daughters of men and the flood which follows. One connection is provided by the word גברים, "the mighty men" who were on the earth (Gen 6:4). In the flood narrative, the same verbal root, גבר, to prevail, is used multiple times to describe the action of the floodwaters that prevail (גבר) over the earth. The word appears in Gen 7:18, 19, 20, 24. See Brown, et al., *The New Brown Driver Briggs*, 149B. Dorothy Peters also notes the repetition of this verbal root and that its frequency would "not escape the attention of the story's interpreters." See Peters, *Noah Traditions*, 20; also 17, 18, 27. On p. 27, Peters summarizes the prevailing (גבר) of the water as "water as the enemy." Certainly the water is enemy to the life that it takes and in the sense of being a destroyer of creation. However, it seems in the narrative that water actually functions in the sense of the word גבר, as a "champion" or "mighty" force wreaking the destruction the Deity intends by sending the flood. Peters's point, though, that the wordplay on גבר would provide material for later interpreters (20), is an important one.

6. Reed, *Fallen Angels*, 1. Parts of the *Book of the Watchers* have been found on six manuscripts from Qumran cave 4. Milik dates the oldest to the first half of the second century BCE (Milik, *Books of Enoch*, 5). See also Nickelsburg, *1 Enoch 1*, 7.

7. Nickelsburg dates *1 Enoch* 6–11 to the end of the fourth century BCE. He connects the wars of the Diadochi (323–302 BCE) with the warfare of the giants in this section of *1 Enoch*. Nickelsburg, "Apocalyptic and Myth," 383–405. On the interpretation of Genesis within *1 Enoch* see VanderKam, "The Interpretation of Genesis," 129–48; and Stuckenbruck, "The Origins of Evil," 88–117, especially 99–110.

8. Reed, *Fallen Angels*, 1.

9. Nickelsburg, *1 Enoch 1*, 140.

10. The etymology of the name *watcher* is problematic. In Aramaic the name is

angels that correspond to their designation as watchers: they "are on twenty-four hour duty attending God"; they "supervise aspects of the universe, that is, they are on night and day duty overseeing the functions of creation"; they "keep watch over the functions of the celestial beings in charge of the seasons"; and, they constantly guard the righteous.[11] However, in *1 Enoch*, the watchers go astray, abandoning their prescribed duties to pursue women as wives. These rebel angels, then, are those reported by Genesis as begetting children with humans. But in *1 Enoch*, unlike the imprecise Genesis account, this angelic-human interaction is unambiguously a bad thing.

Adding to the problem, in an element not found in the Genesis story, sexual interaction between watchers and women is not the only illicit interaction between them. According to the *Book of the Watchers*, the proliferation of evil in the world is caused by a combination of angelic sexual interaction with women and the teaching of forbidden arts. Annette Yoshiko Reed calls this latter motif "illicit angelic instruction"[12] and "illicit pedagogy."[13] First, I will examine the former cause of evil, sexual congress between watchers and women. Then I will examine the subject of illicit pedagogy.

The subject of angelic sexual interaction with women is introduced in *1 Enoch* 6:2 when the angels notice the beautiful daughters of men and say, "Come, let us choose wives for ourselves from among the daughters of men, and let us beget children for ourselves." The watchers swear an oath and bind themselves by a curse that they will carry out this deed, even though they know it to be a "great sin" (*1 En.* 6:3).[14] The

עירין. Perhaps עיר comes from עור, "to arouse oneself," "to be awake," as mentioned above, and means that these angels are constantly awake, always on duty attending God. Nickelsburg, *1 Enoch 1*, 140. See also Nickelsburg, *Ancient Judaism*, 98.

11. Nickelsburg, *1 Enoch 1*, 140–41.

12. Reed, *Fallen Angels*, 6. In this book, Reed considers the redaction-history and reception-history of the *Book of the Watchers*. Reed provides evidence for the development of the theme of the problematic angelic and human interaction within the *Book of the Watchers*, as well as tracing the influence of the *Book of the Watchers* on subsequent early Jewish and Christian texts. Although both motifs are present in the *Book of the Watchers*, when the watchers are referred to in Second Temple Jewish sources and in the New Testament, the motif of sexual deviance predominates. The motif of illicit angelic pedagogy is virtually absent in later references to the *Book of the Watchers*, even though the motif of illicit angelic instruction plays a central role in the book.

13. Ibid., 30.

14. The knowledge of the sinfulness of their plan and the guilt it would incur is ex-

narrator does not disclose any response or reaction on the part of the women. Clearly in this account it is the angels who are initiating the action in full knowledge that they are transgressing and leading humans with them into transgression.

The event is also narrated in the *Animal Apocalypse* in *1 En.* 86:1–4, an allegorical narrative of the sexual interaction between the watchers and the women.[15] In the allegory, first one star (watcher) falls from heaven and pastures among cattle (humans) (86:1). Then other stars also fall (86:3). They have sexual relations with the cows and beget offspring unnatural to their species: elephants, camels, and asses (86:4). Destruction and fear follow as the animals devour and gore one another (86:6; 87:1). "All the sons of the earth began to tremble and quake before them, and to flee" (86:6) and "the earth began to cry out" (87:1). The connection between the fallen angels' sexual relations with women and the multiplication of evil in the world is made explicit in *1 Enoch*. The watchers transgress their heavenly boundaries, involve women in their wrongdoing, and all creation suffers. As in *1 Enoch* 6, the sexual interaction is narrated, but there is no mention in the *Animal Apocalypse* of the rebellious angels teaching forbidden knowledge to the women.

However, immediately following the sexual interaction narrated in *1 Enoch* 6, one hears of the other cause of the proliferation of evil, the illicit instruction of women by their watcher husbands. The motif of illicit angelic instruction will be examined in more detail below. But first I look at how each of the three accounts in *1 Enoch* 7–9 combines the motif of sexual interaction with the motif of illicit pedagogy. In each passage, illicit pedagogy that corrupts humankind is narrated as concomitant with sexual relations.

Two of the accounts, *1 En.* 7:1–6 and 9:7–10, narrate the sexual union between watchers and women and its disastrous aftermath. In *1 En.* 7:1–2 one reads,

---

pressed by Shemihazah, their chief, who does not want to be the only watcher who follows through on the deed. He says to his cohort, "I fear that you will not want to do this deed, and I alone shall be guilty of a great sin" (*1 En.* 6:3; *1 Enoch: A New Translation*, 23). The other watchers suggest an oath as the way to guarantee the watchers' collusion.

15. Nickelsburg dates this section in its present form to ca. 165 BCE. Nickelsburg, *1 Enoch 1*, 8. On the *Animal Apocalypse* see also Tiller, *A Commentary on the Animal Apocalypse*; VanderKam, *Enoch and the Growth of an Apocalyptic Tradition*, 160–70; VanderKam, *Enoch*, 72–89.

> These and all the others with them took for themselves wives
> from among them such as they chose. And they began to go in
> to them, and to defile themselves through them, and to teach
> them sorcery and charms, and to reveal to them the cutting of
> roots and plants.
>
> And they conceived from them and bore to them great gi-
> ants. And the giants begot Nephilim . . .[16]

Chapter 9:8–9 provides the archangels' summary of events, saying
of the watchers,

> They have gone in to the daughters of the men of the earth,
> and they have lain with them, and have defiled
> themselves with the women.
> And they have revealed to them all sins, and have taught
> them to make hate-inducing charms.
> And now look, the daughters of men have borne sons from
> them, giants, half-breeds.
> And the blood of men is shed on the earth,
> And the whole earth is filled with iniquity.[17]

In each passage, between the sexual interaction and the birth of the
resultant offspring comes the illicit pedagogy. In both cases, the order
of narration is this:

1. sexual interaction between watchers and women

2. watchers teach women

3. women give birth to giants.

The teaching of illicit skills to the women comes after their sexual interaction with the angels and before their unnatural unions result in
unnatural offspring. That is, the sexual interaction and the teaching are
somehow, but not explicitly, related.

Sexual interaction as overture to the teaching of women provides
a contrast with the teaching of men by one of the watchers, Asael, in
chapter 8. Chapter 8 also narrates the teaching of forbidden skills to
humans combined with sexual interaction. Reed suggests that seeing
8:1–2 "as a flashback" rather than a subsequent event of pedagogy may
be the best reading of the text.[18] In this reading, Asael first teaches cul-

16. *1 Enoch: A New Translation*, 24–25.

17. Ibid., 27.

18. Reed, *Fallen Angels*, 35–36. See Nickelsburg, *1 Enoch 1*, 191, who views chapter

tural arts to men, and this causes the events of *1 En.* 8:2–4, namely, the descent of the watcher Shemihazah and his companions who then do more illicit teaching.[19] Whether a summary statement, a flashback, or a continuation of action previously narrated, in this version, the teaching of men is narrated first, with no sexual interaction as prelude to the teaching. Rather, the text reports,

> Asael taught men to make swords of iron and weapons and shields and breastplates and every instrument of war.
>
> He showed them metals of the earth and how they should work gold to fashion it suitably, and concerning silver, to fashion it for bracelets and ornaments for women. And he showed them concerning antimony and eye paint and all manner of precious stones and dyes. (*1 En.* 8:1)[20]

However, the men put their newly acquired skills to work, share the results of their skills with their daughters, and sexual interaction between watchers and women results: "And the sons of men made for themselves and for their daughters, and they transgressed and led the holy ones astray. And there was much godlessness on the earth and they made their ways desolate" (*1 En.* 8:1–2).[21]

When knowledge is taught to men, as it is in chapter 8, the illicit pedagogy is mentioned first, outside of the narrative arc of sexual interaction between watchers and women, the teaching of women (related in 8:3), and resultant violence and death. That is, the account in chapter 8 adds the instruction of men to the beginning. Only then is the pattern found in chapters 7 and 9 repeated. The order in chapter 8 is:

1. angels teach men

2. sexual interaction (women lead the angels astray)

---

8 as an interpolation or expansion, added sometime between ca. 300 BCE, when the myth developed in which Shemihazah is the chief of the watchers (as in *1 En.* 6:3), and ca.165 BCE, the latest probable date for our present full text.

19. Reed, *Fallen Angels*, 35. This "flashback" and two-step descent, in which Asael descends first and teaches, then Shemihazah and his companions descend and teach, also fits the narrative in the *Animal Apocalypse* in which first one star (watcher) falls, then later other stars fall. *1 En.* 86:1–2.

20. *1 Enoch: A New Trasnlation*, 25.

21. Ibid.

3. angels teach women (the skills taught are related to what is taught in chapter 7).

4. destruction and death follow.

Here, rather than watchers initiating the sexual interaction with women, the sexual interaction is the result of the men having learned from the watcher Asael the arts of adornment of the body, both metallurgic and cosmetic.

In chapter 8, humans have more agency in what goes wrong on earth. Men are taught by the watchers and, in sharing the product of their knowledge with their daughters, disaster results: women become responsible for the wandering of the watchers, "and they [the women] transgressed and led the holy ones astray" (*1 En.* 8:1).[22] The watchers, seeing the now adorned and ornamented women cannot help but be seduced by them. The blame in this chapter for the transgression of the watchers falls squarely onto the women who make use of the illicit arts taught by Asael. The emphasis here is on the women's initiative in beautifying themselves, rather than, as in chapters 6, 7, and 9, the angels' initiative in deciding to take wives for themselves. Asael initiates the trouble with his illicit pedagogy, but once humans know the angel's secrets, humans participate fully in bringing about the corruption of heavenly orders and godlessness on earth. Women, in particular, participate by making themselves physically attractive to men and to the watchers.

Later Jewish and Christian accounts will share this indictment of the women for leading the angels astray. *Testament of Reuben*,[23] for

22. Ibid.

23. Part of the *Testament of the Twelve Patriarchs, Testament of Reuben* has been variously dated between the second century BCE to the second century CE. VanderKam believes that the challenge with dating the work comes from the fact that the work as it now exists is a Christian work. He writes, "Given the small number of demonstrably Christian passages, it seems more likely that the *Testaments of the Twelve Patriarchs* is a Jewish work with some Christian additions. Moreover, at Qumran texts that may be related to two of the testaments have been found: the Aramaic Levi text has a large amount of the material that appears in the *Testament of Levi*, and a *Testament of Naphtali* (4Q215) shares some points with the Greek work of the same name" VanderKam, *An Introduction to Early Judaism*, 100–101). See also Kugler, *The Testament of the Twelve Patriarchs.* Kugler provides a summary of what he calls "three general approaches to the related questions of the *Testaments'* provenance, date, compositional history and purpose" (ibid., 31). Kugler finds the approach of de Jonge most satisfactory, namely

example, not only assigns responsibility to the women for the watchers' fall, but also provides an interesting explanation for how angels and humans, beings of such different realms, could actually procreate. The fall of the watchers is actually described to illustrate how powerful are the wily ways of women. Reuben warns his sons,

> Evil are women, my children,
> because, having no power or strength over man,
> they use their wiles trying to draw him to them by gestures;
> and whom she cannot overcome by strength,
> him she overcomes by craft.
> For also concerning them the angel of the Lord told me,
> and he taught me
> that women are overcome by the spirit of impurity more than man,
> and in their heart they plot against men,
> and by their adornment they deceive first their minds,
> and by their glance they sow the poison,
> and then they take them captive by the (accomplished) act.
> For a woman cannot force a man.[24]

And then, explaining the watchers' fall, he says,

> For thus they bewitched the Watchers before the Flood:
> as these looked at them continually,
> they lusted after one another,
> and they conceived the act in their mind,
> and they changed themselves into the shape of men,
> and they appeared to them when they were together with their husbands. And they, lusting in their mind after their appearances, bore giants;
> for the Watchers appeared to them as reaching unto heaven.[25]

---

that the *Testaments* are essentially Christian compositions, dating to 190–225 CE, although they incorporate "considerable Jewish source material" (ibid., 35–36). See also Hollander and de Jonge, *The Testaments of the Twelve Patriarchs,* see pp. 82–85 on the date and provenance of the text. On the Jewish material within the *Testaments,* Hollander and de Jonge state, "This may represent a thorough and to a considerable degree consistent reworking of an earlier Jewish writing. It is, however, clear that the quest for an earlier stage (or stages) in the history of the Testaments will have to start with the text as we have it before us" (ibid., 83).

24. *T. Reu.* 5:1–4. The translation, here and in all other uses of *T. Reu.* is by Hollander and de Jonge, cited above, 101.

25. *T. Reu.* 5:6–7 (trans. Hollander and de Jonge, 101–2).

Women, in other words, stirred up the lust of the watchers for them. As the women were engaged in sexual relations with their human husbands, but lusting after the angels, somehow "the object of the women's desire (the angel) becomes the father of the child she is in the process of conceiving with her human husband, and the child thereby becomes a mixture of the two natures."[26] Women are thus responsible for the watchers' fall and the introduction of giants into the world.[27] That women are still capable of such transgression, especially when using the arts of adornment, is the patriarch Reuben's larger and ongoing concern. In regard to the subject of the relationship between sexual interaction and illicit pedagogy in *1 Enoch*, angelic teaching of men leads to sexual immorality, as in chapter 8, but the teaching of men is not itself predicated on sexual activity between the men and their angelic teachers. Where angels and women are concerned, the "knowing" of sexual encounter and the "knowing" of forbidden arts, secrets, and skills are related. [28]

There is one other variation on the theme of pedagogy and sexuality found in *Jubilees*. The motif of angelic instruction of humans is not found in the Genesis account, but it is known elsewhere, for example in the second century BCE book of *Jubilees*.[29] In this retelling of stories

26. Jackson, *Enochic Judaism*, 64–65.

27. See also *Tg. Ps. -J.* Gen 6:2 for a tradition in which it is the women's self-adornment that attracts the watchers and causes their fall: "the sons of *the great ones* saw that the daughters of men were beautiful, *that they painted their eyes and put on rouge, and walked about with naked flesh. They* [the watchers] *conceived lustful thoughts,* and they took wives to themselves from among all who pleased them" (*Targum Pseudo-Jonathan*, 37–38).

28. I would like to know more about the relationship between the sexual interaction and the sharing of knowledge. Is this an exchange? *Quid pro quo?* Is the granting of the knowledge of skills and secrets a reward? Part of the watchers' plan—if we're going to be a family, there are a few things you should know . . . ? Did the women try to gain knowledge? In the version where they lead the watchers astray, do they do so knowing they have something to gain by it? Is it another take on Eve's disobedience in order to gain knowledge? Did the women initiate the transfer of knowledge? Did they somehow deceive the angels, beyond seducing them beyond the boundary between heaven and earth? The Greek myth of Pandora features a woman who opens forbidden box and unleashes disastrous knowledge into the world, but are there other myths that focus on the kinds of knowledge associated with women in particular?

29. On *Jubilees*, see *Jubilees: A Critical Text*, translated by James C. VanderKam. This is the translation that I use for all references to *Jubilees* in this book. See also Endres, *Biblical Interpretation in the Book of Jubilees*; Halpern-Amaru, *The Empowerment of Women*; VanderKam, *The Book of Jubilees*.

from Genesis and Exodus a different take on the watchers is found. In *Jubilees* the watchers descend to earth not because they find women attractive, but because the watchers' very job is to instruct human beings. For the watchers in *Jubilees,* teaching humans is not a byproduct or afterthought of sexual interaction with humans. Teaching humans is their purpose. Specifically, the watchers are to instruct humans in ways of righteousness. *Jubilees* 4:15 says, "during [Jared's] lifetime the angels of the Lord who were called Watchers descended to earth to teach mankind and to do what is just and upright upon the earth."[30] Thus, according to *Jubilees*, the watchers were to teach humans licit knowledge rather than forbidden skills. However, as in the Genesis and *1 Enoch* accounts, the watchers find the women attractive, and rather than persist with their righteous task, the watchers "sinned with the daughters of men because these had begun to mix with earthly women so that they became defiled. Enoch testified against all of them" (*Jub.* 4:22).[31] As in the Genesis and *1 Enoch* accounts, the offspring of the rebel angels and the women are giants (*Jub.* 5:2). As mentioned above, in *1 Enoch*, sexual interaction with women occurs first, and illicit instruction comes second. *Jubilees* reverses the order found in *1 Enoch*. In *Jubilees* (licit) instruction comes first, then sexual interaction follows. In both cases the sexual interaction is wrong.

I now examine more closely the motif of illicit pedagogy and the specific forbidden skills taught in the three accounts found in *1 Enoch* 7, 8, and 9. All three passages describe the second cause of evil in the world, the teaching of forbidden arts. I revisit each passage briefly, noting particularly what knowledge was transmitted from the rebel angels to the humans.

1 Enoch 7:1 says, "These and all the others with them took for themselves wives from among them such as they chose. And they began to go in to them, and to defile themselves through them, and to teach them sorcery and charms, and to reveal to them the cutting of roots and plants."[32] The passage supplements what one reads in Genesis 6, adding the sharing of knowledge as attendant to the sexual interaction of the watchers and women. Specifically, the angels teach their wives "sorcery

30. *Jubilees: A Critical Text*, 25.

31. Ibid., 28.

32. *1 Enoch: A New Translation*, 24.

and charms, . . . the cutting of roots and plants" (1 En. 7:1).[33] William Loader writes that the "sorcery and charms" taught "will have been understood as including activities related to sexual behavior."[34]

In the very next chapter, a second account is found of what the angels teach the women. Here more detail is given, including the names of the instructors and what they teach. But in this passage, women are not the only recipients of forbidden pedagogy. As noted above, men also are recipients of corrupting knowledge:

> Asael taught men to make swords of iron and weapons and shields and breastplates and every instrument of war.
> He showed them metals of the earth and how they should work gold to fashion it suitably, and concerning silver, to fashion it for bracelets and ornaments for women. And he showed them concerning antimony and eye paint and all manner of precious stones and dyes.
> And the sons of men made for themselves and for their daughters, and they transgressed and led the holy ones astray. And there was much godlessness on the earth and they made their ways desolate.
> Shemihazah taught spells and the cutting of roots.
> Hermani taught sorcery for the loosing of spells and magic and skill.
> Baraqel taught the signs of the lightning flashes.
> Kokabel taught the signs of the stars.
> Ziqel taught the signs of the shooting stars.
> Arteqoph taught the signs of the earth.
> Shamsiel taught the signs of the sun.
> Sahiel taught the signs of the moon.
> And they all began to reveal mysteries to their wives and to their children.
> (And) as men were perishing, the cry went up to heaven.
> (1 En. 8:1–4)[35]

In this account, Asael teaches metallurgical arts, and then other watchers add to the list of illicit subjects taught: pharmacology, magical skills, and divination from astral and other heavenly entities. Here there is also a reference to the reality of the connection between war and sexual conquest or violence. The watchers, or Asael specifically, teach men

33. Ibid.

34. Loader, *Enoch, Levi, and Jubilees on Sexuality*, 19.

35. *1 Enoch: A New Translation*, 25–26.

metalworking for both making weapons of war and for making means of beautification. Both war and physical attraction are conditions under which transgressions related to sexuality occur. Men learn some of the skills directly from the angels and women receive the products of those forbidden skills. Sin results. The now beautifully adorned women lead the angels astray, and humans engage in "godlessness" amongst themselves, which may also include adultery and fornication.

After the description of the forbidden skills taught to men and the negative outcomes of that teaching, the texts gives a list of various watchers and the specific skills they teach, now to women and their offspring. To summarize the record of skills taught in chapter 8, in this passage the angels transmit the knowledge of metalworking for weaponry, metalworking for adornment of the body, cosmetic beautification of the body, dyes, precious stones, alchemy, spell-binding, cutting of roots, the loosing of spells, and cosmologically related augury.

A third account of the problematic interaction of angels and women is found in *1 En.* 9:6–10. This account is a retelling by archangels Michael, Sariel, Raphael, and Gabriel of what has happened, their summary of the disastrous interaction between the watchers and humans. Verses 6–8 describe the combination of the illicit transmission of knowledge and the sexual interaction between angels and women:

> You see what Asael has done,
> who has taught all iniquity on earth,
> and has revealed the eternal mysteries that are in heaven,
> which the sons of men were striving to learn.
> And (what) Shemihazah (has done) to whom you gave
> authority to rule over them who are with him.
> They have gone in to the daughters of the men of the earth,
> and they have lain with them, and have defiled
> themselves with the women.
> And they have revealed to them all sins, and have taught
> them to make hate-inducing charms.[36]

As the righteous archangels recapitulate the events thus far, in their summary, also, forbidden knowledge comes to the fore. In the two verses which follow this passage, the disastrous results of both the illicit teaching and deviant sexual mixing of angelic and human are reported once again: the birth of the giants, sin ("the whole earth is filled with

36. Ibid., 26–27.

iniquity," *1 En.* 9:9),[37] and the outcry to heaven of the spirits of the souls of those who have died as a result of the violence on the earth.

In all three accounts, then, there is mention of two elements: the teaching of forbidden knowledge and sexual interaction. The knowledge given in each case differs, as do the recipients. In chapter 7 the angels teach their wives. In chapter 8 both men and women are the recipients. In chapter 9, men learn the eternal mysteries, and women learn "all sins" (9:8).[38] Table I brings together all three chapters, showing subjects taught, by whom, to whom, and the passage in which the illicit art is referenced.

Table I: Summary of Illicit Pedagogy in *1 Enoch*

Knowledge	Teacher	Recipient	Reference
Sorcery, spells, cutting of roots and plants	Watchers	Watchers' wives	7:1cd
Metalworking for making weaponry [materials of war: attack and defense]	Asael	Men	8:1a
Metalwork for the adornment of women [bracelets, decorations]; Cosmetic adornment; precious stones and dyes	Asael	Men [who use them for themselves and women, "their daughters"]	8:1b–2
Incantation and the cutting of roots	Shemihazah	Watchers' wives	8:3a
The undoing of spells, magic, and skills	Hermani	Watchers' wives	8:3b
Cosmological or heavenly augury Astrological skills	Baraqel, Kokabel, Ziqel, Arteqoph, Shamsiel, Sahriel	Watchers' wives	8:3c–h

37. Ibid., 27.
38. Ibid.

(Summary of the subjects taught) iniquity and eternal heavenly secrets	Asael	Humans ("the sons of men")	9:6
(Summary) All sins	Shemihazah and the Watchers	Women	9:8

Reed provides this summary of the knowledge taught: "[1] cultural arts connected to metalworking and ornamentation (8:1–2), [2] magical skills such as sorcery and pharmacology (7:1 cd; 8:3ab), and [3] divination from cosmological phenomena (8:3c–g)."[39] Devorah Dimant suggests that the subjects taught reflect the sins forbidden by the Noachic laws—shedding blood, illicit sexual intercourse, and idolatry—which were binding for all people, and were behind the later rabbinic interpretation of such laws.[40] I will return in the section on Matthew's genealogy to the subjects taught. For now I note that with every skill taught the result is linked in *1 Enoch* to destruction, oppression, pain, and crying out by the earth and humanity for relief.

The summary of the nature of deceit in these passages is this: angels abandon their heavenly station and duties in order to have sexual relations with women, although the angels know this to be a great sin. Their need to swear an oath and bind themselves together with a curse heightens the sense that the watchers are disobedient as a group. This is not the action of one wayward angel. This is rebellion, which has disastrous consequences for the entire created order. The watchers also have a teaching function. They instruct men in skills that lead humans into warfare and godlessness. Some skills lead to sexual sins, but there is no sexual liaison between men and their angelic teachers first. Women are likewise taught skills, but the teaching of women is connected with sexual relations. In the case of women, "knowing" in the sexual sense and "knowing" in the sense of knowledge of skills and arts are related.

What Are the Consequences?

The consequences of the illicit unions between watchers and women and the ensuing illicit pedagogy are several. They include the destructive behavior of the monstrous offspring, the sinful behavior of the

39. Reed, *Fallen Angels*, 37.
40. Dimant, "1 Enoch 6–11," 227–28.

humans now using the illicit arts, and the punishment of the various parties involved. The monstrous offspring from the unions of watchers and women bring death and destruction. The offspring are violent enemies of humankind. Their insatiable appetites and violent behavior bring death to humans and other living beings (*1 En.* 7:3–5). Adding to the violence and sin on the earth are humans who are now skilled in arts perceived as dangerous: skills for war-making, seduction, sorcery, and astrology. As the archangels state to the Lord of the Ages in *1 En.* 9:9, "the whole earth is full of iniquity."[41] The archangels plead that something be done.

Their plea is answered by the commissioning of the archangels to punish the watchers, destroy the giants, prepare for the flood, and renew the earth. First, Sariel is commissioned to inform Noah about the coming deluge and about Noah's selection as the seed from which humanity will have hope of survival for coming generations (*1 En.* 10:1–3).[42] Next Raphael is commissioned to punish Asael, by binding him and holding him prisoner in a dark hole in the earth until the final judgment when he will be "led away to the burning conflagration" (*1 En.* 10:4–6).[43] Gabriel is commissioned to destroy the giants. Their destruction, although set in motion by Gabriel, will actually come by their own hands, as the archangel is to send them "against one another in a war of destruction" (*1 En.* 10:9).[44] Michael is sent to subject Shemihazah and his associates to a similar fate to that which Asael received: they are to be bound for seventy generations, until the day of their judgment when they, too, will be imprisoned in a fiery abyss (*1 En.* 10:11–15). Finally Michael receives the commission to restore the earth, removing all impurities, defilement, godlessness, and lawlessness (*1 En.* 10:16–22). This restoration is a future event that will take place at the final time of judgment.

The watchers, however, do not simply submit to their fate. They ask Enoch to make petition for them to God to release them from their punishment. In *1 Enoch* 15 God responds to the petition, and reveals one more detail about the offspring of the wayward angels and women:

41. *1 Enoch: A New Translation,* 27.

42. On Noah traditions in *1 Enoch* see Peters, *Noah Traditions.*

43. *1 Enoch: A New Translation,* 28.
   On the binding and imprisoning of Asael and parallel traditions, see Nickelsburg, *1 Enoch 1,* 191–93; 221–22.

44. *1 Enoch: A New Translation,* 29.

even after the death of the giants, their spirits will continue to harm humans (*1 En.* 15:9, 10–11, 16:1) and will be called "evil spirits" (*1 En.* 15:9). The giants will be destroyed, but their spirits will plague humankind until "the great judgment" (*1 En.* 16:1). The evil spirits "lead astray, do violence, make desolate, and attack and wrestle and hurl upon the earth and cause illnesses" (*1 En.* 15:11).[45] According to *1 En.* 19:1, they also "bring destruction on men and lead them astray to sacrifice to demons as to gods."[46] Violence, desolation, physical pain, illness, and idolatry are all attributable to the work of the evil spirits. Such devastating outcomes are the legacy of the giants, and will remain potent until the great judgment.

Adding the ongoing work of the evil spirits to the transgressions of the watchers results in the following evil realities for human life according to the Enochic template: illicit sexual relations (through humanity's knowledge of illicit arts involving adornment), bloodshed and violence (through illicit arts involving weapons and warfare), idolatry, pain, and sickness (through the ongoing work of the evil spirits of the giants).

The consequences of the mixing of heavenly and earthly are clearly dire for the watchers, their leaders, the monstrous offspring, those who suffer through arts and skills taught by the watchers, and all who will be damaged by the evil spirits. God acts to restrain watchers and destroy giants, but humans will continue to suffer terrible consequences.

However, one significant group is missing from this summary. What happens to the women most directly involved in the illicit sexual relations and pedagogy?

Not much is said about the women who have illicit sexual relations with fallen angels and receive their illicit teachings. Even what happens to the watchers' wives is at most summed up in a single line, which is now obscure and the subject of scholarly debate. According

---

45. Ibid., 37.
46. Ibid., 39.

to *1 En.* 19:2, the women become "sirens," [47] "peaceful,"[48] or perhaps merely are "brought to an end." [49] The watchers' wives, it seems, despite their pivotal role in the introduction of evil into the world, do not merit much additional comment as the account of the watchers is brought to its conclusion.

47. See Bautch, "Angels' 'Wives,'" 766–80. In the Greek manuscript tradition Panopolitanus, the wives of the fallen angels become sirens. Sirens were known for seducing sailors and leading them to their demise by means of irresistible song in Homer. Later they were connected with mourning, singing dirges for the dead, and perhaps symbolized the souls of the dead (Ibid., 770). Commenting on *1 En.* 96:2, another uncertain text that may mention the weeping of sirens, Nickelsburg notes that the sirens' lament parallels Enoch's role in *1 En.* 95:1, "O that my eyes were a fountain of water, that I might weep over you; I would pour out my tears as a cloud of water, and I would rest from the grief of my heart." (Nickelsburg, *1 Enoch 1*, 465). However, when commenting directly on *1 En.* 19:2, Nickelsburg argues that the women turning into sirens is a continuation of their role of seduction, just as they seduced the watchers, and that "Like their angel husbands, the daughters of men continue to have an evil influence" (Ibid., 288). Neither Bautch nor Nickelsburg points out that in the *Odyssey*, it is not just the sirens' beautiful voices that the sailors find irresistible; the sirens promise wisdom to those who give into their call: "Never has any sailor passed our shores in his black craft until he has heard the honeyed voices pouring from our lips, and once he hears to his heart's content sails on, a wiser man." Homer, *The Odyssey*, 12:202–4. In Homer's version, the sirens lure men and offer them wisdom. If there is a connection between watchers' wives and sirens, their relationship to knowledge and seduction has been reversed: watchers passed illicit knowledge to their wives. Sirens promise wisdom to passing sailors. The relationship between knowledge and seduction is also clearer in the *Odyssey* than in *1 Enoch*: knowledge is part of the seduction. In *1 Enoch* the pedagogy is given after the seduction.

48. In Ethiopian manuscripts the wives of the angels become peaceful (Nickelsburg, *1 Enoch*, 277). Perhaps the translation in the Ethiopian manuscripts comes from the similarity in sound between εἰρηναῖαι (peaceful) and the word found in Greek manuscripts, σειρῆνας (sirens). The Ethiopian translator may have heard εἰρηναῖαι rather than σειρῆνας and translated accordingly. Bautch claims that the Ethiopian reading, "peaceful," may be supported by the view that it gives a more positive outcome for the women, and in *1 Enoch* 6 the women seem to be exonerated from their role in the angels-human wives debacle. It is the angels' lust alone that caused this illicit mixing of angelic and earthly. Bautch, "Angels' 'Wives,'" 772. However, the interpretation that to be peaceful is necessarily more positive than to be one who laments depends on how one values the role of lamenting. To be peaceful may be better for the wives themselves. It may be a more pleasant idea to us. However, if the wives' role is to lament for humanity, they get to perform a useful and appropriate service for humankind, rather than merely enjoying a little peace and quiet. That is, they may have roles as agents in something useful for humanity, rather than slipping back into an, albeit calm, oblivion.

49. That is, "the wives are simply dispatched." Bautch argues that this possibility is most fitting given that, in her estimation, the wives are just not that important in the account of the watchers. Ibid., 778.

However, according to the stories of the women in the genealogy of Matthew, the women, who in the Enochic story received the legacies of the watchers' fall, are very important.

3

Transgression Reassessed

Questionable Means, Suspicious Motherhood, Righteous Results: Jesus' Great-Grandmothers in Matthew, Foreshadowing Redemption

In Chapter 3 I examine how the women named by the evangelist in the genealogy (Matt 1:1–17) function to foreshadow the reversal of the transgression introduced by the watchers in the Enochic typology of the origins of evil. By examining the women in terms of their foreshadowing function, I also provide an answer to the vexing question of why Matthew includes these four women in his genealogy of Jesus.

Transgression looms large in the stories from the now canonical Hebrew scriptures of the four women included in Matthew's genealogy (Matt 1:1–17): Tamar, Rahab, Ruth, and the wife of Uriah as she is called in Matthew, known from the Hebrew scriptures as Bathsheba. Aspects of the watchers' transgression and its consequences are present in the stories of each of the women named as an ancestor of Jesus. First, each woman makes use of the illicit skills and arts taught by the fallen angels in the Enochic tradition. Each of the women named in the genealogy participates in sexual activity considered suspicious at best and unrighteous at worst. Each of their stories involves use of the arts of seduction or beautification. Two of the stories, the story of Rahab and the story of the "wife of Uriah," involve both the arts of beautification and the arts of war. Each of their stories, then, includes the combination seen in the watchers' descent myth: "knowing" as sexual activity and "knowing" as understanding illicit arts. Second, each of the stories involves echoes[1] of additional elements of the Enochic template. These elements include the following: interaction with angels, sometimes with hints of sexual activity, questions about the paternity of the women's offspring, and questions about the unusual nature of their offspring.

Now, in the case of the use of the illicit arts, perhaps the reader is to think that this is just exactly what one should expect from any group of women. After all, the story from *1 Enoch* functions aetiologically, explaining where women obtained their abilities to use cosmetics, jewelry, perfumes, and the like, in the first place. But, according to the aetiology, these are not ambivalent skills. The use of these skills, along with the voracious appetites of the gigantic offspring of the rebellious angels and women, are responsible for the spread of evil, immorality, destruction, and death throughout the whole created order. The consequences of the introduction of the forbidden skills amongst humans, and women in particular, are entirely bad. And while the archangels are able to restrain the perpetrators of the illicit pedagogy, the episode ends with the readers' knowledge that the evil spirits of the giants still roam the land and, just look around—imagine the narrator telling us— humans still use the forbidden skills and arts to destructive and immoral ends. In fact, it is the continuing use of those skills and the immoral results that patristic writers made use of in their appeals to *1 Enoch*. For example, Clement uses the example of the watchers to appeal to men that they not be enticed by women's beauty and fall like the rebel angels

1. Steve Moyise provides this summary of how scholars have defined references to texts within later texts, specifically references to the Hebrew Bible in the New Testament: "generally a quotation involves a self-conscious break from the author's style to introduce words from another context . . . An allusion is usually woven into the text rather than 'quoted', . . . Naturally, there is considerable debate as to how much verbal agreement is necessary to establish the presence of an allusion. An echo is a faint trace of a text and might be quite unconscious, emerging from minds soaked in the scriptural heritage of Israel" (Moyise, "Intertextuality and Biblical Studies," 419). I refer to "echoes" in this book, but wish to expand beyond Moyise's definition to include not just texts, but also traditions, especially since the textual history of the Enochic traditions is complex. I am arguing that a tradition that appears in one text may be echoed in another, rather than that one text necessarily contains the echo of a particular text. Allusions to texts may, in fact, be present in the material with which I am dealing. However, following Moyise's observation about debates over "how much verbal agreement is necessary to establish the presence of an allusion," I will make the more cautious claim that echoes of Enochic themes, rather than allusions, are detectable in Matthew's Gospel.

did.[2] Both Tertullian and Cyprian make use of the story of the watchers' illicit pedagogy in their appeal to Christian women to cease using cosmetics and other means of beautification which came from such a corrupted source.[3]

I suggest in this section that it is not the Gospel readers' ability to point to the illicit sexual encounters or the ongoing use of the illicit instruction which is of importance to Matthew. Rather, it is the consequences of all that illicit "knowing"—sexual and skillful—that are under scrutiny in Matthew's naming of the four great grandmothers of Jesus in his genealogy. In the Enochic story, the consequences are thoroughly negative: death, destruction, and mayhem. But in the stories of Matthew's four women—Tamar, Rahab, Ruth, and the wife of Uriah—the consequences of their knowing through sexual activity and their use of the forbidden arts are life, lawfulness, and salvation. The stories of each of the four women shows these women engaging in questionable sexual activity and use the fruits of illicit pedagogy not only to their own advantage, but to the wholesome advantage of their kith and kin as well.

Chapter 3 will proceed in this way: first, I review briefly how others have attempted to solve the puzzle of Matthew's unusual inclusion of women in his genealogy. I then examine each woman's story, looking at both the Hebrew Bible narratives and other non-canonical traditions that may have been available to Matthew's audience, and see how the mention of each woman suggests the reversal of the consequences of the watchers' transgression.

2. See Clement, *Paedagogus* 3.2; The instructor against embellishing the body, "the mind is carried away by pleasure; and the unsullied principle of reason, when not instructed by the Word, slides down into licentiousness, and gets a fall as the due reward of its transgression. An example of this are the angels, who renounced the beauty of God for a beauty which fades, and so fell from heaven to earth" (*ANF* 2:274).

3. See Tertullian, *On the Apparel of Women* 1.2. (*ANF* 4:15); Tertullian. *Disciplinary, Moral and Ascetical Works*, 118–21. In *On the Veiling of Virgins* 3.7, Tertullian argues that virgins should be veiled on the basis of the illicit sexual relations between the fallen angels and women. He reasons that the women whom the angels desired and consequently married must have been virgins. Therefore, virgins should be veiled (*ANF* 4:32); Cyprian, *De Habitu Virginum* 14. Cyprian, *Treatises*, 43–44.

Why These Women?

Matthew's unusual inclusion of four women from the Hebrew Bible in his genealogy[4] of Jesus has generated many explanations for the inclusion. These explanations generally are based on one of four theological themes that would link the women with Matthew's portrayal of Jesus: (1) the women were all Gentiles, and their inclusion shows that Gentiles would be included in the salvation offered by Jesus; (2) the women were all sinners, and their inclusion shows that Jesus would be the savior of sinners; (3) the women engaged in questionable sexual relationships with men, and their inclusion sheds light on the unusual birth circumstances of Jesus; (4) the women were all part of God's unfolding plan of salvation in history. I will briefly summarize each of these four explanations and then state how my thesis differs from these solutions already offered.

First, the suggestion has been made that all the women were Gentiles, or associated with Gentiles, and therefore foreshadow God's inclusion of Gentiles as well as Jews in God's salvific activity in Jesus.[5] This view has been challenged on the basis that only Ruth and Rahab are clearly identified in the Hebrew Bible as Gentiles.[6] Tamar might also

---

4. Women are not usually included in biblical genealogies except in some cases in which the mention of them helps to distinguish among different groups with the same patriarchal figure, or, in a couple of examples in which there was something extraordinary about them. For example, Gen 16:15; 21:1–5; 25:1–6 names the wives and concubine of Abraham and the sons born to them; 22:20–24 names the wife and concubine of Abraham's brother Nahor and their sons; 1 Chr 2:18–20; 46–49 names Caleb's concubines and their sons. Johnson thinks that Aaron's wife is named in Exod 6:23 because she was a Judahite, daughter of Amminadab and sister of Nahshon, head of the tribe during the exodus (Johnson, *The Purpose of the Biblical Genealogies*, 153 n. 2). Raymond Brown notes that 1 Chr 3:1–10 lists David's wives, including Bathsheba, in its list of generations (Brown, *The Birth of the Messiah*, 71 n. 21).

5. This suggestion is supported by Bauckham, "Tamar's Ancestry," 313–29; Gundry, *Matthew*, 14–15; Lohmeyer, *Das Evangelium des Matthäus*, 5; Schweizer, *The Good News according to Matthew*, 25; Hare, *Matthew*, 6; Luz, *Matthew 1–7*, 85, though "in a spirit of a degree of uncertainty"; and Senior, *Matthew*, 38.

6. Ruth, in Ruth 1:4, is identified as one of the Moabite wives of Naomi's sons. She is called "Ruth the Moabite" in Ruth 1:22; 2:21; 4:5, 10, and "the Moabite" in 1:6. Rahab, in Josh 2:1, is identified as a prostitute living in Jericho. Her verbal interaction with the Israelite spies clearly identifies her as a Canaanite who professes faith in the God of Israel, and who needs Israelite protection when the Israelites eventually take over her people's land (see Joshua 2).

have been a Gentile since her story is set in Canaan, although her ancestry is not clearly disclosed in the Hebrew Bible. When Judah "took a wife for Er his firstborn" (Gen 38:6) while Judah and his family are living in Canaan, it makes sense that the wife would be a Canaanite.[7] However, two early traditions about Tamar, *Testament of Judah* 10:1–2, 6 and *Jubilees* 41:1–7, contrast Tamar with Judah's Canaanite wife and identify Tamar as a daughter of Aram from the family of Nahor, Abraham's brother and son of Abraham's father Terah. Tamar therefore secures the racial purity of Judah that is important to the author of these texts.[8] Technically, however, as the descendant of Nahor rather than Abraham, Tamar would be as Gentile as Sarah, Rebekah, Leah, and Rachel, who are not named in Matthew's genealogy. Targum Pseudo-Jonathan (Gen 38:6), *Gen. Rab.* 85:10, and *Num. Rab.* 13:4, texts much later than Matthew's Gospel,[9] record the tradition that Tamar was the daughter of Shem-Melchizedek, "the only worshipper of the true God, apart from the family of Abraham, who could then have been found in Canaan."[10] Arguing for Tamar's identity as a Gentile and the equivalent of a Canaanite, Philo held that she was a woman from Palestinian Syria.[11] So Tamar, along with Ruth and Rahab, could have been consid-

7. Below, I will examine the identification of Tamar as a קדשה, sometimes translated as "temple prostitute," as in the NRSV and NASB. The role of the קדשה is disputed, but its use as a term describing Tamar seems to indicate her identity as a Canaanite since the term was used to describe Canaanite practices abhorrent to the Israelites. See, e.g., Deut 23:18; 1 Kgs 14:24; 15:12; 22:47; 2 Kgs 23:7; Hos 4:14; Job 36:14.

8. Bauckham, "Tamar's Ancestry," 318.

9. Michael Maher believes that *Targum Pseudo-Jonathan* did not reach its final form until the seventh or eighth century CE, although it certainly contains many ancient traditions. Maher, *Targum Pseudo-Jonathan: Genesis*, 11–12. Roger Le Déaut provides a summary of ancient traditions contained within *Ps.-J.* in *Introduction à la Littérature Targumique*, 92–96. Albeck suggests that *Gen. Rab.* took its basic documentary shape in the late fourth and early fifth centuries CE, although it contains traditions from many centuries earlier. C. Albeck, מבוא לבראשית רבא [Introduction to *Genesis Rabba*]. In vol. 3 of *Midraš Berešit Rabba*, 1–138; 93–96. Strack and Stemberger date *Gen. Rab.* to the first half of the fifth century CE. Strack and Stemberger, *Introduction to the Talmud and Midrash*, 279. The final form of *Num. Rab.* is much later still. Strack and Stemberger state that although there was an earlier, shorter version, the version of *Num. Rab.* that we now know is a compilation from and expansion upon a variety of halakhic and haggadic works, and cannot be dated before the twelfth century CE. Strack and Stemberger, 311.

10. Bauckham, "Tamar's Ancestry," 319.

11. Philo, *Virt.* 40.220–22 (*Colson*, LCL); Bauckham, 320.

ered a Gentile. In the case of Bathsheba, her (first) husband, Uriah the Hittite, is a Gentile, but her own ethnic identity is not disclosed. So it is correct that Gentiles are included in Jesus' family tree, and the evangelist will portray Jesus' mission as extending to "all nations" (Matt 28:19 NRSV). However, the claim that all four women are included because they are Gentiles who foreshadow the inclusion of Gentiles amongst the followers of Jesus does not bear up under scrutiny: it is not certain that Matthew would have regarded all four to be Gentiles. Even if it could be shown conclusively that Matthew regarded all four as Gentiles, their Gentile identity would not negate my theory that the Enochic watchers' template is behind Matthew's naming of these four women in his genealogy. The women's connection with themes from the watchers' template does not depend on their identity as Gentiles or Jews.

A second suggestion is that the women named in the genealogy were all sinners and their inclusion shows that Matthew intends to portray Jesus as the savior of sinners.[12] These women provide examples of the very kind of people Jesus will save. As the angel explains to Joseph in Matthew 1:21, "She will bear a son, and you are to name him Jesus, for he will save his people from their sins" (NRSV). This explanation has come under attack by many scholars,[13] primarily because it depends on the reader's judgment that the woman portrayed is sinful, rather than how the woman is actually regarded within the story that records her actions or the tradition that remembers her actions. Thus, although some see the women as examples of how God can exalt even those of "disreputable origin to positions of the highest honor," Schweizer comments, "Jewish tradition lauds the 'righteousness' of Tamar (Gen 38:26), the actions of Rahab (cf. also Heb 11:31; Jas 2:25), and Ruth as ancestor of the Messiah; and in the case of Bathsheba, only David is ever blamed."[14] Jesus' function as savior of sinners is a concern of Matthew's

12. This interpretation is offered by Plummer, *An Exegetical Commentary*, 2–3; Lohmeyer, *Das Evangelium des Matthäus*, 5; Robinson, *The Gospel of Matthew*, 3; Rienecker, *Das Evangelium des Matthäus*, 15; and Morris, *The Gospel according to Matthew*, 23. See also Parambi, *The Discipleship of the Women*, 73; and Weren, "The Five Women in Matthew's Genealogy," 288.

13. For example, Beare, *Gospel according to Matthew*, 64; Davies and Allison, *Matthew*, 5; and Luz, *Matthew 1–7*, 83–84.

14. Schweizer, *The Good News according to Matthew*, 25.

Gospel, but this does not provide a satisfactory answer to the riddle of why the women are included.

A third suggestion is a variation on the previous suggestion; it uses the argument that the women engage in activity that could be considered sinful. However, this suggestion focuses on the scandalous sexual behavior of the women, and holds that Matthew uses these women to foreshadow the scandalous situation of the fifth woman named in Jesus' family, Mary, who is pregnant but not yet married to Joseph, her betrothed.[15] That is, according to this suggestion, it is not that the women were regarded as sinful generally, but rather that their scandalous sexual behavior nevertheless results in the vindication of the women and good for the people of Israel. Some scholars specify that Matthew includes these women with their questionable sexual activities as part of his polemic against "the Jewish accusation that Jesus was the illegitimate son of Mary."[16] Jesus' family tree included several people whose birth stories or behavior were marked by scandal and nonetheless God had used them to bring about good ends for the Israelite people; God was doing something similar through Mary, despite what the neighbors might think.

However, while scandalous sexual behavior or efforts to avoid suspicions of such behavior do mark all the women's stories, my criticism of this suggestion is that it falls short in a significant way: Mary's pregnancy by the Holy Spirit does not stand in easy succession with the four earlier women, or any women named in the Hebrew Bible whose pregnancy was suspect. The evangelist wants to make the point that not only is there a good explanation for Mary's pregnancy, but her pregnancy oc-

---

15. This suggestion is supported by Freed, *Stories of Jesus' Birth*, 32–52; D'Angelo, "(Re)Presentations," 177; Johnson, *Purpose*, 158; Corley, *Public Women Private Meals*, 151–52. Corley argues that it is not only concern with Mary's reputation that occupies Matthew, but also the reputation of Jesus' followers as promiscuous sinners that prompts the evangelist to highlight the four great-grandmothers as well as Mary with their suspect reputations. Corley, *Public Women Private Meals*, 151–52.

16. Freed, *Stories of Jesus' Birth*, 32. See also pp. 46 and 51; Schaberg, *Illegitimacy of Jesus*, 20–34; and Beare, *The Earliest Records*, 30. Johnson believes that the women are included because of polemics, but not polemics about the virgin birth. Rather, Johnson thinks that Matthew includes the women because of polemics "within Judaism itself" in regards to the ancestry of David, that is, whether a Davidic or Levitical Messiah should be expected. Matthew responds to the argument by including the four women to show that Jesus fulfills the Pharisaic expectations of a Davidic Messiah. Johnson, *Purpose*, 177–78.

curs in a way that marries the watchers myth with a righteous outcome rather than a disastrous outcome. In other words, Joseph's suspicion that Mary's pregnancy is born of unrighteous behavior is wrong, but not in the way one would expect. According to the Enochic template, it actually is horribly wrong for a human woman to beget a child with a celestial being. However, according to Matthew, this is exactly what happens. Mary becomes pregnant by the Holy Spirit and gives birth to Jesus. But in Matthew the conception of Jesus happens without sexual intercourse and happens according to God's purposes rather than the machinations of the watchers. Much more will be said about this subject in chapter 4 of this book.

A last and more general attempt to explain the presence of the women in Matthew's genealogy of Jesus also connects the four named women with Mary, and holds that all five of the women are instrumental as agents of God's providence in bringing about the future God desires, often by means of "alternative pathways."[17] Raymond Brown uses rabbinic sources that connect each of the four Hebrew Bible women with God's providence or Holy Spirit.[18] Wim Weren argues that each of the women plays a pivotal role in Israel's history, a history that would otherwise have been derailed had not the woman in each case acted wisely and creatively on behalf of the Israelite people. In each case their creativity has something to do with provisions in the law, or their status in the eyes of the law.[19] Irene Nowell makes the intriguing suggestion that Matthew includes the four Israelite women in order to bring to mind all the women in the ancestry line of Jesus.[20] That is, the four women named do not stand out from the rest of the women Matthew could have included; they represent all of them. In her argument, then, Nowell describes all of the women who are ancestors of Jesus. Nowell's summary includes aspects listed in the other suggestions, including that amongst Jesus' ancestors there are women who are "Sinners, Foreigners, and [who have] Pregnancy/Childbirth Issues."[21] However, Nowell fo-

17. Weren, "Five Women," 290.

18. Brown, *Birth*, 62–64. Freed also cites these rabbinic stories in order to link Hebrew women with Mary and as part of his thesis that Matthew is trying to refute the attack of illegitimacy. See Freed, *Stories of Jesus' Birth*, 37–40, 51.

19. Weren, "Five Women," 301–5.

20. Nowell, "Jesus' Great-Grandmothers," 1–15.

21. Ibid., 10.

cuses in her summary of the women on their roles as "Guarantors of the Future."[22] Nowell summarizes the women who are ancestors of Jesus, including those unnamed in the genealogy and Mary as "women who have endured discrimination and false judgment, who have suffered through difficult pregnancies and childbirth, and who know how to use devious means to achieve their purposes. These women are courageous, hospitable, and creative, and they have risked life and reputation to ensure our future."[23]

Thus Brown, Weren, and Nowell are representative of scholars who stress the connection of the four great-grandmothers of Jesus with Mary his mother and see all five women as courageous, creative vehicles for God's plans for salvation.

This interpretation does not go far enough in showing the specific nature of the surprising creativity involved in the women's activities. As will be shown below, the women's actions are not merely creative; they all include aspects of the Enochic template. To be sure, the women use what may be described as "alternative pathways," but none of these scholars note the distinctive Enochic characteristics of their actions.

Having summarized the four prevalent explanations for Matthew's unusual inclusion of four women amongst the ancestors of Jesus and Jesus' immediate family, I now remind the reader of my thesis of why Matthew includes the four women in the genealogy. Matthew names these four women as part of Jesus' genealogy because they foreshadow the overturning of the transgression of the watchers, the Enochic template for the origins of evil in the world. The women engage in, or are suspected of, transgression themselves by illicit or suspect sexual relations; they make use of the illicit arts taught by the watchers; they are associated with traditions in which they interact with celestial beings; and they give birth to offspring in which paternity is questioned or who have unusual or exceptional attributes. And yet, unlike in the watchers' descent narrative and its horrific consequences, these women bring about righteous results. The argument that the women all have in common sexual scandal as part of their stories is correct. However, the nature of their scandalous and in the end helpful behavior corresponds with aspects of the watchers' narrative. To say that their stories are scan-

22. Ibid., 11.
23. Ibid., 15.

dalous is only the half of it: their stories actually flout the watchers' narrative, showing that the redemption of the world can be brought about by the use of the very arts originally forbidden and destructive. It is the combination of transgression, scandalous sexual interaction, and the illicit arts that brings all four women's stories together. That other elements of the Enochic template are present in their stories also supports my claim that the Enochic template stands behind Matthew's mention of these four women. Thus, for example, Bathsheba is referred to as "the wife of Uriah the Hittite," even though the child by which she is actually included in the genealogy is not fathered by Uriah. This mention of Uriah serves to remind the reader of the combination of the illicit arts of war and the illicit arts of attraction which appears in the Enochic template.[24] Matthew uses these women and the stories recalled by their names to show that God was already foreshadowing the full redemption that would come in Jesus' unusual birth circumstances in these women in the genealogy. The beginnings of redemption were underway, and God would use the very things that had brought destruction to set that redemption underway.

I turn now to a discussion of each of the women named in Matthew's genealogy.

Tamar: Always Save Your Receipts

Tamar appears in Matthew's genealogy in Matt 1:3, the first of the women to be mentioned. I will focus on transgression as a theme in Tamar's story in Genesis 38, and note how she makes use of the illicit pedagogy to reach her goal of becoming a mother: the fact, after all, which earns her a place in the genealogy. Transgression in Tamar's story hinges on her deception of Judah. Her actions lead Judah to think that Tamar has transgressed the law. In actuality, she has used the illicit arts to deceive Judah into participating with her in a scandalous sexual encounter. Her transgression of societal norms results in good for herself and for Judah as well. Although Tamar is not the first person named in the genealogy to be involved in deception, she is the first, because she is the first woman, to make use of the illicit arts, and to bring good results from

24. Much more on this and other elements of the Enochic template and how they appear in the stories of the women in Matthew's genealogy will appear below.

their use. In this section, I examine Tamar's deception of Judah and transgression of societal norms and describe how her story connects with additional themes in the Enochic typology.

Tamar is not alone among the ancestors of Jesus in engaging in deception. Each of the ancestors mentioned in the Matthean genealogy, up through and including Tamar, is involved in some deceptive scheme involving identity. Abraham (Matt 1:2) passes his wife Sarah off as his sister, not just once, but twice, for his own protection or advantage (Gen 12:10–20 and 20:1–18). Isaac (Matt 1:2) does the same, passing his wife Rebekah off as his sister in order to protect himself (Gen 26:6–16). Isaac is the victim of deception as his wife Rebekah hatches a scheme to have Isaac give his blessing to her favorite son Jacob (Gen 27:1–45), rather than the first-born, and Isaac's favorite, Esau. Third in the genealogy is Jacob (Matt 1:2), who is deceived by his father-in-law Laban. On what was to be Jacob's wedding night with Rachel, Laban substitutes his older daughter Leah (Gen 29:21–26). Jacob works an additional seven years to obtain marriage with Rachel (Gen 29:28). Although Jacob loves Rachel more than Leah (29:30), it is Leah's son Judah who is mentioned in the genealogy. Certainly, already in these generations mentioned, there is plenty of deception driving the drama, indeed the outcome, of the family line. But Tamar is the first woman mentioned in Matthew, and the first woman in the genealogy, including those implied but not named, to be the agent, object, and beneficiary of deception.

Tamar's story is found in Genesis 38. She is also mentioned by name in Ruth 4:12 and 1 Chr 2:4, in each case as part of a genealogy. Her begetting of children by Judah is also referred to in Gen 49:9–12, as part of Jacob's testament to his sons. Judah marries a Canaanite woman, and with her has three sons, Er, Onan, and Shelah. Judah takes Tamar as a wife for Er, the eldest, but he "was wicked in the sight of the Lord" (NRSV) and God kills him, leaving Tamar childless. Following Levirate custom,[25] Onan is to beget a child for Er by Tamar, but he refuses. His refusal is duplicitous: he gives the appearance that he will carry out his duty, but he prevents conception by withdrawing from her. God kills Onan as well, and Tamar remains childless. Judah promises his third son, Shelah, to Tamar, but Judah tells Tamar she must wait until Shelah

25. For more on levirate marriage, see Pressler, *View of Women*, 63–74; Marsman, *Women in Ugarit and Israel*, 312–18; Coats, "Widow's Rights," 463; and Davies, "Inheritance Rights," 138–44.

is of age before he will be given to her. However, the narrator tells us that Judah is nervous that this third son also will die while married to Tamar and that Judah has no intention of following through on his duty as a father-in-law. Judah does not want to lose Shelah as well to this dangerous daughter-in-law. Tamar returns to her father's house as a widow and waits.

Time passes, Judah does not make good on his word, and Tamar decides to take matters into her own hands. She sees her opportunity when Judah goes up to Timnah to shear his sheep. Tamar takes off her widow's garments and puts on a veil. She sits on the road to Timnah and when Judah sees her wrapped in a veil, he does not know it is Tamar, but thinks instead that the woman before him is a prostitute. He propositions her. She asks for payment. He offers a kid from his flock. She asks for a pledge until the kid can be delivered. At this point Judah is almost passive in the story. He asks her what pledge she would like, and she asks for his signet, cord, and staff—all things which would readily identify him as their owner.[26] Judah is happy to hand over these markers of his identity to someone whose identity is unknown to him. He sees her only as someone who offers a service he desires. He does not realize it is his service to her that is the goal in this transaction and it is Tamar who is getting her way. Judah has intercourse with Tamar, and she conceives. Tamar leaves, puts off her veil and puts back on her widow's garment, and resumes her identity as widow. Judah has been twice deceived by Tamar: she was no prostitute and she wanted no payment; she wanted the child that he was obliged to give her by his son. For her double deception of Judah she is rewarded by pregnancy with twins.

Later in Genesis, as part of his testament the patriarch Jacob engages in wordplay about Judah's encounter with Tamar. Jacob remarks,

> The scepter shall not depart from Judah,
> nor the ruler's staff from between his feet, [ומחקק מבין רגליו]
> until tribute comes to him; [עד כי־יבא שילה]
> and the obedience of the peoples is his. (Gen 49:10)[27]

26. Robert Alter calls these the equivalent of his driver's license and credit cards, symbols of his patriarchal authority, in *Genesis*, 221; and in *Art of Biblical Narrative*, 8–9.

27. NRSV; the Hebrew follows the *BHS*.

Calum Carmichael points out the double entendre in the word "scepter" that Tamar asks of Judah as part of his pledge. The scepter "symbolizes the headship of a line and also connotes generative power . . . the staff between the feet or legs alludes to the male sexual organ."[28] Specifically Tamar asks to have as a pledge the "staff that is in your hand" (Gen 38:18 NRSV). In return, she is granted the "staff from between his legs," to use Jacob's words. When Tamar receives Judah's staff, in both senses of the word, she ensures that there will be a next generation to whom Judah's heraldic staff may be passed.[29]

28. Carmichael, *Women*, 61. Carmichael builds on Good, "The 'Blessing' on Judah," 427–32. Good points out that רגל is used as "a euphemism for the sexual organ" (for example in 2 Kgs 18:27; Isa 7:20; Ezek 16:25). Also, in Deut 28:57, the phrase מבין רגליה, that is, רגל with the preposition ב as it appears in Gen 49:10, refers to a woman giving birth (ibid., 429). As Good also notes, the LXX, *Tg. Onq.*, *Tg. Ps.-J.*, and Vulgate all read this verse as referring to a generative function, Judah's producing an heir who would be a ruler (see Carmichael, *Women*, 61 n. 15). The LXX reads, καὶ ἡγούμενος ἐκ τῶν μηρῶν αὐτοῦ, "and a ruler from his thigh." *Tg. Ps.-J.* states, "Kings and rulers shall not cease from those of the house of Judah, nor scribes teaching the Law from his descendants" (Maher, *Targum Pseudo-Jonathan: Genesis*, 159). *Tg. Onq.* states, "The ruler shall not cease from those of the house of Judah, nor the scribe from his children's children" (Aberbach and Grossfeld, *Targum Onqelos on Genesis 49*, 13). In the Targums, then, the מטה, "staff," is related to חק, "law," and "from between his feet" is interpreted as children who will be born. The Vulgate has, "*et dux de femoribus eius*," "and a ruler from his thigh." Good sees the phrase as an ironic description of Judah's actions: when Judah's "staff" departed from him, Tamar became pregnant (Good, "The 'Blessing' on Judah," 429). Wenham also accepts the interpretation of Judah's staff between his feet as a reference to his sexual organ (Wenham, *Genesis 16–50*, 477). Robert Alter does not accept the interpretation of staff as a euphemism, but believes that the reference is suggestive: "There is no reason to construe it . . . as a euphemism for the phallus, though the image of the mace between the legs surely suggests virile power in political leadership" (Alter, *Genesis*, 295). However, when commenting on the story of Sisera and Jael, Alter notes that when Jael kills Sisera, Sisera is "lying shattered between her legs in a hideous parody of soldierly assault on the women of a defeated foe" (Alter, "From Line to Story," 633). In other—more graphic—words, Jael is "standing over the body of Sisera, whose death throes between her legs—he's kneeling, then prostrate— may be, perhaps, an ironic glance at the time-honored martial custom of rape" (ibid., 635). It seems in this context that Alter grants the possibility that the position of being "between the legs" may be a euphemism related to the sexual organs.

29. Jacob's further comment is translated in the NRSV as "until tribute comes to him" with the note that "tribute" may also be translated "Shiloh." Carmichael gives the translation instead as "until Shelah (*šlh*) would go in [to Tamar]." This line, according to Carmichael, is thus about Judah's dilemma regarding Shelah's being next in line as the male who can raise up an heir for Er. Carmichael, *Women*, 61. Also, the scene between Judah and Tamar provides an interesting contrast with the scene between Joseph and Potiphar's wife in Genesis 39. In the case of Tamar, she asks for and receives a pledge

When Tamar is noticeably pregnant, and still noticeably unmarried, Judah plans to respond in the way considered appropriate: Tamar is to be burned. As she is brought out for her punishment, Tamar produces the items given in pledge to her, identifying their owner as the one who has made her pregnant. "Recognize, please, whose these are, the signet, the cord, and the staff," (Gen 38:25),[30] she says. Her words, "Recognize, please" (הכר־נא), are the same words Judah and his brothers had used (in Gen 37:32) to deceive their father Jacob into believing his beloved son Joseph had been killed when they showed him Joseph's bloodstained robe. Tamar uses the words to reveal truth to Judah concerning the life within her; Judah had used the same words to conceal truth and feign death.

When Tamar shows Judah his pledge, he acknowledges his role in her pregnancy and declares, "She is more righteous than I"[31] (צדקה ממני) "because I did not give her to my son Shelah" (Gen 38:26). Tamar has exacted from Judah himself the pregnancy that Judah should have made possible through Shelah.[32] Tamar is the only woman called "righteous" in the Hebrew Bible. As if to seal doubly her righteous status and prove her worthiness to be a mother, Tamar gives birth to the twins, Perez and Zerah. Thus Tamar, through disguise and deceit, accomplishes what Judah should have made happen, but did not. She has been accused of transgression but instead Tamar ensures her own security and Judah's hereditary line.

---

from Judah when he approaches her for his own sexual gratification. In the case of Potiphar's wife, she takes an article of clothing from Joseph and uses it to imply, falsely, that he has used her for his sexual gratification. The pledge in Tamar's case results in her vindication, the false "pledge" in the case of Potiphar's wife, results in Joseph's imprisonment.

30. My translation.

31. My translation. The NRSV translates, "She is more in the right than I." The NASB and RSV also translate, "She is more righteous than I."

32. Judah's unrighteousness may also be seen in his, albeit anachronistic, violations of the Holiness Code in Lev 18:15. By engaging Tamar for sex, he "uncovered the nakedness of [his] daughter-in-law." Lev 20:12 repeats the prohibition and identifies it as a capital offense: "If a man lies with his daughter-in-law, both of them shall be put to death" (NRSV).

Connections with the Enochic Typology

USE OF THE ILLICIT ARTS

But Tamar's deceit was not just any form of trickery. Tamar engages in the illicit arts, those, according to the Enochic template for the origins of evil in the world, that were forbidden for the watchers to share. Once the illicit arts were taught to humans, humans' activity spiraled into violence and evil that would only be completely corralled and corrected at the end of time. Specifically, Tamar uses the arts related to seduction, making herself appear as a prostitute to attract Judah's attention. While in the Hebrew she wraps herself in a veil (יתכס בצציף ותתעלף, Gen 38:14), the LXX translates her action as "she put a covering around herself and she beautified her face" (περιεβάλετο και εκαλλωπίσατο).[33] Whether by obfuscation, as in the Hebrew Bible, or beautification, as in the LXX, it is by making herself sexually attractive and available to Judah that Tamar is able to carry out her plan.

That Judah would be susceptible to falling prey to such a plan may have been hinted at by the way the entire episode began. Judah's actions, with which Genesis 38 opens, are reminiscent of the way in which the narrative of the watchers' fall begins: "Judah saw [וירא] there the daughter of a Canaanite man, whose name was Shua; he took her [ויקחה] and went into her [ויבא אליה], and she conceived [ותהר] and bore [ותלד] a son, and he called his name Er" (Gen 38:2–3).[34] The watchers "see" (1 En. 6:2) the daughters of men; they "take" wives from among them; they "go into them" (1 En. 7:1); the women "conceived" and "bore" the giants (1 En. 7:2). Gunn and Fewell point out that in the case of Judah, the narration is very abrupt, even missing the conventional Hebrew phrase "take for a woman (wife)."[35] Another parallel with the watchers' transgressive action is that Judah is in a place called כזיב ("Chezib" NRSV) when his wife bears their second son (Gen 38:5). The meaning

---

33. In T. Jud.12.3 Judah likewise says that Tamar's "beauty enticed me because of her manner of tricking herself out" (Howard C. Kee's translation in Charlesworth (ed.), *Apocalyptic Literature and Testaments*, 798. The Greek uses διὰ τοῦ σχήματος τῆς κοσμήσεως. In the LXX and the T. Jud. Tamar does not merely cover herself; she changes her appearance in order to be more appealing.

34. My translation.

35. Gunn and Fewell, *Narrative in the Hebrew Bible*, 35.

of כזיב is "falsehood" or "lie."[36] That Judah is in a place called falsehood when his wife is giving birth to their child does not bode well for his abilities in ethical decision making. In terms of the actions of Judah and his wife—seeing, taking, going into, conceiving, bearing—and Judah's connection with falsehood, Judah bears more than a passing resemblance to the watchers and their actions with the women. The watchers also see, take, go into, and cause to conceive and bear offspring—even though they know this to be a "great sin" (*1 En.* 6:3).

Judah's actions toward his wife are reminiscent of those of the watchers; Judah's naming of his eldest son also reflects a connection with the watchers: Judah names him "Er" (ער, Gen 38:3). Martin Noth[37] and William F. Albright[38] state that the name Er means "watchful" or "watcher" by connecting it with עור, "to be awake."[39] Er's name thus derives from the same root as the name of the rebel angel watchers of *1 Enoch*. According to Gen 38:6, Judah again takes (ויקח) a wife, Tamar, this one for his son Er. Tamar's first husband, Er, for whom she is taken, just as the watchers take (*1 En.* 7:1)[40] those who appeal to them, is also a watcher, at least by name. Because of his evilness in the Lord's sight, the Lord kills Er (Gen 38:7), setting in motion the quest of Tamar to have a child by another man, which leads her to Judah.

Judah's interaction with Tamar includes an element with connections to the illicit arts, specifically with the art of metallurgy.[41] Judah participates in his own humiliation by giving Tamar his signet ring as part of his pledge to the "prostitute" who turns out not to be one.

36. Ibid., 35. Gunn and Fewell also point out that "almost the same set of verbs—see, take, and lie with—are the terms used only a few chapters earlier to preface Shechem's rape of Dinah" in Gen 34 (ibid). Judah's taking of the Canaanite woman, the rape of Dinah, and the watchers' rebellion all share the same narrative pattern. That the chain of events leads to the conception of offspring in the case of Judah and the daughter of Shua adds to the similarities between Judah and the watchers. In the case of the watchers and Shechem's rape of Dinah, the aftermath is violence and destruction. In the case of Judah, his first two sons die as punishment for wickedness, but the end of the story is redeemed because of Tamar's action.

37. Noth, *Die israelitischen Personennamen*, 228.

38. Albright, "The Egyptian Empire," 238.

39. Albright identifies "Er" as the Qal participle of עור, "wakeful, watchful, alert, vigilant" (ibid).

40. *1 Enoch: A New Translation*, 24.

41. The art of metallurgy is found in the list of watchers' teachings in *1 En.* 8:1.

Metallurgy for human decoration is also one of the arts taught illicitly by the watchers. Judah does not himself engage in metallurgy, but his action of handing over an object crafted by one who participated in the metallurgical arts may serve as a reminder of the forbidden art.[42] In Tamar's story, however, as in the others seen below, the use of illicit arts

---

42. An echo of the illicit arts of making dyes and eye paint (*1 En.* 8:1) may be attached to Judah in the testament of Jacob in Gen 49:11. First, in Gen 49:11, Jacob says of Judah, "he will wash his garments in wine, his robes in the blood of grapes." 1 Chron 4:21 notes that Judean families were linen-workers at Beth-ashbea; that is, they were engaged in weaving and dyeing. Sarna points out that excavations at Tell Beit Mirsim, in the territory of Judah, revealed "a major and well-organized dyeing and weaving industry." Wine would either be figurative speech for red dye or would have been used in the dye itself. Nahum M. Sarna, *Genesis* בראשית (JPS Torah Commentary 1; Philadelphia: Jewish Publication Society, 1989), 337. *Tg. Onq.* on this verse also contains the theme of dyed garments, "Let his [the Messiah's] raiment be of fine purple, and his garment all woolen, crimson and multi-colored (or: of bright, sparkling colors)" (Aberbach and Grossfeld, *Targum Onqelos on Genesis 49*, 16). Second, in Gen 49:12, Jacob continues his statement about Judah, "His eyes will be darker than wine." *Tg. Ps.-J.* and *Tg. Onq.* to Gen 49: 12 treat this statement as a further description of the Messiah. *Tg. Ps.-J.* declares, "How beautiful are the eyes of King Messiah, like pure wine, for they have not seen the uncovering of nakedness or the shedding of innocent blood . . . His mountains and his press will be red from wine . . ." *Tg. Onq.* more briefly says, "His mountains shall be red with his vineyards; his vats shall overflow with wine . . ." Michael Maher, in his comments on *Tg. Ps.-J.* notes, "The Targums of this verse, like those of the preceding verse, bear little relationship to the text being translated" (Maher, *Tg. Ps.-J.*, 159n34). What do eyes, wine, overflowing vats—in the Targums, attributed to the Messiah—have to do with Judah? The Targums' concern is to avoid providing a license for drunkenness which could be gained from Jacob's statement about Judah in Genesis (Aberbach and Grossfeld, *Targum Onqelos on Genesis 49*, 26). Therefore, the Targums instead speak of mountains and vats overflowing with wine, rather than eyes darkened or reddened by wine, in the Messianic age, as is described in Joel 2:24, "the vats shall overflow with wine and oil." But what is the connection with mountains? As Aberbach and Grossfeld point out, the root חכל, used in Gen 49:12, חכלילי עֵינַיִם מִיַּיִן, "his eyes will be darker than wine," "could, by metathesis, become כחל 'to paint', especially the eyes or eyelids." (Aberbach and Grossfeld, *Targum Onqelos on Genesis 49*, 26). The same root is used in *Tg. Ps.-J.* 2 Kgs 9:30, "and she painted her eyes with eyepaint (or antimony)" and *Tg. Ps.-J.* Jer 4:30, "you paint your eyes with eyepaint (or antimony)." As painting [כחל] drips, so do mountains with wine in Joel 4:18 ("the mountains shall drip [יטפו] sweet wine") and Amos 9:13 ("and the mountains shall drip [והטיפו] sweet wine"). Aberbach and Grossfeld thus propose the connection of dripping eyepaint with the dripping wine of mountainside vineyards. What they do not note is that Judah is connected with eyepaint, not just through metathesis, but through his adventure with Tamar who changes her appearance to attract Judah, as in LXX and the *T. Jud.*, noted above.

brings not the demise of the characters, but rather righteousness and the flourishing of God's people.

In addition to the concern with transgression and the use of the illicit arts, the story of Tamar may be connected by the time of the writing of Matthew's Gospel with other Enochic themes. Therefore next I note two themes: first, the theme of sexual relations with celestial beings, and second, the theme of heavenly mediators and messages.

TAMAR—SEXUAL INTERACTION THAT CONNECTS THE EARTHLY TO THE HEAVENLY REALM

An Earlier Form of Tamar's Story

There is one detail in Tamar's story that ought not be passed by too quickly, namely, the use of two different terms to identify Tamar's false identity in Genesis 38, זונה, in 38:15 and 24, and קדשה, in 38:21 and 22. The first word, זונה, usually means prostitute in the sense of a woman who exchanges money for sexual activity. The second, קדשה, is often translated as "temple prostitute," as in the NRSV and NASB.[43] The word means "consecrated one."[44] The subject of "sacred prostitution" or "temple prostitution" is a complex one, and beyond the scope of this book.[45] However, a brief overview of the matter is warranted in preparation for a look at the occurrence of קדשה in the story of Tamar.

What is a קדשה, and what is a "sacred prostitute"? Scholars disagree about the nature of the activity and role of the women referred to by this term, whether in Canaanite culture, or in earlier Mesopotamian contexts. Scholars have used "sacred prostitution" to describe a variety of practices they claim existed at times in Mesopotamian culture, including "a priestess whose caring for the gods included offering them

43. RSV translates both זונה and קדשה as "harlot." The NIV translates קדשה as "shrine prostitute."

44. Kornfeld and Ringgren, "קדש," *TDOT* 12:542.

45. Even on the subject of prostitution in general, Phyllis A. Bird cautions, for example, "Attempts to compare attitudes and incidence of prostitution in Canaanite and Israelite society or in different periods of Israelite history are futile, because the data do not permit statistical comparison and because the different literary genres in which the references are preserved display quite different pictures of the harlot and attitudes toward her" (Bird, *Missing Persons*, 201 n. 8).

sexual services,"[46] and "a laywoman who participated in organized, ritual sexual activities."[47] Others, however, object to the use of the term "sacred prostitution" at all. For example, Joan Goodnick Westenholz translates קדשה as "holy one" in her argument that given what scholars know of how the word is used in the Hebrew Bible, it is "impossible to arrive at the conclusion of illicit sexual activity."[48] Westenholz surveys the use of the word *qadištu*, the Akkadian etymological equivalent of קדשה, and the Sumerian lexical equivalent, NU.GIG, and concludes that the duties, roles, and activities of the women to whom these words refer never include prostitution.[49] Rather, their duties seem to have included presiding over childbirth and wet-nursing,[50] officiating in exorcistic rituals and sorcery,[51] and in the case of the NU.GIG, participating as the personification of the goddess Inanna[52] during the ritual coupling of the king and the goddess during the New Year Festival,[53] often called "sacred marriage." Like the Enochic watchers' transgression story, sa-

46. Lerner, "The Origin of Prostitution," 239.

47. Fisher, "Cultic Prostitution," 230.

48. Westenholz, "Tamar," 248.

49. Ibid., 260.

50. Ibid., 252.

51. Ibid., 253. Note that sorcery and the casting and breaking of spells are illicit arts taught by the watchers.

52. Inanna was the Sumerian deity of sexual love, fertility, and warfare. Her name in Sumerian means, "Queen of Heaven" (Wolkstein and Kramer, *Inanna*, xvi). See also Kramer, *Sumerians*; Jones, "Embracing Inana," 291–303. Inanna shares with the watchers of the Enochic template the task of transferring the arts of civilization from one realm to another through transgressive means. In the case of Inanna, two stories are told of her gaining the divine laws or decrees of civilization, called *me's*. *Me's* "either embody or symbolize the divine archetypes of the individual elements that comprise Mesopotamian culture in its widest sense" (ibid., 294). In one of the stories, Inanna takes the *me's* from Enki, the lord of wisdom, after Enki becomes drunk at a banquet and offers them to her. When Enki becomes sober again, he realizes his error and tries to recover them, but to no avail (Kramer, *Sumerians*, 160–61). In the other story, Iddin-Dagan A, Inanna gains the *me's* through her sexual relations with the royal incarnation of Dumuzi (Jones, "Embracing Inana," 294). Also, as are the watchers in the Enochic story, Inanna is associated with demons. In the story of her descent to the netherworld, she returns with a band of demons who pose a threat to the living (Jones, "Embracing Inana," 294).

53. Westenholz, "Tamar," 257. "This ritual intercourse seems to have been performed once a year during the New Year's festival in the latter half of the third millennium and the beginning of the second millennium as symbolic of the union of the divine and human realms" (ibid., 262).

cred marriage served to bridge the gap between the heavenly realm
and the earthly realm. One of the major sources for scholars' views
on sacred marriage is Iddin-Dagan A, an Old Babylonian royal hymn.
The narrative of the hymn describes the goddess Inanna (or "Inana,"
as in Jones's discussion) descending from the heavens to consummate
marriage with the king. The king, by means of the sacred marriage, is
marked as the mediator between the earthly and heavenly realms. [54]

Westenholz differentiates between prostitution, which she defines
as "occurring outside the cultural bounds of controlled sexuality," [55] and
"controlled coitus within the sacred sphere." [56] Westenholz joins scholars Fisher and Lerner in differentiating "cultic sexual service" from
"commercial prostitution," [57] and therefore does not agree with use of
the term "sacred prostitution" for even the very limited sexual activity in which the *qadištu*, NU.GIG, and קדשה may have been involved.
Through her examination of the evidence of the *qadištu*, NU.GIG, and
קדשה, Westenholz provides a much fuller picture of the role of the
women with these titles, one in which sexual activity is much more
limited—indeed, in most cases, non-existent. Her research gives pause
to those who would limit the activity of such women to sexual interaction with men or within a cultic sphere, with or on behalf of, celestial
beings. Given the linguistic, geographic, and chronological complexi-
ties involved in the issue of the קדשה and her[58] Mesopotamian roots, I
proceed to talk about Tamar, the supposed קדשה, with some caution.
Tamar's story does include the interesting detail of the word קדשה.
Examining the use of the term קדשה in her story, one may see connec-

54. Jones, "Embracing Inana," 291. On Sacred Marriage, see Black and Green,
Gods, Demons and Symbols, 157–58. The human participants in the sacred marriage,
king and priestess, seem to have been enacting the roles of the god Dumuzi and the
goddess Inanna. Black and Green also mention the possibility of a ritualized sexual
union between an *entu* priestess and a local storm god, probably Adad or Wer, known
from Emar (Syria) in the fourteenth century BCE. Black and Green, *Gods*, 158. See also
Wakeman, "Sacred Marriage," 21–31; and Bottéro, *Religion in Ancient Mesopotamia*,
155.

55. Westenholz, "Tamar," 257.

56. Ibid.

57. Ibid.

58. קדשה is the female person identified by the term. That there were also males
identified by a similar term is seen by the use of the masculine version קדש (in the
singular or plural) in Deut 23:18; 1 Kgs 14:24; 15:12; 22:47; 2 Kgs 23:7; Hos 4:14; Job
36:14.

tions between the Tamar story, Enochic legends, and the gospel writer Matthew's interest in Canaanite women.

When Judah encounters the veiled Tamar sitting at the entrance to Enaim on the road to Timnah, Judah mistakes her for a prostitute, זונה. When Judah's friend Hirah the Adullamite goes to exchange the promised kid for the pledge from the woman Judah had encountered, Hirah inquires into the whereabouts of the prostitute, קדשה. He is told that there has been no קדשה in this location, a fact which he passes on to Judah, using again the word קדשה. About three months later, when Judah learns of Tamar's pregnancy, he is told that Tamar's pregnancy is the result of prostitution. That is, she has been engaging in sexual activity as a זונה. In Tamar's story both words are applied to Tamar, although in reality in the narrative she is neither. But why would קדשה be used at all? If what Judah thinks he sees, in the beginning of the deception to his advantage, and at the end of the story, to Tamar's disadvantage, is a זונה, why does קדשה come into the story?

Some have suggested that Judah's friend is trying to cover for Judah's lack of morals by asking for the local קדשה, "sacred prostitute," rather than the local זונה, common prostitute.[59] Westenholz suggests that since a קדשה ought not to be identified as a woman available for any kind of indiscriminate sexual activity, Hirah is instead denying the affair altogether. He is, rather, "pretending to take the kid for a sacrifice, as in Hos 4:14."[60] However, Hirah is looking for the woman with whom his friend left his pledge for the kid in exchange for sexual services. Further, he believes that by identifying the woman as a קדשה, he will find that woman. In other words, to Hirah, and to readers of the story, זונה and קדשה share at least one thing in common: their availability for sexual activity. Westenholz asks, "If the ostensible outward behavior of Tamar could be subsumed under this title of female cultic functionary, what had she done to elicit such a response?" The answer to this question is: she had sexual intercourse with Judah. That is the hub around

---

59. See Speiser, *Genesis*, 300. Gerhard Von Rad, despite the statement in the text that Judah "thought she was a prostitute" (זונה, Gen 38:15), thinks that Tamar was pretending to be a "devoted one" (קדשה) and that "Judah too thought of her in this way." Von Rad, *Genesis*, 360. Von Rad says that it is "noteworthy" that Judah uses an intermediary to settle "the rather delicate situation," but does not comment on the difference in the terms used between what Judah thought of Tamar (זונה), and what Hirah asked for (קדשה). Ibid.

60. Westenholz, "Tamar," 248.

which this story turns. If Hirah doesn't know that a קדשה would have sexual relations with his friend Judah, then asking where she is doesn't guarantee he will find the supposed זונה who is still holding Judah's staff, cord, and ring. Despite Westenholz's efforts to rehabilitate the reputation of the קדשה and her Mesopotamian counterparts, what is at stake in the story is not the reputation of the "sacred prostitute." Even if what is said of her by later scholars might make her blush, it none-theless may be the case that her Hebrew opponents might join in the derision, unfair though it may be. That is how it goes with enemies. As Westenholz herself says, "the Hebrews saw all forms of religion except their own as depraved and full of debauchery. To the Hebrew author, the pagan priestess must be a harlot, and vice versa."[61] While Westenholz helps us understand the role of the קדשה better and beyond what the Hebrews despised, the fact remains that the Israelites do not esteem the Canaanites and see what may have even be a noble profession within the Canaanite milieu as instead the world's oldest. This disrespect for Canaanite ways is part of what makes Tamar's story pack its punch: when at its conclusion, Judah says, "She is more righteous than I," he is really saying something. So, having established that קדשה does indicate a woman available for sexual activity outside of marriage in the eyes of Judah, Hirah, and the Hebrew readers of Tamar's story, but that קדשה and its Mesopotamian counterparts may have indicated a much more complex and often non-sexual role for women, what ought one make of the use of קדשה in Tamar's story?

Michael Astour has written that the Tamar story includes not only the designation קדשה but also enough other details connected with, as he calls it, much to Westenholz's chagrin, "temple prostitution" in Babylonia that the story may yet divulge its original form as a story about a Canaanite קדשה who becomes pregnant by her father-in-law.[62] Although Tamar's ethnic background is not explicitly disclosed, her story is set in Canaan. It begins with Judah leaving his brothers for the land of Canaan, marrying a Canaanite wife and raising half-Canaanite sons. Judah will take some grief in his father's testament in Genesis 49

---

61. Ibid.

62. Astour, "Tamar the Hierodule," 185–96. As one might expect, given our brief review above of Westenholz's conclusions, Astour's argument has received negative criticism on many sides. Some of the objections to his argument will be noted below.

for his interaction with Canaanites,[63] and efforts were made by later interpreters to separate Tamar from identification as a Canaanite.[64] It makes sense, then, that the story of Tamar would change over time to separate Judah and Tamar from Canaanite ways. However, Astour argues that if the story is read as if Tamar was in fact in the original form of the story a Canaanite קדשה, some of the more curious details of the story make sense. In particular, all of the following details fit the context of a temple prostitute, at least as there is evidence from Babylonia, especially the Old Babylonian period: Tamar's not being impregnated by her husbands, her wearing a veil, Judah's visiting a prostitute at the time of the sheep shearing, and the punishment of burning for Tamar when it is discovered that she is pregnant.[65] Temple prostitutes could be

63. Genesis 49:11–12, part of Jacob's testament about Judah, states, "Binding the foal to the vine and his donkey's colt to the choice vine, he washes his garments in wine and his robe in the blood of grapes; his eyes are darker than wine, and his teeth whiter than milk." Carmichael points out that Canaanites were derisively compared to asses, so the reference to Judah's foal, עיר, echoes the name of Judah's son, Er, ער, and reminds readers of his Canaanite connections. Also the parallel reference to the son of the she-ass (בני אתן) echoes the name of Judah's second son (בן) Onan (אונן) born by his Canaanite wife. Tamar was supposed to be the means by which Judah's vine would grow and put forth new shoots. "However, if one tethers asses to a vine, it is destroyed" (Carmichael, "Women, Law, and the Genesis Traditions," 61–62). Judah's eyes (עינים) have been darkened—better, perhaps, "dimmed" or "dulled by wine," which brings to mind the place name Enaim (עינים) where Judah encountered Tamar and took her to be a prostitute. Judah's white teeth recall the Song of Songs 4:2, in which the bridegroom describes the teeth of his beloved as "like a flock of shorn ewes that have come up from the washing, all of which bears twins, and not one among them is bereaved" (NRSV). As Carmichael writes, Judah "was on his way to his sheep-shearing when he lay with her, and he promised her a kid from his flock for her services. What came instead were the twin children who kept his family stock on the increase" (ibid., 61).

64. For example, in some later rabbinic material Tamar is identified as the daughter of a merchant rather than a Canaanite. See b. Pesaḥ. 50a and Tg. Onq. to Gen 38:2. In an effort to clear up any confusion over Tamar's ethnic identity, in the Testament of the Twelve Patriarchs, Tamar is described specifically as not Canaanite. In fact, it is because she is not from Canaan that "he [Er] was in a difficulty concerning Tamar," and Er refuses to have intercourse with Tamar "on account of the craftiness of his mother" (T. Jud. 10:2–3). The xenophobia of Er's mother is likewise the cause of Onan's refusal to have intercourse with the non-Canaanite Tamar: Onan "went into her, but spilled the seed on the ground, according to his mother's command" (T. Jud. 10:5). Test. 12 Patr. (trans. Hollander and de Jonge, 201). For more on early Jewish interpretation of the story of Tamar, see Menn, Judah and Tamar.

65. Sharon Pace Jeansonne thinks that Astour "goes beyond the evidence of the story when he argues that Judah's decree of punishment shows that Tamar was considered a member of the cult personnel" (Jeansonne, The Women of Genesis, 141–42 n. 18).

married, but were forbidden to bear children.[66] They were required to wear veils in order to distinguish themselves from common prostitutes (in the Old Babylonian period) and from unmarried temple prostitutes (according to Middle Assyrian law).[67] Judah's engaging the services of a sacred prostitute at the time of the shearing of the sheep fits the context of the pre-exilic period when feast times, such as sheep-shearing, would be accompanied by rituals to encourage the increase of fertility amongst the herds.[68] The punishment for misconduct on the part of a sacred prostitute as a member of temple personnel according to Babylonian law was burning.[69] Prostitution in Israel was never punishable as such,[70] and only in the case of a priest's daughter engaging in prostitution, by burning (Lev 21:7).[71] Yet Judah sentences Tamar to be burned. These details, curious in the story of Tamar as recorded in the Hebrew Bible, make more sense if Tamar originally was a temple prostitute, able to

---

She does not comment on the other details Astour mentions or whether the story may contain what he calls "vestigially preserved details that evoke associations with the legal and ritual prescriptions for temple harlots in Babylonia." Astour, "Tamar the Hierodule," 185.

66. Ibid., 188. However, Westenholz notes that from Ugarit there is evidence that the *qdšm* (the Ugarit equivalent to Astour's "sacred prostitute") could marry and have children. Westenholz, "Tamar," 249.

67. Astour, "Tamar the Hierodule," 187. Bird, however, insists that it is "useless to argue from the Middle Assyrian Laws . . . to practices in Canaan/Israel, since dress is a matter of local or regional custom." Bird, *Missing Persons*, 204, n.17. Westenholz notes that in Assyria, from the Old Assyrian period onwards, there is evidence that the *qadištu*-woman could marry and, if married, could wear a veil in public, and therefore "Tamar could have been considered by the Canaanite inhabitants as a veiled, married *qadištu*-woman." Westenholz, "Tamar," 254.

68. Astour, "Tamar the Hierodule," 193.

69. Ibid., 194.

70. There are no laws against men in Israel marrying or using the services of prostitutes, with one exception: priests were not allowed to marry prostitutes (Lev 21:14). See Street, *The Strange Woman*, 43.

71. That burning was prescribed for priest's daughters who engaged in prostitution is not mentioned by Astour. He considers the existence of an earlier form of the story in which Tamar is a Canaanite hierodule, but not one in which she is the daughter of a priest of Israel. *Tg. Ps.-J.* (Gen 38:6, "Judah took a wife for Er his first-born, the daughter of Shem the Great, whose name was Tamar," and the later *Gen. Rab.* 85:10 and *Num. Rab.* 4:8 identify Tamar as the daughter of the priest Shem-Melchizedek. In *Tg. Ps.-J.* Gen 38:24, upon learning that Tamar is pregnant, Judah says, "Is she not the daughter of a priest? Bring her out and let her be burned" [see *Targum Pseudo-Jonathan: Genesis*, trans. by Maher, 128–29]). See also Bauckham, "Tamar's Ancestry," 319.

be married, and therefore needing to be veiled, forbidden from having children, engaged for her services at festival time, and sentenced to be punished by burning for becoming pregnant.

Astour's thesis may go beyond the weight of the evidence, and both his thesis and the arguments against it suffer from a paucity of evidence and our inability to bridge both the geographic and temporal distance between Canaan and Mesopotamia, and Tamar's story as known in the biblical text. Tamar is clearly not a cultic functionary in the story as we have it. However, it is worth considering that there may be some residual, or "vestigial," as Astour prefers to call them,[72] aspects of Tamar's story that link her with practices involving women in sexual interaction connected with celestial beings. In this way, the story of Tamar, through its earlier form, contains within it echoes of the watchers' transgression. The phenomenon of the קדשה may involve, and the watchers' story certainly involves, sexual activity between heavenly and earthly beings. Both were without a doubt considered wrong—the watchers' transgression within the Enochic story, and the existence of the קדשה within temple-sanctioned religion in Israel. Israelites are forbidden from becoming a קדשה or קדש in Deut 23:18 (17). According to 1 Kgs 14:24, the קדש (the male form of the word) "committed all the abominations of the nations" (NRSV); 1 Kgs 15:12 reports that Asa expelled them from the land. According to 2 Kgs 23:7, Josiah broke down the houses of the קדשים who were in the house of YHWH "where the women did weaving for Asherah." It is logical to see why that aspect of Tamar's identity would be excised from the story. However, if Astour is correct, some evidence of the story's early form remains.

Celestial beings are also present in a later interpretation of Tamar's story.

Interactions with Angels and the Bat Qol

The story of Tamar shares some elements in common with the Enochic template, namely the theme of transgression and the use of the illicit arts. The identification of Tamar as קדשה, while raising issues about the precise nature and role of the קדשה, raises the possibility that Tamar may have been linked to a tradition in which humans engaged in sexual

---

72. Astour, "Tamar the Hierodule," 185.

relations in order to participate in a bridging of earthly and heavenly realms. This tradition of sacred marriage, while uncertain and complex, seems to have involved a human king engaging in ritualized sexual behavior with a woman playing the role of a celestial being in order to mark the king as the mediator between the two realms. If there was a connection between Tamar and traditions in which humans and celestial beings interact, and if this connection may be seen even vestigially in her story as it exists in the biblical story, is there any evidence that in Matthew's time traditions existed in which celestial beings are connected with Tamar and her story?

One way to answer this question is to trace the trajectory of the interpretation of Tamar's story by looking at traditions earlier than Matthew (which I have done above) and by looking at traditions later than Matthew. If later traditions also share common elements, then it is possible that at the time of the evangelist's activity similar elements may have been known. A review of the traditions concerning Tamar shows that as Tamar's story was retold and reinterpreted various details were added to the story that include the participation of celestial beings in the narrative. Specifically, in later retellings of Tamar's story angelic mediators and the voice of God, or *Bat Qol* are present.

In rabbinic and other later traditions, efforts are made to exonerate Tamar and Judah from the appearance of unseemly behavior in the episode. These efforts include inserting the guidance of angels and the heavenly voice into the narrative.[73] For example, the archangel Michael

---

73. Other efforts include turning Tamar into an example of modesty and removing Tamar's identity as a Canaanite, mentioned above. In the case of the former, Tamar's veiling herself becomes a mark of her modesty in *Tg. Neof.* Gen 38:15, rather than her efforts to conceal her true identity. When she sits on the road to Timnah, she wraps herself in a veil, and when Judah sees Tamar, he does not know who she is because she had kept her face covered when she had been in his house. Thus Tamar is doubly covered: on the road to Timnah and, previously, when she was resident in Judah's house as the wife of his first two sons. In the Babylonian Talmud Tamar is also said to have kept her face covered in Judah's house and is praised for her modesty: "Every daughter-in-law who is modest in her father-in-law's house merits that kings and prophets would issue from her. Whence is this? From Tamar" (*b. Seder Naš.* 10b). Another approach was to explain Tamar's behavior in disguising herself is explained as customary for her people: "For it was a law of the Amorites that she who was about to marry should sit in impurity by the gate for seven days" (*T. Jud.* 12:2). In the *Testament*, it is clear that Tamar's pregnancy is in accordance with God's will ("it was from the Lord." *T. Jud.*12:6). Likewise, in *Gen. Rab.* 85.11, R. Jeremiah says, in the name of R. Samuel b. R. Isaac, that the Holy Spirit said, "Through Me (*mimmeni*) did these things occur."

is sent by God to help Tamar when she is dragged before the court.[74] In one rabbinic tradition told to exculpate Judah from guilt, it is Judah who is assisted by an angel: Judah would have passed by the disguised Tamar on the road, but an angel from God persuaded him to engage her services.[75] In other words, an angel made him do it. But the angel knew beforehand what Judah did not: the "prostitute" the righteous Judah wished to avoid was really the future mother of his own descendants and therefore Judah must have intercourse with her. In an effort to clear both Judah and Tamar of wrongdoing, following Judah's acknowledgment of his guilt and Tamar's innocence, a voice from heaven declares them both innocent.[76] Later traditions thus exculpate Judah and Tamar by introducing into the story heavenly messengers who mediate divine truths about the situation that would have remained hidden from humans had not the angels and heavenly voice intervened. In the trajectory of traditions about Tamar traditions both earlier and later than Matthew involve celestial beings.

Next I examine the possibility that within the Gospel of Matthew itself, Matthew includes a woman foreshadowed by Tamar, the Canaanite woman of Matt 15:21–28.

MATTHEW AND THE CANAANITE WOMEN

That the next woman named after Tamar in Matthew's genealogy, Rahab, has some things in common with the Canaanite woman in Matt 15:21–28 has been noted by scholars, and will be revisited in the section on Rahab below. But Tamar also has significant similarities with the Canaanite woman Jesus encounters in Matthew[77] and may be the

74. In *Tg. Neof.* Gen 38:25–26, when Tamar has been sentenced to be burned, she searches for the three pledges but is unable to find them. She prays to God, and God sends Michael to bring them to her. In the Babylonian Talmud, the evil angel Samael takes the pledges, but Gabriel comes to Tamar's rescue and gives her the items (*b. Seder Naš.* 10b).

75. *Gen. Rab.* 38:15: R. Johanan said, "He wanted to pass by, but the Holy One Blessed be He assigned the angel in charge of desire to him. He said to him, 'Where are you going, Judah? From whence are kings and redeemers to arise?' 'And he turned aside to her' (Gen 38:16) under compulsion and not of his own free will."

76. *Tg. Neof.* Gen 38:25–26.

77. There is, to begin with, the fact that Matthew, alone of the synoptic gospel writers, uses the designation *Canaanite* to describe the woman, which links Matthew's

woman who influences Matthew's telling of the encounter. Tamar, in some significant ways, not only shows the reassessment of the Enochic transgression template, but also foreshadows the role that the Canaanite woman plays in Matthew's Gospel.

What Tamar and her later Matthean counterpart have in common is this: Tamar and the Canaanite woman both meet in a public setting the man they believe can give them what they need; this meeting in a public setting brings with it an association with prostitution;[78] both are praised for their behavior, Tamar for having great righteousness (Gen 38:26), the Canaanite woman for having great faith (Matt 15:28); both obtain what they need from the man they encounter: Tamar, children from Judah, the woman, healing for her daughter from Jesus; both are clever in their interaction with the man: Tamar in deceiving Judah to get what was rightfully hers, the Canaanite woman in her theological dialogue with Jesus which convinces him of her faith; and both are concerned about children: Tamar about becoming pregnant, the Canaanite woman about her daughter's affliction by a demon. Tamar and the Canaanite woman both risk public shame in order to get their needs met; both are praised for their actions. Further, the Canaanite woman in Matthew builds her argument to Jesus around his statement, "It is not fair to take the children's food and throw it to the dogs" (Matt 15:26 NRSV), words that have caused much consternation amongst scholars of Matthew.[79] It is worth examining this statement in detail. In doing

---

Canaanite woman to her biblical predecessors such as Tamar and Rahab. The word Canaanite carried with it associations with Israel's enemies (see Davies and Allison, *Matthew 8–18*, 547), and also connections with prostitution and sexual sin (see Corley, *Private Women*, 166). Further, Matthew's use of the term stands out because it is anachronistic. By the first century CE, the nationality Canaanite had ceased to exist (ibid.). Mark's designation of the woman as Syro-Phoenician (in Mark 7:26) reflects the designation of Jesus' day (O'Day, "Surprised by Faith," 115).

78. Tamar, as has been shown, encourages Judah to think of her as a prostitute. Already associated by her ethnic designation with Tamar the one-time prostitute and Rahab the prostitute by trade, the Canaanite woman in Matthew, by "coming out" (ἐξελθοῦσα) to meet Jesus "heightens the impropriety" of her actions (Corley, *Private Women*, 166).

79. See the summary of attempts to explain Jesus' words in Beare, *Matthew*, 342. Beare thinks that the words belong to some members of the early Jewish Christian community. Calling the Gentile woman a dog while "completely out of keeping with everything else that is reported of him," would "reflect not unfairly the attitude of some zealous members of the Jewish Christian communion of the apostolic age" (ibid., 343). Luz believes that the image is of a household pet, rather than "despised wild dogs" (Luz,

so, another connection between Tamar and the Canaanite woman in Matthew becomes apparent.

In addition to the notion, offensive for some, that Jesus would insult the Canaanite woman by calling her a dog, there is the issue of how the verbal repartee between Jesus and the Canaanite woman results in his great praise for her faith. How is it that his reference to dogs leads to her reference to the activity of dogs, and results in Jesus' affirmation of her great faith? What do dogs and Canaanite women have in common?

One of the few occurrences of the word "dog" in the Hebrew Bible is in a passage that brings together dogs, and the two words applied to Tamar, as shown above, קדשה and זונה. Deuteronomy 23:18–19 (17–18 MT) states, "None of the daughters of Israel shall be a קדשה; none of the sons of Israel shall be a קדש. You shall not bring the fee of a זונה or of a male prostitute (NRSV) (כלב, literally "dog"; κυνὸς in LXX) into the house of the Lord your God in payment for any vow, for both of these are abhorrent to the Lord your God."[80] The word "dog" in this passage may function as a hook-word (or *Stichwort*) that links this passage with Matt 15:26. According to the *gezera sheva* rule for biblical interpretation,[81] when two texts share a word or words, the texts are "perceived to be in fact similar or related."[82] The texts sharing the similar word or words "are linked and used to explain, clarify, or amplify one another."[83] The word *gezera* refers to "law."[84] If the same word appears in two passages from the Pentateuch, then the law applying in one should be applied to the other.[85]

Matthew 8–20, 340).

80. Based on the NRSV and MT.

81. One of the Thirteen Rules of R. Ishmael for biblical interpretation. R. Ishmael's rules amplify the seven rules of R. Hillel, which may predate Hillel (Jacobs, "Hermeneutics"). Although identification of *gezera sheva*, or comparison of similar expressions, is not codified as a rabbinic rule until after New Testament texts were recorded, there is evidence within the New Testament for the use of this form of interpretation. See, for example, Stockhausen, *Moses' Veil*, in which Stockhausen argues that Paul used this method in 2 Cor 3:1–4:6.

82. Stockhausen, *Moses' Veil*, 26.

83. Ibid.

84. According to Jacobs, *gezera* probably means "law," "as in Dan 4:4, 14—so that *gezerah shavah* would mean a comparison of two similar laws" (Jacobs, "Hermeneutics," 367–78).

85. Stockhausen, *Moses' Veil*, 26.

That Jesus is insulting the woman in his use of the word "dog" seems clear, even if not to those who want to protect Jesus from that problematic speech.[86] But in calling the woman a dog,[87] Jesus may be disparaging her not only as a Gentile, but also as a loose woman, perhaps even as a prostitute. Matthew alone of the evangelists identifies the woman as a Canaanite. As noted above, Canaanites were hated in part because of their practices, including the practices of their קדשות and קדשים By having Jesus call the Canaanite woman a dog, the evangelist may be bringing to mind Deut 23:18–19, which disparages Canaanite קדשות (in Deut 23:18), זונה (in Deut 23:19), and dogs (there a reference to male prostitutes). Given Deut 23:18–19 as background, Jesus does not intend "to take the children's food and throw it to the dogs" (NRSV). However, the Canaanite woman, in reference to the same passage from Deuteronomy, can hear in it not only the word "dog," but also the words קדשה and זונה. That is, she hears both of the words applied to Tamar in Genesis 38. When the woman counters, "Yes, Lord, yet even the dogs eat the crumbs that fall from their masters' table," (Matt 15:27 NRSV), she may be recalling Tamar, who despite being identified as the female equivalent to the male prostitute (a "dog" in Deut 23:18), is vindicated and called "righteous" (Gen 38:26). Tamar waited on Judah, the man who was supposed to give her what she needed to sustain her. When her "master" did not, she took matters into her own hands, and obtained what he casually "let fall" by the side of the road to Timnah. Tamar, the Canaanite woman's ancestor in faith, was called both קדשה and זונה, no better than a dog, and in Deut 23:18, the equivalent of a dog. But at the conclusion of the story, Tamar has what she went to Judah for, pregnancy, and Judah's statement, "She is more righteous than I" (Gen 38:26).

Jesus has called the Canaanite woman a dog, the equivalent of קדשה and זונה. But the Canaanite woman, like Tamar, seeks a righteous cause, the healing of her daughter. In the woman's response to Jesus, in which she accepts the identification of herself as a dog willing to accept what falls from the master's table, she may also be claiming identifica-

86. See above n. 79.

87. The word here is κυναρίοις, the plural accusative form of κυνάριον. O. Michel thinks that in using this diminutive form of κύων, "house dog," Jesus recognizes the historical privilege of Israel, but, like the little house dog, Gentiles also may be "tolerated in the house" (Michel, "*kýōn*," *TDNT* 3:1104).

tion with Tamar who was called righteous. Jesus' response, "O woman, great is your faith"[88] (Ὦ γύναι, μεγάλη σου ἡ πίστις, Matt 15:28) and granting her desire for her child would be a fitting conclusion to the encounter, even as Judah's response and Tamar's giving birth to twins was a fitting conclusion to Tamar's story.

What Tamar and the Canaanite woman have in common, however, highlights the distinction between them: Tamar obtains what she needs by engaging in apparently illicit sexual activity with Judah; the Canaanite woman achieves her goal by engaging in theological discussion with Jesus. The difference is of the utmost importance when discussing the Enochic template, its partial overturning in the stories of the Hebrew women, and its complete redressing in Matthew's Gospel. The watchers transgress through illicit sexual activity and illicit teaching and it results in disaster. Tamar uses sexual activity and illicit teaching and it results, not in disaster, but in a proclamation of righteousness for Tamar and good for Judah. In Matthew, Jesus is approached by a woman who is associated by the name "Canaanite" and her location in the street, as was the case with Tamar, with illicit sexuality. This woman obtains her goals, and it results in a proclamation of great faith for the woman, healing for the daughter, and the expansion of Jesus' ministry beyond the borders of Israel. However, and importantly, the woman, although associated with sexual availability, does not use sexual activity to get what she needs. She uses affirmation of faith and theological discussion. Corley writes, "the association of the woman with harlotry allows her to be easily compared to the πόρνει who also 'believe' and enter the messianic kingdom before the Pharisees (Matt 21:31–32)."[89] However, I think the Canaanite woman who believes, and uses words, not sexuality, to approach Jesus, also may be compared to those who "have made themselves eunuchs for the sake of the kingdom of heaven" (Matt 19:12 NRSV).[90] She does not use the sexuality or sexual im-

88. My translation.

89. Corley, *Private Women*, 167.

90. While these words, spoken by Jesus in the text, follow Jesus' teaching on divorce and marriage, some scholars, such as Davies and Allison, argue that Jesus is speaking here about celibacy rather than referring back to marriage and divorce (Davies and Allison, *Matthew 19–28*, 27; Fenton, *Gospel of St. Matthew*, 311; Harrington, *Matthew*, 274). Jesus seems to be opposing the disciples' general application in Matt 19:10, ". . . it is better not to marry," by his qualifying remarks, "Not everyone can accept this teaching, but only those to whom it is given," and "Let anyone accept this who can"

propriety that is naturally associated with her as a Canaanite woman to approach Jesus. Sexuality has nothing to do with her faithfulness. Regardless of her (unknown) marital status (she has a daughter, but we do not know if she has a husband), her acting in a way that is surprising for a Canaanite woman meeting Jesus in the street (i.e., with no sexual advances) demonstrates her acceptance of Jesus' teaching. There is no sexual activity in her pursuit of the wholeness of the kingdom.

The story of the Canaanite woman in Matthew's Gospel shows the third movement of the trajectory from transgression to redemption of transgression that this book demonstrates. The first movement is the transgression itself, the watchers' fall and illicit pedagogy in the Enochic template. The second movement is the partial redemption—the fore-shadowing of redemption—of transgression in the story of Tamar, in which her transgression—use of illicit pedagogy and association with elements found in the Enochic template—results, not in tragedy, but in righteousness and moving the story of salvation forward. The third movement, which will be discussed in more detail in the next chapter, is the full redemption of transgression as Matthew shows it in the life and ministry of Jesus.

In the story of the interaction of the Canaanite woman and Jesus in Matthew's Gospel this redemption is at work. The Canaanite woman is foreshadowed by the mention of Tamar in the genealogy. As a Canaanite woman who meets Jesus on the street and whom he calls a dog, she brings with her to the encounter associations of the transgressions of her foremother, that is, associations of being a Canaanite prostitute. However, when confronted by Jesus about her transgressive identity, she counters with a hermeneutical move that shows her faithfulness: she is like Tamar, who was declared righteous and whose children continued the heritage of Israel. She worships Jesus—"she knelt" (προσεκύνει), in Matt 15:25 and calls him "Lord" (κύριε), in Matt 15:22, 25, 26—and she addresses him as the one who can grant her request. In response, Jesus declares that her faith is great and grants healing to her daughter.

(Matt 19:11–12 NRSV). The Canaanite woman, though associated with impropriety of a sexual nature, demonstrates faith through her words and dialogue. She acts in such a way to counteract the expectations of others that in the act of approaching Jesus in public, she is approaching him as a possible sexual partner. Instead, she engages in dialogue based on her faith in his ability to see that she is righteous, as Tamar was, and has a righteous cause, as did Tamar.

Significantly, the interaction between Jesus and the woman, which begins with the statement that Jesus cannot transgress the boundaries of his mission ("I was sent only to the lost sheep of the house of Israel," Matt 15:24 NRSV), brings a crossing of that boundary.[91] Further, the transgression that originated in the fall of the rebel angels and their desire for sexual relations with human woman and the ensuing illicit pedagogy is redeemed in Matthew's Gospel without sexual relations between the woman and Jesus.

Summary

Tamar is accused of transgression by her father-in-law. In fact, Tamar has transgressed the social mores of her time by dressing as a prostitute and tricking her father-in-law into giving what he was obliged to give all along. However, Judah had promised to give Tamar her due through his son and certainly had not anticipated that he himself would personally fulfill his obligation through his own actions. Not only is Tamar's transgression revealed to be righteous, but it guarantees that Judah will not be the last male in his line. Tamar makes use of the illicit arts to achieve this righteousness-through-transgression. Other echoes of the Enochic template are present in Tamar's identity as a קדשה, a veiled married woman without children, punishable by burning when she is found to be pregnant. As a קדשה she would be engaged in sexual activity with a sacred purpose and in connection with celestial beings. Later rabbinic traditions also associate Tamar with the apocalyptic motifs of association with celestial beings and the *Bat Qol*. Tamar's presence in

---

91. Commentators point out that Jesus' mission does not change: he does not himself go again into Gentile territory, and "the priority of Israel in salvation-history remains uncontested" (Davies and Allison, *Matthew 8–18*, 556). However, this encounter gives permission and affirmation for the Matthean community's mission to Gentiles. Beare asserts that although Jesus himself rarely heals Gentiles (he does so here, in Matt 8:5–13, the healing of the centurion's child or servant, and in Matt 8:28–34, the healing of the Gadarene demoniacs), the story shows that through faith the healing powers of Christ are available to Gentiles as well as Jews (Beare, *Matthew*, 344). Luz: "Jesus has not confined God within the borders of Israel, but has let himself be moved by the faith of the Gentile woman." This action of Jesus confirms for the Matthean community that they may seek "a new life and a new field of endeavor among the Gentiles" (Luz, *Matthew 8–20*, 341). Hagner states that Jesus' mission remained limited to Israel, "but the time of the blessing of the Gentiles was indicated by Jesus explicitly and is foreshadowed here" (Hagner, *Matthew 14–28*, 442).

Matthew's genealogy may also serve to foreshadow the Canaanite woman who confronts Jesus in a public space to get her needs met. However, in stark contrast to Tamar, she gets what she needs not through sexual interaction, but rather through conversation with Jesus that reveals her faith in his teaching.

I look next at Rahab, a woman whose multiple transgressions bring about a new beginning for an entire people.

Rahab: Transgression as Faithfulness

Rahab is named in Matthew's genealogy in Matt 1:5. In the story of the Israelites, Rahab is instrumental in the entry of the Israelites into the land of Canaan (see Joshua 2).[92] It is her transgression of ethnic loyalty and her willingness to deceive her own people that enable her to provide safe passage for Israelite spies and helpful intelligence to their leaders, setting in motion the entry into Canaan. While Tamar's transgression took the form of acting like a prostitute just once in order to achieve her goal, Rahab makes a profession of prostitution. Stephenson Humphries-Brooks calls prostitution "one of the most detested professions within Torah-centered Judaism."[93]

As a prostitute, Rahab lives quite literally on the boundary of Canaan, on the city wall of Jericho. She is quite used to providing hospitality to men who visit her in her home. Her identity as a prostitute is straightforward in the text, as is her identity as a Canaanite. However, it is the assumed clarity of her identity that allows her to conceal strange men and her allegiance to their God from her Canaanite ruler. That is, she is a prostitute: it is logical that strange men would lodge in her home. And she is a Canaanite: it is expected that she would obey the king of Jericho by turning these strangers over to the king and telling him the truth. But she does neither. Instead, she protects the foreigners and lies to her earthly king. Rather than show loyalty to the king of Jericho, she exclaims her loyalty to the God of Israel, "The Lord your God is indeed God in heaven above and on earth below" (Josh 2:11b NRSV). So, her fellow Canaanites know who she is: a prostitute and

92. Rahab is also a place name in Psalm 87:4 (ρααβ, in LXX Psalm 86:4).

93. Humphries-Brooks, "The Canaanite Women in Matthew," 141. For others on prostitution in Israel, see Baskin, "The Rabbinic Transformation," 141–57; Bird, *Missing Persons*; Streete, *Strange Woman*; Marsman, *Women in Ugarit and Israel*, 431–35.

Canaanite. But they do not really know who she is: a protector of spies and faithful to the God of Israel.

There is, however, an element of play with Rahab's true identity that goes on with the Israelite spies as well as the king. The narrative in Joshua 2 is delightfully vague about the Israelite men's intentions when they go to Rahab's house. [94] Joshua sends two men "secretly from Shittim as spies" (Josh 2:1a). He gives them instructions to "view the land, especially Jericho" (Josh 2:1a). However, despite these clear instructions, they get no farther than "the house of a prostitute whose name was Rahab, and spent the night there" (Josh 2:1b). Perhaps these unnamed spies are to be congratulated for successfully infiltrating the borders of Jericho by entering the prostitute's home on the city wall. Perhaps their spending the night in the prostitute's home provided an opportunity for a good night's rest before an active day of espionage. The text does not tell.

94. That is, the text does not state specifically why the men go to Rahab's house, allowing the reader to provide a reason for the men's actions, or, in other words, to fill in a gap in the narrative. Meir Sternberg describes the reality of the filling in of gaps by the reader of any literary work in this way: "the literary work consists of bits and fragments to be linked and pieced together in the process of reading: it establishes a system of gaps that must be filled in. This gap-filling ranges from simple linkages of elements, which the reader performs automatically, to intricate networks that are figured out consciously, laboriously, hesitantly, and with constant modifications in the light of additional information disclosed in later stages of the reading" (Sternberg, *The Poetics of Biblical Narrative*, 186). Sternberg suggests that in order to understand a literary work, the reader must answer a number of questions in the course of reading, such as "What connects the present event or situation to what went before, and how do both related to what will probably come after? What are the features, motives, or designs or this or that character?" However, Sternberg notes, it is the reader who supplies many of the answers, rather than the author who explicitly supplies the answers. The reader then engages in filling the gaps in the narrative in order to construct the world of a literary work and make meaning of the text. "Biblical narratives," Sternberg observes, "are notorious for their sparsity of detail" (ibid., 191). The story of Rahab is no exception. So the reader must fill in the gaps. To do so legitimately, according to Sternberg, the reader must use "the text's own norms and directives," including: (a) the different materials—actional, thematic, normative, structuring—explicitly communicated by the text; (b) the work's language and poetics; (c) the perceptual set established by the work's generic features; (d) the special nature and laws and regularities of the world in projects, as impressed on the reader starting from the first page; (e) basic assumptions or general canons of probability derived from "everyday life" and prevalent cultural conventions. There is an "appeal of the hypothesis that organizes the maximum of elements in the most cohesive patterns," as well as "the attraction of the gap-filling that presents things in the most interesting light" (ibid., 188–89).

The text does tell, however, that the spies' cover has already been blown on the first day of their mission. Someone informs the king of Jericho, "Some Israelites have come here tonight to search out the land" (Josh 2:2). If the Israelites thought that visiting Rahab's house would conceal their true purpose, they were mistaken. The king knows just where to look for the Israelite moles. He sends orders to Rahab to bring out her foreign visitors and adds a message to inform her of their true purpose: "they have come only to search out the whole land" (Josh 2:3 NRSV). Again, the narrative gap in the text allows the reader to fill it in with a couple of possibilities. The king, viewing Rahab only as a Canaanite prostitute, does not want her to be deceived: the one thing these men have on their mind is a different kind of undercover work than she provides. The Israelites' visit to her home, all other activities aside, is for the purpose of gaining entrance to the whole land. Or perhaps the king's statement, "they have come only to search out the whole land," provides the reader with a moral identity check for the Israelites: that really is their only purpose. Neither the prostitute nor the reader should be confused. However, when the king is being made a buffoon of by Rahab, are his words to be trusted? He knows the truth: the men are spies. But the king's informing of Rahab, who will prove to be smarter than he, contains in it the seeds of irony. She already knows better than he. She will deceive the king because she knows more than he about the God of Israel. Does she know more than the king about the spies' intentions at her home as well? If the king's message to her includes the subtext, "They're here for one thing only, and it's not you," might she reply, "That is what you think"?

Rahab is also clearly more intelligent than the Israelites. They have been found out. She has not. Whether or not the spies knew Rahab would be willing to cooperate with them when they entered her house, they were fortunate in their choice of hosts. Rahab provides a subterfuge, sending the king's men on a wild goose chase and hiding the Israelite spies until she sends them out with instructions that will guarantee their safety. It is likely that the spies did not know that their safety would depend on Rahab when they came to her, since her declaration of faith in the God of Israel comes only after the spies have found themselves in the awkward position of having been found out by the king. Rahab hides them and then tells them that she knows "that the Lord has given you the land" (Josh 2:9 NRSV) and declares her own faith, "The

Lord your God is indeed God in heaven above and on earth below"
(Josh 2:11 NRSV). With this statement, Rahab gives the acknowledge-
ment Moses enjoins on the Israelites in Deut 4:39, "So acknowledge
today and take to heart that the Lord is God in heaven above and on the
earth beneath; there is no other" (NRSV). The Israelite spies may have
thought they were visiting a Canaanite prostitute, regardless of the nature of the one thing on their minds. What they find is that they are in
fact being saved by a woman whose faith is aligned with that demanded
of true Israelites. And just as the Israelites were urged by Moses in the
same speech to keep God's statutes and commandments "so that you
may long remain in the land that the Lord your God is giving you for
all time" (Deut 4:40), so Rahab's faithful actions toward the spies result
in her remaining in the land: "she has lived in Israel ever since. For she
hid the messengers whom Joshua sent to spy out Jericho"[95] (Josh 6:25).
The spies came to the house of a Canaanite prostitute, but found they
were in the company and safe-keeping of a faithful proselyte. Without
Rahab's faith in Israel's God, the spies would not have been able to be
faithful to their mission to view the land.

But Rahab's identity as a Canaanite prostitute is not forgotten,
by Rahab or the Israelite spies. As Rahab has shown her loyalty to the
God of Israel by saving the Israelite spies, she demands their loyalty to
her and her family (Josh 2:12–13). She knows that as a Canaanite, she,
along with her Canaanite family members, will need protection from
the Israelites when the Israelites take the land. Rahab asks the men for a
sign of good faith that they will spare the lives of her family and herself.
The men reply, "Our life for yours! If you do not tell this business of
ours, then we will deal kindly and faithfully with you when the Lord
gives us the land" (Josh 2:14 NRSV). Considering how the narrative
began, one wonders, about which business, exactly, is Rahab to keep
quiet? Is it the fact that they still had hopes to fulfill their spying mission? Or, the fact that their business was "to view the land, especially
Jericho," and they had, thus far, got no farther, than a prostitute's—at the
story's most innocent interpretation—roof? Perhaps both are allowed
by the narrative.[96] In any case, their words are enough for Rahab, and

95. My translation.

96. The MT seems to allow for both interpretations. The phrase, "we will deal kindly and faithfully with you" comes at the end of the sentence. A more literal translation
would have "if you do not tell this deed of ours when YHWH gives us the land to us

she lowers them through a window into the city with instructions on how they can escape their pursuers.

Apparently, though, Rahab's identity as a friend to Israel and Israel's God is not enough reassurance for the spies. Once they are safely on the ground, no longer dangling by Rahab's rope, they call up to her about two matters dealing with identity. The first is a practical matter: how will the Israelites identify the dwelling of Rahab and her family? The solution is for Rahab to tie a crimson cord in the window through which she has just released the two men. The crimson cord provides an echo of the blood painted on the door lintels when the Israelites were preparing for God's rescue of them from Egypt. Just as the angel of death passed over the Israelites' dwellings, so the Israelites will pass over Rahab's dwelling place, and she and her family will be spared the killing that will sweep through the land.

But in addition to the practicality of identifying Israel's friends in the time of the conquest, the spies reiterate their concern that Rahab not "tell this business of ours" (Josh 2:20 NRSV). No longer dependent upon her rooftop hiding place, her rope leading them down to safety, or her words of wisdom concerning their flight plan, the spies reassert their identity as spies and their suspicions of her as a Canaanite. Despite the fact that she has already shown herself faithful to their God and helpful to them, they want reassurance that she will not disclose their actions. As if to assert that they now have the upper hand despite their recent dependence upon her, they call up to Rahab who peers down

---

then we will deal kindly and faithfully with you." Perhaps Rahab is to keep quiet now and also when YHWH gives them the land and the spies' superiors also arrive in the land. In rabbinic tradition, any ambivalence is cleared up. Rahab had an unwholesome past, but it is over by the time the Israelites come to her home that night. Rahab is a model proselyte whose disgraceful history as a prostitute gives way to faithful repentance, demonstrated by her hiding of the spies (Baskin, "Rabbinic Transformation," 144). See, for example, *b. Zebah.* 116a–b in which Rahab's knowledge of YHWH's saving of Israel at the Red Sea come from the fact that "There was no prince or ruler who had not possessed Rahab the harlot." That is, her knowledge came from the princes and rulers whom she served as a prostitute. However, the same passage then relates, "At the age of fifty she became a proselyte. Said she: May I be forgiven as a reward for the cord, window, and flax." In some traditions, even her past as a prostitute is denied. According to *Sipre Num.* 78, for example, Rahab is not a prostitute, but rather an innkeeper. Baskin explains that the rabbis interpreted *zônāh* as coming from the root *zûn*, "to prepare food," "to sustain," rather than from the root *znh*, "to act as a prostitute." However, as Baskin notes, "innkeepers were not above suspicion of sexual promiscuity" (Baskin, "Rabbinic Transformation," 150).

upon them from her window, and demand that she keep her oath. She reassures them that she will and once again drives the action forward by sending them away (Josh 2:21). Because of Rahab, the Israelite spies safely complete their mission.

Rahab's story is a mix of faithfulness and deceit, straightforward appearances and surprises. She is willing to deceive her Canaanite king in order to carry out the plans of the God of Israel. She is faithful in deed and word to the Israelite spies, taking action to hide them and deliver them safely, and keeping her word not to disclose their purpose in spending time with her. As spies, the Israelites initially fail miserably; their identity is discovered immediately by their adversaries. Conversely, Rahab's identity as faithful to the God of Israel is kept from her fellow citizens. Her identity as anything more than a Canaanite prostitute may in fact have been revealed to the spies only once Rahab takes action to hide them and speaks the words of a faithful Israelite, the words Moses told the people of Israel to use.[97] Rahab's deceit to her fellow citizens is faithfulness to the God of Israel. By her faithfulness she transgresses her own transgressive identity (a Canaanite prostitute) by proving her-self to be more than a one night companion to the Israelite spies who enter Canaan. In the words of Frymer-Kensky, a Canaanite prostitute becomes, "the 'midwife' of the embryonic Israel."[98]

Connections with the Enochic Template

USE OF THE ILLICIT ARTS

While Tamar used the illicit arts to play the role of a prostitute and gain offspring to guarantee her future and a future for Judah, Rahab was a prostitute. Her use of the illicit arts in order to have sexual relations with men provided her with her livelihood and her identity ("a pros-titute whose name was Rahab," Josh 2:1). By the time of the rabbis, it was said that "even the sound of her name evoked sexual excitement."[99]

97. Deut 4:39.

98. Frymer-Kensky, *Reading the Women of the Bible*, 36.

99. *b. Meg.* 15a: "The Rabbis taught: there have been four women surpassing beauty in this world—Sarah, Rahab, Abigail, and Esther . . . Rahab inspired lust by her name . . . R. Isaac said: Whoever says, 'Rahab, Rahab', at once has an issue . . . Said R. Nahman to him: I say Rahab, Rahab and nothing happens to me!"

Although the narrative does not tell, the Israelite spies may have come to her house specifically because of her identity as a prostitute and hence her sexual availability to them. The reader is certainly given no information that the Israelite spies knew her as anything other than a prostitute with a home on the edge of the city wall when they paid her a visit at night. Their initial attempts at intelligence into the city of Jericho ended at the city wall and perhaps with an attempt to gain "knowledge" of Rahab alone. However, if Rahab's practice of the illicit arts connected with seduction is what attracts the spies to her house, their attraction to her is what saves them. Had they not come to Rahab's house, they might not only have been found out but also apprehended, and their mission thwarted. Once again, as with the case of Tamar, the woman's use of the illicit arts results not in disaster, but in the movement forward of God's plan of salvation.

Not only does Rahab engage in illicit arts connected with seduction, but she also helps spies gain access to Canaan as part of Israel's military conquest of the land. While Rahab herself does not take up weapons of war, her actions make way for the Israelites to do so. Therefore her story is connected with the illicit arts of war. Clearly in this context, these arts are not perceived within the narrative as negative for Rahab or the Israelites who engage in them directly. Rather, they are the necessary means by which Israel enters the promised land. Rahab's story, then, makes use of two categories of illicit arts identified in *1 En.* 8:1, arts concerned with the making of war and the beautification of women.

In addition to the concern with transgression and the use of the illicit arts, the story of Rahab may be connected with other Enochic themes. These themes are seen in three connections with angels, her hiding of God's messengers, and connections with giants.

Entertaining Angels

Like Tamar, Rahab also is associated with angels by later tradition. In the New Testament Letter of James, Rahab is paired with Abraham as an example of one justified by works and not by faith alone (Jas 2:24). Rahab is named specifically in Jas 2:25: "was not Rahab the prostitute also justified by works when she welcomed the messengers [ἀγγέλους;

ἄγγελος in the nominative singular][100] and sent them out by another road?" The ambiguous word ἄγγελος, translated in many English translations of Jas 2:25 as "messenger,"[101] is also the word used in the LXX for "angel." The ambiguity is present in Hebrew as well, and in Josh 6:25 the word מלאכים is used to explain why Joshua spared the lives of the Canaanite Rahab and her family when the Israelites conquered the land and committed all other Canaanite people and animals to the ban: "But Rahab the prostitute, with her family and all who belonged to her, Joshua spared. She lives in Israel to this day for she hid the messengers (מלאכים) whom Joshua sent to spy out Jericho." It is interesting that the LXX does not use ἄγγελος in Josh 6:25, but κατάσκοπος ("spy") instead. In other words, the writer of James is not quoting the LXX text, but rather makes use of the ambiguous ἄγγελος which may connote "messenger" or "angel," and thereby preserves the ambiguity of the Hebrew version of Josh 6:25 with its מלאכים.

It is their hospitable treatment of messengers/angels that links Abraham and Rahab as positive examples in James, according to Robert W. Wall.[102] The epistle mentions Abraham's offering of Isaac as the irrefutable proof of Abraham's justification by works (Jas 2:21; See Gen 22:1–14). However, Wall, citing R. B. Ward, notes the epistle's repeated reference to "works" in the plural. The single example given, of the *Akedah*, functions as a synecdoche, referring to all of Abraham's spiritual tests.[103] The action of Abraham that most clearly links the patriarch with Rahab is Abraham's merciful treatment of the three strangers who visit Abraham and Sarah and promise the birth of Isaac (Gen 18:1–15). The strangers turn out to be angels on their way not only to bring good news to righteous Abraham and Sarah, but also to wreak destruction on unrighteous Sodom and Gomorrah. Abraham shows hospitality to the angels, a theme further emphasized by the inhospitable treatment with which the angels are threatened by the residents of Sodom. Abraham's hospitable treatment of the angelic strangers leads to the promise that "Abraham shall become a great and mighty nation, and all the nations of the earth shall be blessed in him" (Gen 18:18).

100. There are a few texts, however that have κατάσκοπος(spy), as in LXX, instead of ἄγγελος, the earliest of which is C, from the fifth century CE.

101. For example, in the NASB, RSV, and ASV.

102. Wall, "Intertextuality," 217–32.

103. Ibid., 224.

In the time of Rahab, Israel's entry into the promised land of Canaan is dependent upon another act of hospitality, Rahab's merciful treatment of the two spies. However, James does not praise Rahab for hiding the spies, but rather for "receiving the messengers" (ὑποδεξαμένη τοὺς ἀγγέλους, Jas 2:25). The use of ἄγγελος here, as in Josh 6:25, provides a parallel of Abraham's righteous behavior in Genesis 18 towards his angelic visitors. Further, James praises Rahab because she "sent them out by another road" (ἑτέρᾳ ὁδῷ ἐκβαλοῦσα, Jas 2:25). Wall points out that Rahab's sending (ἐκβάλλω) may be a hook-word linking Rahab's actions towards the messengers she received with Abraham's actions toward his guests. Abraham sends the messengers away (לשלחם) in Gen 18:16 and Rahab sends her visitors away (ותשלחם) in Josh 2:21.[104] The combination of receiving and sending away the unexpected guests, says Walls, "frames the hospitable works that authenticate the faith of each."[105] And in each case, the blessing by God of Israel is at stake— Abraham will become a great nation, and Rahab's hospitality enables the conquest of the land and allows her family to have a place in the land that is a blessing to the Israelites. More will be said about Rahab's "receiving" and "sending away" the "messengers" below in a discussion of parallels with Matthew's Gospel.

It appears, then, that by the time of the writing of the epistle of James the story of Rahab has been reinterpreted so that the spies are now understood as angels in disguise, just as the strangers who first visited Abraham were initially seen as men and turned out to be angels. Some parallels between Rahab's story and the story of Moses have been noted in the overview of Rahab's story above. Another connection between Moses and Rahab may be that the Lord promised Moses that he would send an angel (ἄγγελος) ahead of him into the promised land. According to Wall, "Rahab's positive response to them [the "messengers/angels"] is, in effect, an affirmative response to God's plan of salvation, which is typically monitored by the agency of angelic messengers."[106] According to James, both Abraham and Rahab have "entertained angels unawares"

---

104. The hook-word connection works only in the MT. In the LXX two different words are used: συμπροπέμπων ("escorted") in Gen 18:16 and ἐξαπέστειλεν ("she sent") in Josh 2:21.

105. Wall, "Intertextuality," 226.

106. Ibid., 228.

(see Heb 13:2, where ἄγγελος is used), and for this hospitable behavior they obtained blessing for Israel.

The context in James for the examples of Abraham's and Rahab's justification through works of hospitality is the discussion in James 2 of the treatment of one's neighbor. Those who show mercy towards their neighbors do the works without which faith is dead. For James this ethical behavior has eschatological consequences as well: "For judgment will be without mercy to anyone who has shown no mercy" (Jas 2:13). This theme, of eschatological judgment based on the treatment of one's neighbor, is of interest to Matthew's Gospel as well. In fact, James's examples in 2:14–16, clothing the naked and feeding the hungry, are also Matthew's in 25:35–36 ("I was hungry and you gave me food, I was thirsty and you gave me something to drink, I was a stranger and you welcomed me, I was naked and you gave me clothing, I was sick and you took care of me, I was in prison and you visited me" NRSV). Merciful treatment of the neighbor leads to welcome into God's "kingdom prepared for you from the foundation of the world" (Matt 25:34 NRSV). In James, as Wall says, hospitable treatment of strangers "heralds a new creation where such 'mercy will triumph over judgment'"[107] (Jas 2:13).

I will revisit the theme of Rahab's foreshadowing of Matthew's Gospel below. For now, I note that the ambiguous meaning of the word ἄγγελος to describe the spies whom Rahab received has been interpreted by James to indicate that Rahab showed hospitality to angels by receiving and sending them out by another way. Her merciful treatment of celestial beings parallels Abraham's and gains both of them their status as exemplars of those justified by works.

CONNECTIONS WITH LOT—HEAD FOR THE HILLS

Rahab's story contains another echo of an earlier story concerning angels and directions for safety. When Rahab lowers the spies out her window she gives them fairly specific instructions. She tells them, "Go to the hills" (ההרה לכו, Josh 2:16). Rahab's advice to go to the hills and stay there three days saves the men, but gives more information than the reader needs in order for the story to move forward. The command to go to the hills for safety is an echo of the instructions given by the angels

107. Ibid., 227.

to Lot when they are about to destroy Sodom and Gomorrah, "flee to the hills" (ההרה המלט, Gen 19:17). In Lot's case, the messengers/angels direct him. In Rahab's case, she gives the angelic advice to the messengers/angels. The parallel is noted by *1 Clement* (written between 80 and 140 CE),[108] in which Abraham, Lot, and Rahab are all connected by the theme of exemplary hospitality and faith. The three are named in succeeding chapters. Abraham is praised in *1 Clement* 10 for "his faith and hospitality";[109] Lot in chapter 11 for "his hospitality and godliness";[110] and of Rahab, *1 Clem.* 12:1 remarks, "Because of her faith and hospitality Rahab the harlot was saved."[111]

Echoes of the events of Sodom and Gomorrah in Rahab's story may also serve Matthew's interest in apocalyptic eschatology, especially in the theme of judgment for inadequate hospitality shown to the envoys of the Deity. Sodom and Gomorrah serve as an important trope in apocalyptic literature for those who were, or will be, destroyed for their wickedness.[112] In his study of the reuse of the Sodom tradition in the

108. According to Welborn, *ABD* 1:1060.

109. In *1 Clem.* 10:7.

110. In *1 Clem.* 11:1.

111. Details of Rahab's instructions to the spies are not given in *1 Clem.* However, her hanging of the crimson thread in her window is given so as to foreshadow that "through the blood of the Lord redemption will come to all who believe and hope in God" (*1 Clem.* 12:7). Rahab is heralded not just for hospitality and faith but also prophecy: "You see, dear friends, not only faith but also prophecy is found in this woman" (*1 Clem.* 12:8). Rahab was also held in rabbinic tradition to be the mother of prophets and priests: "R. Eliezer said: she was rewarded with eight prophets and priests being her descendants, Jeremiah, Hilkiah, Seraiah, Ma'aseiah, Baruch the son of Neriah, Hanane'al, Shalum as it is written: 'And the families of the house of Rahab the harlot . . .'. R. Judah said: Even Huldah the prophetess was a descendant of Rahab as it is said, 'So Hilkiah the priest and Ahikam and Achbar, and Shaphan, and Asaiah went to Huldah the Prophetess, the wife of Shulum the son of Tikvah' (*Yal. Joshua* 9). In *Ruth Rab.* 2:1 Ezekiel and Buzzi are added.

112. In apocalyptic literature, language reminiscent of the destruction of Sodom and Gomorrah is found, for example, in 1 QM 1.1;9.1;16.5–6,7; and 17.12–14; and 1QpHab 10.5, 13; 1 QpHab 9,13 echoes Jer 49:16–18 in which *Edom* will be like Sodom and Gomorrah. In *T. Abr.* 6:13 and *Gk. Apoc. Ezra* 2.19, Sodom is an example of a place destroyed because of its sin. In *T. Isaac* 5.26, the punishment of sinners who "committed the sin of Sodom" is shown to the seer, but the nature of the sin is not described. See Carden, *Sodomy*, 43–60. In the *Testaments of the Twelve Patriarchs*, the example of Sodom occurs repeatedly and sometimes is combined with the fall of the watchers. For example, *T. Benj.* 9:1 says, referring to sexual promiscuity with loose women: "from the words of Enoch the righteous; you will act impurely with the impurity of Sodom, and

canonical Hebrew Bible, Weston Fields argues that "the destruction of Sodom is seen as prototypical of divine judgment upon wicked cities, nations, or peoples with regard to its (a) suddenness and spectacular nature, (b) totality, and (c) perpetuity."[113] Sodomites are "archetypical instances of wickedness," especially with regard to their arrogance, inhospitality, unconcern for the weak or socially disadvantaged, and for sexual transgressions of various kinds.[114] Divine judgment against Sodom and Gomorrah is mentioned in Matthew's Gospel in a passage which also brings together the theme of welcome/reception of those sent by Jesus. In Matthew 10, Jesus sends out the twelve with instructions to do his mission. He tells them, "If anyone will not welcome you (μὴ δέξηται ὑμᾶς) or listen to your words, shake off the dust from your feet as you leave that house or town. For truly I tell you, it will be more tolerable for the land of Sodom and Gomorrah on the day of judgment than for that town" (Matt 10:14–15 NRSV). In other words, not to welcome Jesus' messengers is to court a judgment worse than that which befell Sodom and Gomorrah. Rahab provides an example of one who receives messengers from God hospitably and therefore will escape judgment. In James, she provides an example, by receiving the messengers, of one who "receives the implanted word (δέξασθε τὸν ἔμφουτον

---

you will perish, all save a few; and you will renew wanton deeds with women, and the kingdom of the Lord will not be among you, because straightway he will take it away"; *T. Levi* 14:6–7 declares, referring to sexual promiscuity with prostitutes, adultery, and marriage to Gentile women: "[you] pollute married women, defile virgins of Jerusalem, be joined with harlots and take to wives daughters of the Gentiles, purifying them with an unlawful purification, and your union will be like Sodom and Gomorrah in ungodliness"; *T. Naph.* 3:4–5 remarks, linking Sodom and the watchers: "[recognize] the Lord who made all things, so that you do not become as Sodom which changed the order of its nature. In like manner also the Watchers changed the order of their nature." All three refer to Enoch for their knowledge: *T. Levi* 14:1, "the writing of Enoch"; *T. Naph.* 4.1, "the holy writing of Enoch"; and *T. Benj.* 9:1, "the words of Enoch the Righteous." In *Jubilees*, the sexual nature of Sodom's sin is described: they "commit filthy acts in their flesh, and do abominable things on the earth," (*Jub.* 16:5, 6); and commit "sexual impurity, uncleanness and corruption among themselves" (*Jub.* 20:5; VanderKam, *Jubilees*, 339, 117). In 2 Pet 2:4–10, the judgment of the rebellious angels of *1 Enoch*, "cast them into hell and committed to chains" (NRSV), is combined with Sodom and Gomorrah, "by turning the cities of Sodom and Gomorrah to ashes he condemned them to extinction and made them an example of what is coming to the ungodly" (NRSV).

113. Fields, *Sodom and Gomorrah*, 158.

114. Ibid., 158.

λόγον) that is able to save your souls" (Jas 1:21 NRSV).[115] Rahab received the Israelite messengers (ὑποδεξαμένη τοὺς ἀγγέλους), and then
gave them the same warning the angels gave to Lot to help him and
his family avoid the punishment assigned to Sodom and Gomorrah.
Thus Rahab provides an example of one whose own soul will escape the
judgment of a figurative Sodom and Gomorrah, even as she mirrors the
angelic help given to help Lot and his family to avoid the judgment of
the original Sodom and Gomorrah.

SENDING THEM AWAY BY ANOTHER WAY

But Rahab performs another function that in Matthew's Gospel has
angelic overtones as well. In Joshua, Rahab's sending away of messengers is recorded in two ways. First, she sends them with the advice to
go into the hills. Second, after the spies repeat their desire that Rahab
not tell anyone their "business," she "sent them away" (ותשלחם, MT;
ἐξαπέστειλεν, LXX; Josh 2:21). In James' summary, she "sent them out
by another road" (ἑτέρᾳ ὁδῷ ἐκβαλοῦσα, Jas 2:25 NRSV). In Matthew's
infancy narrative, magi are unwittingly sent as Herod's spies to see the
child "born king of the Jews" (Matt 2:2) and report back to him (Matt
2:8). However, they found the child and worshipped him, "having been
warned in a dream not to return to Herod, they left for their own country by another way" (δι' ἄλλης ὁδοῦ ἀνεχώρησαν εἰς τὴν χώραν αὐτῶν,
Matt 2:12 NRSV). To receive warning and direction in a dream is not an
unfamiliar occurrence in Matthew. In the Matthean infancy narrative
angels appear in dreams with information, warnings, and directions to
Joseph in Matt 1:20 and 2:19. In Matt 2:22 Joseph also has a divinely
inspired dream of warning that guides his geographical destination,
although, as in the magi's nocturnal divine visitation, the presence of
an angel in the dream is not noted. In Rahab's story, she gives warning
to the messengers, giving them instructions for what route they should

---

115. In Matt 13:3–9, Jesus tells a parable in which a sower casts seeds on the ground
to various effect, often called the Parable of the Sower. In the interpretation of the
parable, Matt 13:18–23, the seed is the word of God sown in various kinds of hearers,
a parallel to James's "implanted word." The seed which falls on good soil and produces
fruit is "the one who hears the word of the kingdom and understands it" (ὁ τὸν λόγον
ἀκούων καὶ συνιείς, Matt 13:23 NRSV). Rahab, in receiving the "implanted word," as
evidenced in her action of receiving the messengers, is like the seed falling on good soil,
hearing and understanding and bearing fruit.

take. Her warning to them is interpreted in James as "sending them out by another way." Also, in the Rahab narrative in Joshua, she gives her instructions to the messengers at night, instructions which will save them also from an enemy king. In Matthew's Gospel, the magi receive instructions in a dream to go home by another way in order to prevent them from aiding the enemy king Herod (Matt 2:12).[116] Matthew, by naming Rahab in his genealogy, may have intended his readers to recall Rahab's nighttime warning to the messengers, delivering them safely from an enemy king and giving them alternate directions for their route, and to remember Rahab and her warning when he tells the story of the celestial messengers who appear in dreams and do the same for the magi and Joseph.

Hiding the Elect

Rahab's role as one who hides those who have a divinely mandated mission links her with canonical and Enochic traditions of the same theme. These traditions sometimes also involve angelic intervention.

I noted above some parallels between Rahab's role in the entry into Canaan and the Exodus from Egypt under Moses's leadership. Yet another parallel is seen in the theme of hiding. The relatively rare word for "hide," from the root צפן, is used in the Rahab story when Rahab hides the spies under the flax.[117] Specifically, the third person imperfect feminine form of the verb is used with a surprising suffix, the third person masculine singular (ותצפנו) "she hid him" (Josh 2:4). Why would the singular form of the suffix be used when Rahab conceals two men under the flax?[118] The only other use of the third-person feminine imperfect

---

116. The narrative is careful to point out that the verbal exchange between Rahab and the spies takes place "before they went to sleep" (Josh 2:8 NRSV) although there is no mention of their actually going to sleep and the action of their being lowered out the window and fleeing to the hills follows directly on their conversation. Perhaps the mention of these events "before they went to sleep" is an attempt to distance the spies from any implication that they were not at the home of a prostitute for the purpose of sleep. However, as noted, there is no mention of actual sleep.

117. Frymer-Kensky, *Reading*, 36.

118. In *Num. Rab.* 8.9, the rabbis solve the problem of the singular ending by saying that when Rahab hid the two spies, "the Holy One, blessed be He, accounted it unto her as though she had performed the act for *Him*, and He gave her reward. In confirmation of this it says, *And the woman took the two men, and hid* Him' (Josh. 2:4).

of this verb in the Hebrew Bible is when Moses's mother saves her baby by hiding him (תצפנהו, "she hid him")[119] for three months (Exod 2:2).[120] Rahab conceals the Israelite spies (ותצפנו) who would play an instrumental role in the entry into Canaan just as Moses' mother concealed the one (תצפנהו, "she hid him") who would lead the Exodus from Egypt.

In Enochic traditions, leaders are hidden while they receive knowledge that will help them survive and persevere and, in so doing, save a group of people. For example, the angel Sariel is sent to tell Noah to hide himself, to "reveal to him that the end is coming" and to "teach him what he should do, the son of Lamech [Noah], how he may preserve himself alive and escape forever" (*1 En.* 10:1, 3).[121] Through hiding and receiving knowledge, Noah would benefit all generations to come since

> From him a plant will be planted,
> and his seed will endure for all the generations of eternity.
> (*1 En.* 10:3)[122]

Enoch is also hidden and his whereabouts are unknown to humans while he is sent on missions to the watchers and holy ones (*1 En.* 12:1–2).[123] His time of being hidden from humanity is a time during which he gains knowledge he records for the benefit of future generations. In the *Book of the Parables* (*1 Enoch* 37–71), notoriously difficult in regard to dating,[124] it is said of the Son of Man (revealed in *1 En.* 71:14 as Enoch himself),

> For this (reason) he was chosen and hidden in his presence

119. Frymer-Kensky, *Reading*, 36.

120. Is Rahab's sending the spies she concealed to the hill country for three days an echo of Moses' mother hiding her baby for three months?

121. *1 Enoch: A New Translation*, 27–28.

122. Ibid., 28.

123. Knibb translates this passage: "And before everything Enoch had been hidden, and none of the sons of men knew were he was hidden, or where he was, or what had happened. And all his doings were with the Holy Ones and with the Watchers in his days" (Knibb, *The Ethiopic Book of Enoch*, 2:92). The translation by Nickelsburg and VanderKam has "Before these things, Enoch was taken; and no human being knew where he had been taken, or where he was, or what had happened to him. His works were with the watchers and with the holy ones were his days" (*1 Enoch: A New Translation*, 31).

124. See chapter 1, above.

before the world was created and forever.
And the wisdom of the Lord of Spirits has revealed him to the
holy and the righteous;
for he has preserved the portion of the righteous.
(1 En. 48:6–7)[125]

The theme of hiding and while being hidden receiving knowledge that leads to safety and the well-being of the elect is paralleled in Rahab's story.

Comparing Rahab's story with other traditions shows Rahab as one who receives angelic messengers and acts herself as angelic messengers do. She receives and sends angels, as does Abraham (noted in James). She gives messages that parallel those of angelic messengers, sending her messengers to the hills, as in the case of Lot (noted by 1 Clement). She warns and directs the spies at night, sending them to a different destination in order to save them from an enemy king, as the angels do with the magi in Matthew.[126] She hides her messengers as the mother of Moses and Enochic angels do of the elect, thereby protecting people whose well-being will benefit an entire group.[127]

OFFSPRING—ECHOES OF GIANTS

The narrative about Rahab's hiding and directing the spies does not include any information about her status as a mother. Her family is mentioned (father, mother, brothers, and "all who belonged to" her; Josh 2:18; 6:23), but no child. It is Matthew's genealogy that makes Rahab the mother of Boaz, or preserves another tradition which does so.[128] In so doing, Matthew ties Rahab with traditions about the גברים and, by association, with traditions about giants, another Enochic theme.

---

125. *1 Enoch: A New Translation*, 62.

126. And as they do with Joseph as well. The spy element is missing in the case of Joseph, although Joseph, like the magi, finds himself traveling to a foreign country by divine mandate.

127. As many have noted, the hiding of Jesus from Herod by taking him to Egypt provides a parallel to the hiding of Moses as well. More will be mentioned on this subject in the next chapter.

128. Others beside Matthew have desired a man to make an honest woman of Rahab. The Talmud reports that Rahab married a man who is perhaps her equal in heroism on behalf of Israel, no less than Joshua himself. *b. Meg.* 14b–15a (trans. Epstein).

Matthew's connection of Rahab and Boaz will be examined first, followed by the גברים –giants connection.

It is ostensibly Rahab's status as a mother which qualifies her for
mention in Matthew's genealogy, as mother of Boaz by Salmon (Matt
1:5). However, the chronology of the Hebrew Bible would separate
Rahab and Salmon by about two centuries.[129] That Salmon is the father
of Boaz is supported by the genealogy with which the book of Ruth
concludes. No women, however, are mentioned in Ruth's genealogy.
There are no other extant sources in which Rahab and Salmon are
linked to each other. Davies and Allison suppose that this pairing is
"the product of Matthean fancy."[130] Bauckham, however, argues that the
marriage of Rahab and Salmon "must surely have been an already accepted exegetical tradition"[131] in order for Matthew to include it in his
genealogy, expecting, as he did, that it would carry weight with his audience. In looking for the roots of the tradition, Bauckham points to the
practice of Jewish exegetes at the time of the New Testament of linking
biblical figures with the same names[132] or similar names[133] whenever
possible. Bauckham then identifies the Salma of 1 Chron 2:51, 54, the
father of Bethlehem, with the Salma of 1 Chron 2:11 who is identified as the father of Boaz. This Salma is the Salmon named by Matthew
as the father of Boaz. Bauckham then identifies the Rechab (רכב) of
1 Chron 2:55 with Rahab (רחב). The two, Salma and Rahab, could be
understood as married because 1 Chron 2:55, usually translated as
"These are the Kenites who came from Hammath (מחמת), the father
of the house of Rechab,"[134] could be understood as meaning, "from the
family-in-law of the father of Rahab."[135] The "family-in-law" connection
is made if "Hammath" (חמת) is understood not as a place name but as
a relationship, because of its similarity with חם, "father-in-law," (as in
Gen 38:13, 25; 1 Sam 4:19, 21)[136] and חמה, "mother-in-law" (as in Mic
7:6). According to 1 Chron 2:55, then, the Kenites, Salma's descendents,

129. Davies and Allison, *Matthew 1–7*, 173.
130. Ibid.
131. Bauckham, "Tamar's Ancestry," 322.
132. Ibid., 326.
133. Ibid., 327.
134. Ibid.
135. Ibid.
136. Ibid.

came from the family-in-law of Rahab's father because Rahab had married Salma.[137]

Whether a product of "Matthean fancy," or of an extant Jewish exegetical tradition, Rahab in Matthew's genealogy has a husband named Salmon and is the mother of Boaz. Boaz figures prominently in the life of Ruth, the next woman named in Matthew's genealogy. With Boaz comes a connection with giants, present in the Enochic template. An examination of this connection shows, not that heroes of the Hebrew Bible were thought of as physically gigantic in the way that the gigantic offspring of wayward angels and human mothers were. What does become apparent is a trajectory in which both the גברים who are the heroes and legendary figures of the Hebrew Bible and the גברים who are the gigantic offspring find common background.

In Ruth 2:1 Boaz is called גבור חיל, variously translated as "a prominent rich man" (NRSV); "a man of wealth" (RSV); "prominent" (NAB); "a man of standing" (NIV); "a man of great wealth" (NASB), and "a mighty man of wealth" (ASV).The phrase is used of other valiant men or warriors in the Hebrew Bible, including other Israelites, for example, Joshua's soldiers (Josh 8:3), Gideon (Judg 6:12) and Jephthah, (Judg 11:1, also the son of a prostitute), and David (1 Sam 16:18); as well as non-Israelites, for example, the mighty men of Jericho, delivered into the hand of Joshua (Josh 6:2), the Gibeonite mighty men (Josh 10:2), Goliath the Philistine (1 Sam 17:51) and Namaan the Syrian (2 Kgs 5:1).[138] This is the same word used in Gen 6:4 to describe the offspring

---

137. Ibid.

138. In the LXX, words used to translate גבר and גברים often include δυνατὸς ἰσχύι and similar terms. For example, in Ruth 2:1 Boaz is called δυνατὸς ἰσχύι; Joshua's mighty men (Josh 8:3) are called δυνατοὺς ἐν ἰσχύι; Gideon (Judg 6:12) is δυνατὸς τῇ ἰσχύι (in A) and ἰσχυρὸς τῶν δυνάμεων (in B); Jephthah, (Judg 11:1) is δυνατὸς ἐν ἰσχύι (in A) and ἐπηρμένος δυνάμει (B); the mighty men of Jericho defeated by Joshua (Josh 6:2) are δυνατοὺς ὄντος ἐν ἰσχύι; the mighty Gibeonite opponents of Joshua and his army(Josh 10:2) are ἰσχροί; Namaan the Syrian (2 Kgs 5:1) is δυνατὸς ἰσχύι. David is an exception. In 1 Sam 16:18 the word in the LXX corresponding to גבר is συνετός, meaning "intelligent," "sagacious," "wise," "with good sense" (Arndt and Gingrich [eds.], Greek-English Lexicon, 796). The word, συνετός looks somewhat similar to δυνατὸς, so perhaps the use of συνετός here is an error. However, David, although called a גבר in the Hebrew text of 1 Sam 16:18, will be revealed in his confrontation with Goliath (another גבר) as wise, rather than as a mighty warrior in the same way that Goliath is a mighty warrior. David relies on the Lord, whereas Goliath relies on weapons: "David said to the Philistine, 'You come against me with sword and spear and javelin, but I come against you in the name of the Lord Almighty, the God of the armies of Israel, whom you have defied'"

of the daughters of humans and the sons of God, "These were the he-roes (הגברים) that were of old, warriors of renown" (NRSV). Thus the Genesis story of the relations between women and the sons of God pro-vides an aetiology for the origin of humans of exceptional strength or valor, people seen later in the Hebrew Bible, Israelite and non-Israelite alike.

Genesis 6:4 also describes the event of the sons of God having sex-ual relations with women and producing the גברים as taking place when "the Nephilim (הנפלים) were on the earth" (NRSV). In the Hebrew Bible the Nephilim and the origins of the גברים are concurrent. However, in the LXX, the relationship between the Nephilim and the warriors of renown is unclear. Both terms, the גברים and the Nephilim, were trans-lated as οἱ γίγαντες ("the giants") in the LXX.[139]

The connection between the γίγαντες /Nephilim and the γίγαντες /offspring of the angels and women is also made in *1 Enoch*. In *1 Enoch*, the offspring of the watchers and the women are "great giants" (*1 En.* 7:2).[140] Nickelsburg notes that the Aramaic word used in *1 En.* 7:2 for the offspring was *gibbārîn*,[141] and that "these offspring correspond to the גברים of Genesis."[142] According to *1 Enoch*, the giants/ גברים then begat Nephilim (*1 En.* 7:2). A third generation of giants also results, called "Elioud" (*1 En.* 7:2). The meaning of "Elioud" is obscure, but may denote that these giants were anti-gods.[143] In 4Q 180–81 (4Q Ages of Creation), there are also two references to the offspring of the watch-ers and women, both using the word translated as "giant" (גברים) to describe them.[144]

(1 Sam 17:45). The LXX in calling David συνετός rather than δυνατός in 1 Sam 16:18, prepares the reader for David's confrontation with Goliath, who is called δυνατός in 1 Sam 17:51, by making a distinction between the wise David and his mighty oppo-nent, a distinction not made in the Hebrew text, which calls them both גברים.

139. Nickelsburg, *1 Enoch 1*, 184. Stuckenbruck points out that the "assimilation of both Hebrew terms into one group" is made by the Aramaic Targums *Onqelos* and *Neophyti* on Gen 6:4, which have גיבריא and גיבריה, respectively (Stuckenbruck, "The Origins of Evil," 89n3).

140. *1 Enoch: A New Translation*, 24.

141. Nickelsburg, *1 Enoch 1*, 185.

142. Ibid.

143. Ibid.

144. "[And] interpretation concerning 'Azaz'el and the angels wh[o came to the daughters of man] [and] sired themselves giants" ("גברים") . . ." (4Q180 1.7–8); "[the

As noted in the section on the watchers above, the gigantic offspring of the watchers and women wreak havoc and destruction in the
world because of their voracious appetites and bellicose natures. The
size of these offspring is described in CD 2:19 (=4Q266 2 II:19): "And
their sons, whose height was like that of cedars and whose bodies were
like mountains . . ."[145] The same text also brings together both terms,
Nephilim and גברים, in a summary of the fall of the watchers, their
monstrous offspring, and the dire consequences for the world of the
watchers' transgressions. The passage attempts to explain not only what
went wrong, but the origins of the word "Nephilim" as well. The passage begins with a description of the legacy of sin left by the fall of the
watchers, namely, "the thoughts of a guilty inclination and lascivious
eyes" (CD 2:16). The passage continues,

> For many have gone astray due to these ["the thoughts
> of a guilty inclination and lascivious eyes"]; brave heroes
> (וגבורי חיל) stumbled on account of them, from ancient times
> until now. For having walked in the stubbornness of their hearts
> the Watchers of the heavens fell (נפלו); on account of it they
> were caught, for they did not heed the precepts of God. And
> their sons, whose height was like that of cedars and whose bod-
> ies were like mountains, fell (נפלו). All flesh which there was
> on the dry earth expired and they became as if they had never
> been, because they had realized their desires and had failed to
> keep their creator's precepts, until his wrath flared up against
> them. (CD 2:16–21)[146]

In other words, the passage reports that even brave heroes (גברים)
throughout time have fallen (from the root נפל) because of lustful
thoughts. First the watchers fell (נפל). Then their gigantic offspring
(גברים) fell (נפל). And mighty warriors (גברים) have been falling ever
since.

In the Hebrew Bible as well, גברים and other words describing giants, Nephilim (נפילים) and Rephaim (רפאים), indicate people of stature
and power and, in some cases, people of bellicose nature who threaten

---

daughters of] man and sired giant[s] ("[גבר]ים") for themselves" (4Q181 2.2). See
García Martínez and Tigchelaar, *Dead Sea Scrolls*, 1:370–75).

145. García Martínez and Tigchelaar, *Dead Sea Scrolls*, 1:553. See also Nickelsburg,
1 Enoch 1, 185.

146. García Martínez and Tigchelaar, *Dead Sea Scrolls*, *Dead Sea Scrolls*, 1:553.

the Israelites long after the primeval narratives in Genesis have come to an end. For example, Num 13:31–33 describes the Nephilim who inhabit Canaan: they are so tall they make the Israelites seem like grasshoppers in comparison. Deuteronomy 3:1–11 tells of King Og of Bashan who came out in battle against the Israelites. King Og was of the remnant of the gigantic Rephaim; his huge iron bed is noted as a curiosity still on display in Rabbah of the Ammonites. Second Samuel 21:16–22 tells of four descendants of giants (Rephaim): Ishbi-benob and Goliath the Gittite, whose size and power are indicated by their dreadfully large weapons (a spear weighing three hundred shekels of bronze and a spear shaft like a weaver's beam respectively), Saph, and the giant of Gath, noted for having an extra digit on each of his hands and feet. Another adversary of Israel named in 1 Samuel is Goliath, mentioned above, the enemy taken on by David, who is called the Philistine's גבר.[147]

The words for "giant" in both *1 Enoch* and the Hebrew Bible have some specific meanings and some meanings which are unclear or overlap. *Rephaim* seems to be a specific term for a race of people gigantic in size, bellicose, and enemies to the Israelites. The נפילים and גברים both get translated as "giants" by the LXX, and the Genesis and Enochic traditions contain efforts to sort out the differences between, and origins of, the two.[148] In the Hebrew Bible, גברים has a broader meaning,

147. 1 Sam 17:51.
148. See Stuckenbruck, "The Origins of Evil," on attempts by authors of apocalyptic traditions to distinguish between them, particularly in regard to myths of the transmission of knowledge, for instance, in the fragmentary accounts preserved by Alexander Polyhistor in the first century BCE in his "On the Jews." In one of the fragments, "Abraham's ancestry is traced to giants 'who lived in the land of Babylonia.'" Abraham is the source of astrological knowledge, which he passed on to the Phoenicians and to Egyptian priests (Stuckenbruck, "The Origins of Evil," 95). In both fragments, giants provide the link between the "pre-diluvian Enoch and the post-diluvian Abraham," that is, they are responsible for the introduction of culture in the world. Only some of the giants are punished for their action, namely those giants who, according to this account, build a tower in Babylon, and are punished by being scattered throughout the earth. The introduction of culture *per se* by the giants is not offensive or punishable (ibid., 96–97). However, in other early apocalyptic texts such as the *Book of the Watchers*, "a clear line of demarcation" is drawn between the watchers who begot giants and introduced illicit knowledge to humans and the angels who instructed Enoch in divine knowledge (ibid., 100). In the *Book of Giants*, dated by Stuckenbruck to the first half of the second century BCE, the giants are regarded as uniformly evil and deserving of punishment (ibid., 105). In summary, ambivalent traditions about giants must have existed that needed sorting out and specifying which were evil and culpable for

indicating people of valor who are worthy of emulation, such as Boaz and his descendant King David, as well as people who are portrayed as merely bellicose and strong, such as Moabite warriors and Goliath, the Philistine champion. In the Genesis tradition, the גברים came into being with the relations between the sons of God and the women, but they clearly live on in Hebrew Bible traditions. In *1 Enoch*, likewise, they are the products of the sexual liaison of watchers and women. While these destructive giants may have been contained through the efforts of the archangel Gabriel (*1 En.* 10:9 and 15), their spirits will plague humankind until "the great judgment" (*1 En.* 16:1). Jackson makes the point that the aspect of the גברים that is most to be feared is not their size, but their ongoing threat to the eschatological generation.[149]

This presentation of the background of גברים is necessary for looking at one further aspect of Rahab's identity, as mother of Boaz. It will also be useful when reviewing traditions related to Ruth and her family members. As mentioned already, Boaz is a גבר חיל, a prominent man, and clearly from his actions that will be reviewed in the next section, a man to be emulated. His characterization as גבר is solely a compliment. However, I wonder if there may be an echo, however faint, in the story of a prostitute who makes use of the illicit arts who has welcomed angels (מלאכים) to her home and becomes the mother of a גבר, of the earlier tradition of angels (מלאכים) who have sexual relations with women and give birth to גברים.

RAHAB AND THE CANAANITE WOMAN IN MATTHEW

As mentioned above, scholars have noted the connections between Rahab, the Canaanite prostitute, and the Canaanite woman in Matthew's Gospel who approaches Jesus and obtains healing for her daughter. Although I argue that Matthew's Canaanite woman has much in common with Rahab's ancestor Tamar, I note the similarities between Rahab and the Canaanite woman in Matthew. It may be that Matthew intends to evoke both Tamar and Rahab in his presentation of the Canaanite woman.

---

destruction and misery on earth, and which could be regarded as good and playing a role in divine revelation.

149. Jackson, *Enochic Judaism*, 40.

In addition to their clear identification as Canaanites, Rahab and the Canaanite woman in Matthew both make statements of faith. These statements of faith set them apart from the other characters in their stories and gain them the life they are seeking. Rahab, in stating her belief in the God of Israel and making her statement using the formula given by Moses, becomes a model of faith for Israelites, despite her Canaanite identity. The Canaanite woman is praised by Jesus for her statement of faith after she says, "Yes, Lord, yet even the dogs eat the crumbs that fall from their masters' (κυρίων) table" (Matt 15:27 NRSV). The woman refers to Jesus as "Lord," in Matt 15:22, 25, and 27. In 15:27, as Stephen Humphries-Brooks points out, the woman also refers to "lords" in the genitive (possessive) plural.[150] Humphries-Brooks believes that the use of κυρίων in 15:27 is a reference to her confessional use of "Lord" earlier in the sentence. It is the bread rather than the table which belongs to the children, according to Jesus' statement in 15:26. By referring to "Lords'" in the plural, the woman's statement of faith is consistent with Matthew's claim that "the eschatological banquet belongs to God and the Son of Man (e.g. Matt 22:1–14; 25:1–13)."[151] Thus, her statement of faith combines "theological, Christological, and eschatological-apocalyptic insight."[152] Both Rahab and the Canaanite woman in Matthew are examples of women outside the boundaries of Israel who make strong statements of faith for which they are rewarded and remembered.

Summary

The story of Rahab, and the various traditions which made use of her story, is the story of a woman who transgressed Israelite social mores by being a prostitute. She also transgressed her Canaanite identity by deceiving her king and compatriots. Through her words of allegiance to the God of Israel and her acts of welcoming and sending out the Israelite spies, she plays a crucial role in the conquest of Canaan by the Israelites. Her story contains not only echoes of the canonical stories of Moses, but also echoes of the Enochic template. In addition to the theme of transgression, Rahab is a woman who earns her livelihood using the

---

150. Humphries-Brooks, "The Canaanite Women," 143.

151. Ibid., 144.

152. Ibid.

illicit arts and illicit sexual interaction. She welcomes men who, at least by the time of the writing of the James, are reinterpreted as angels. She hides them, which serves as an echo of the angels' roles vis-à-vis Noah and Enoch. She protects them by sending them to the hills, echoing the story of Sodom and Gomorrah. She sends them out by another way, instructing them at night, echoing the role of angels in the Matthean narrative. Rahab is identified by Matthew as the mother of one of the גברים, Boaz, a designation with multivalent significance in the Hebrew Bible, but clearer meaning in the Enochic tradition. However, despite her transgressions, her use of illicit arts and engagement in illicit sexual interaction, her connections with celestial beings, and her noteworthy offspring, Rahab's story is one of hope and victory, in her own time and for Israel's future.

I look now at the story of Ruth, who married the גבור חיל Boaz, but not without first committing some transgressions of her own.

Ruth: Under Cover of Night

Ruth is the third woman named in Matthew's genealogy, appearing in Matt 1:5. Her story is the subject of the biblical book of Ruth. She is another non-Israelite, a Moabite in origin. Ruth will, like Rahab, transgress ethnic boundaries in order to become part of the people of Israel and play an important role ensuring their future. Like Tamar, Ruth has found herself widowed with no child, and Ruth also will transgress social mores to gain security and a child. Ruth follows the plan of her mother-in-law Naomi to secure a commitment from Boaz, although Ruth takes the plan into her own hands at the time it is carried out. The target of the plan, Boaz, will not know of the women's machinations until he finds himself in the midst of a situation he had not intended. He may be pleased by the outcome, but he is first surprised to find himself involved. Ruth's story, too, involves use of the illicit arts. Because she is a Moabite, Ruth is connected with three aspects of the watchers' legacy: illicit sexual intercourse, bloodshed, and idolatry. Further, Moabites share with those of illegitimate birth the status of being excluded from the assembly of the Lord. The designation of illegitimate birth is also applied at Qumran to the offspring of the watchers and the women. The story proceeds as follows.

Ruth is a Moabite and widow who goes with her mother-in-law Naomi to Bethlehem where, following a long famine, food is once again available. Naomi tells Ruth to stay in Moab as Naomi has no other son for Ruth to marry. Ruth's sister-in-law, Orpah, in the same situation as Ruth, kisses Naomi goodbye. But Ruth refuses, making her declaration,

> Where you go, I will go;
> where you lodge I will lodge;
> your people shall be my people,
> and your God my God. (Ruth 1:16 NRSV)

Once in Bethlehem, Naomi notices that Ruth has caught the attention of a relative of hers by the name of Boaz, and Naomi hatches a plan to gain him as a husband for Ruth.

Ruth, following Naomi's instruction, takes her place next to Boaz one night on the threshold after "Boaz had eaten and drunk, and he was in a contented mood" (Ruth 3:7 NRSV), coming to him "stealthily" (Ruth 3:7 NRSV). She "uncovered his feet, and lay down" (Ruth 3:7 NRSV). That all of this is done without Boaz's knowledge is apparent when he wakes at midnight startled, rolls over and sees a woman at his feet (Ruth 3:8). He sees her, and yet does not. He has to ask her name. Here she is truthful with Boaz when she reveals her identity, "I am Ruth, your servant" (Ruth 3:9 NRSV). At this point, Ruth departs from Naomi's instructions. Rather than wait for Boaz to tell her what to do (Ruth 3:4), Ruth tells Boaz what to do: "spread your cloak over your servant, for you are next-of-kin" (Ruth 3:9 NRSV). Actually, he is not. There is a man with that identity, but Boaz is impressed enough by Ruth that he promises to stand up publicly for her and gain the right to be her redeemer, even as he has reclined privately with her on the threshing floor and desired this right. What Boaz does tell her to do is to stay the rest of the night with him, but leave before dawn's light can illumine her identity or expose where she spent the night (Ruth 3:13–14). In other words, Boaz also participates in the cover-up. A woman who has spent the night covered by his cloak should not be seen leaving the scene.

The next day, Boaz makes good on his word and in the appropriate public venue openly engages in the customs by which he accepts the obligations of acquiring the field and Ruth as his wife (Ruth 4:7–10). However, there is an actual next of kin who must first give up his right to redeem the land and Ruth. In this detail too, there is the uncovering of the truth in stages: the unnamed man is at first happy to acquire the land (Ruth 4:4). However, when he finds out the whole truth, that he would also be obliged to take on Ruth and further the inheritance of Ruth's dead husband rather than benefit his own financial future, he gives up the right of redemption (Ruth 4:6). Boaz is free to be the redeemer and marry Ruth. Together they have a son, whom they name Obed. The book is completed by a genealogy which begins with Perez, as mentioned above, the son of Tamar, and goes through Obed, to David.

Ruth's story then has a very happy ending for all involved. A story that began with multiple deaths in the land of Moab (Ruth 1:1–5) ends in Judah with many generations leading up to King David. Naomi calls herself "Bitter" (Mara) at the beginning of the story (Ruth 1:20) and is celebrated at the story's conclusion by the women of the neighborhood who say, "A son has been born to Naomi" (Ruth 4:17 NRSV). Clearly, with the story's outcome, Naomi is able to reclaim the meaning of her name, "Pleasantness." But the story ending with pleasantness, prosperity, and posterity comes because of transgression, even if it is transgression for a good cause and with a good outcome. Naomi and Ruth have tricked Boaz by putting him into a compromising position on the threshing floor. Ruth's transgression of social mores and ethnic identity will become even more apparent through an examination of the connections in her story with the Enochic template.

Connections with the Enochic Template

USE OF THE ILLICIT ARTS

Ruth's encounter with Boaz on the threshing floor is orchestrated by the design of Naomi who instructs Ruth in how the night should progress. Specifically Naomi instructs Ruth to "wash and anoint yourself, and put on your best clothes and go down to the threshing floor" (Ruth 3:3 NRSV). At its most innocuous, Naomi is merely telling Ruth to make herself presentable, to "pretty herself up" for her encounter with Boaz. However, since the intended result is to put Boaz in a position of being obligated to marry Ruth, it may be more realistic to see Naomi as encouraging Ruth to make use of the arts of seduction, specifically those named as illicit arts in the Enochic tradition. Accordingly Ruth makes use of cosmetic adornment (ointment, perfume), specifically identified as one of the illicit arts, as well as putting on her finest raiment in order to be more attractive to Boaz. Ruth's physical attractiveness, nowhere claimed in the biblical text, became legendary in later rabbinic interpretations of the story. For example, in *Ruth Rab.* 4:4, the phrase in Ruth 2:3, "as it happened," or "by chance," (ויקר מקרה) is interpreted as a statement about the effect of Ruth's appearance on others, "R. Johanan said: Whoever saw her was sexually excited."[153] Ruth is not only beautiful in an aesthetically pleasing sense. Her appearance is such that she is sexually attractive to men. That this interpretation of Ruth's beauty is a later addition to the story is probably attested to by the fact that Naomi gives Ruth instructions to make herself attractive to Boaz. Someone of Ruth's power as the midrashists remembered it would hardly need help.

But Ruth's connection with the illicit arts and seduction may have as much to do with her ethnic heritage as it does with Naomi's instructions. Ruth is a Moabite, a fact mentioned no less than seven times, in Ruth 1:4, 1:22, 2:2, 2:6, 2:21; 4:5, and 4:10. In Israelite tradition, Moabites were associated with idolatry and their women with sexual wantonness and seduction of Israelite men. This association comes from the episode of the worship of Baal of Peor, recorded in Numbers 25:1–5. This incident of Israelite unfaithfulness began with Israelites having sexual relations with Moabite women who also invited the Israelites to make sacrifices to the Moabite gods, eating and bowing down to them. Later tradition elaborated on the Moabite women's proclivity for harlotry and their ability to seduce the Israelite men, even adding an explanation of their techniques. *Num. Rab.* 20:33, for instance, explains,

> They made booths for themselves and placed in them harlots in whose hands were all manner of desirable objects. An old woman would sit outside and keep watch for the girl who was inside the shop. When the Israelite passed by to purchase an article in the bazaar, the old woman would say to him: 'Young man, would you not like some linen clothing that comes from

153. *Ruth Rab.* 4:4. That is, R. Johanan relates the word מקרה, "happening" קרי, to "semen." (trans. Rabinowitz, 52, n.4). The two words מקרה and קרי are related in the term for nocturnal emissions, as in Deut 23:11, where a man in the camp may be unclean because of מקרה־לילה, "chance of night " or "emission of night." See also *New Brown Driver Briggs Gesenius*, 899B, קרה. R. Johanan is second generation, Palestinian, although, as noted above, *Ruth Rab.* is later, but contains earlier traditions. Strack and Stemberger date it to ca. 500 CE.

Beth-Shean?' She would show it to him and say: 'Go inside and
you will see some lovely articles'...Thereupon she would make
him drink the wine and the Satan would burn within him and
he would be led astray after her; for it says harlotry, wine and
new wine take away the heart (Hos. 4:11).[154]

That Ruth is a Moabite, and therefore an heir to Moabite traditions and
regard amongst the Israelites in Judah would not be lost to the readers
of Ruth's story. The narrator's repetition of her ethnic identity would not
allow it. The fact of Ruth's Moabite heritage, then, provides a witness
to the ability of the divine to work in surprising ways, incorporating
surprising people into the plan of salvation, despite what were seen as
their "natural" inclinations.

In fact, the scandal of having Moabite ancestry as part of the
Davidic line is addressed in later rabbinic tradition. By the time of the
writing of *Ruth Rab.*, Ruth becomes a model proselyte, and Naomi's
instructions to Ruth are not about seduction, but about preparations
for righteousness. Naomi's coaching of Ruth becomes, "Wash thyself
clean of thine idolatry. And anoint thee refers to good deeds and righteous conduct. And put thy raiment upon thee. Was she then naked?
It must refer to Sabbath garments."[155] Likewise, the rabbis wanted to
ensure Boaz's uprightness, despite appearances to the contrary in the
text, and taught that despite Ruth's attractive appearance, Boaz did not
even touch her while they lay together on the threshing floor. The voice
of Boaz's "Evil Inclination" speaks to him and says, "'You are unmarried
and seek a wife, and she is unmarried and seeks a husband. Arise and
have intercourse with her, and make her your wife.'"[156] But Boaz resists:
"And he [Boaz] took an oath to his Evil Inclination saying: As the Lord

---

154. See *Midrash Rabbah Numbers,* trans. by Slotki, 337.

155. *Ruth Rab.* 5:12. In the Targum to Ruth the identity of Ruth as a proselyte is
mentioned repeatedly, beginning with 1:16 where Ruth says to Naomi, "I demand to
be converted" (Levine, *Aramaic Version of Ruth,* 22). See also 2:6 (ibid., 24); 2:13 (ibid.,
28); and 3:10 (ibid., 32).

156. *Ruth Rab.* 6:4. The rabbis corroborate the evidence of Boaz's upright behavior
and protect Ruth's reputation as well. When Ruth returns to Naomi, Naomi asks her,
"Who are you my daughter?" (מי־את בתי) which the NIV translates as, "How did it
go, my daughter?" The rabbis prefer a more literal translation and interpret Naomi's
puzzling question to her daughter-in-law in this way: "Did she then not recognize her?
Yes, but she meant, 'Are you still a virgin or a married woman?' She answered, 'A virgin,'
And she told her all that the man had done to her" (see *Midrash Rabbah Ruth,* trans.
by Rabinowitz, 84).

liveth, I will not touch her,' and to the woman he said, 'Lie down until the morning.'"[157] In fact, it is Boaz' ability to resist this temptation that explains his name: "R. Hunya said: It is written, *A wise man is strong (be'oz); yea, a man of knowledge increaseth strength* (Prov. xxiv, 5): read not *'be'oz'* (strong), but *Boaz; 'A wise man is Boaz, and a man of knowledge increaseth strength,'* for he strengthened himself with an oath."[158]

Thus, in later tradition, the Moabite Ruth puts off her seductive ways, putting on "good deeds and righteous conduct" instead, and Boaz does not fall for the beauty and seductive nature of the Moabite. It seems, though, that such developments in the tradition would only be necessary if Ruth's identity as a Moabite still had some scandal attached to it.

The scandal of a Moabite identity comes not only from the incident at Shittim with the Ba'al of Peor, but also from the commandment of Deuteronomy 23:3–6, "No Ammonite or Moabite shall be admitted to the assembly of the Lord. Even to the tenth generation, none of their descendants shall be admitted to the assembly of the Lord . . . You shall never promote their welfare or their prosperity as long as you live" (Deut 23:3, 6 NRSV). Ruth's claim of faithfulness to the God of Israel becomes very important. Otherwise, she remains part of the accursed Moabite people whose presence in the assembly of the Lord is prohibited and whose prosperity is not to be promoted. Despite her statement to Naomi in Ruth 1:16, "your people shall be my people, and your God my God," Ruth continues to be called "the Moabite" by the narrator of the story.

Moabites, as presented in the Hebrew Bible tradition, are a clear example of a people who have transgressed the Noachic law. Transgression of the Noachic law may be the concern of the Enochic watchers narrative. As stated above, in chapter 2, the three main concerns of the Noachic law and the subjects of the illicit pedagogy taught by the watchers are shedding blood, illicit sexual intercourse, and idolatry.[159] Moabites were considered enemies of Israel who had engaged in all three. Moabite women were responsible for seducing

157. Ibid., 81.

158. Ibid. In the rabbinic tradition, then, Boaz acts in a way opposite to the watchers. Whereas they take an oath to engage in illicit sexual activity (*1 En.* 6:4), Boaz takes an oath that he will not engage in illicit sexual activity.

159. Dimant, "1 Enoch 6–11," 227–28.

Israelite men into participating in the last two, with tragic results and the shedding of the blood of many Israelites (see Num 25:1–5). Perhaps Moabite women's supposed predilection for seducing men for illicit sexual relations comes from their origin. Moab, the eponymous ancestor of the Moabites, was the offspring of Lot's elder daughter and Lot. His daughters had gotten Lot drunk in order to have sexual intercourse with him when they feared they may have been the last humans on earth after witnessing the utter destruction of Sodom and Gomorrah (Gen 19:30–38).[160]

In addition to the incident of Ba'al of Peor, which ends with Moses' command to the judges of Israel to kill any of their people "who have yoked themselves to the Ba'al of Peor," the Moabites went to battle with Israel on other occasions. For example, after Israel "again did what was evil in the sight of the Lord" (Judg 3:12 NRSV), King Eglon[161] and his people the Moabites defeated Israel and held them as subjects for eighteen years (Judg 3:14). Israel defeated the Moabites under the leadership of Ehud and killed about ten thousand Moabites (Judg 3:29). Thus the Moabites could serve as the example of people who transgressed the Noachic code and lived out the legacy of the illicit teaching of the watchers.

A further connection to the watchers tradition may be seen in the beginning of the Deuteronomic command against inclusion of the Moabites in the assembly. The verse preceding the mention of Moabites cautions, "Those born of an illicit union (ממזר) shall not be admitted to the assembly of the Lord. Even to the tenth generation, none of their descendants shall be admitted to the assembly of the Lord" (Deut 23:3 NRSV). The next groups to receive the same level of censure are the Ammonites and Moabites in verse 3. Jackson notes that in the Qumran literature the gigantic offspring of the watchers and women are referred to as ממזר: "We find the concept of 'bastard' (ממזר), drawn from Deut 23.2–4 and Zech 9.6 applied to the offspring of the angels and the women throughout the Qumran literature."[162] That is, there is in

---

160. This may also be the reason behind the tradition that the Moabite women seduced Israelite men at Shittim using aphrodisiac-laced wine as seen in *Num. Rab.*

161. The Moabite King Eglon was held in later tradition to be Ruth's father (*b. So,tah* 42b).

162. Jackson, 62. Jackson gives the examples of ממזר in 4Q394 8 i.10; 4Q396 1.5; 4Q397 5; cf. also 4Q174 i.21, 2, 4. The phrase "the spirits of the bastards" appears in

the Qumran literature a conceptual link between the illegitimate monstrous offspring of the watchers and women and the Torah command to exclude Moabites from the assembly. In the Qumran literature Moabites find themselves in the same category of exclusion as those born of the illicit unions of watchers and women. That the Moabites' legacy of illicit behavior overlaps with what the wayward angels taught their wives may be no mere coincidence. That Moabite women lead Israelites away ("the [Israelite] men began to indulge in sexual immorality with Moabite women, who invited them to the sacrifices to their gods," Num 25:2–3) also parallels the behavior of the unvanquished spirits of the giants who "taking on many forms, will harm humankind and lead them astray, to sacrifice to demons until the great judgment" (*1 En.*19:1).[163]

Interactions with Angels/ the Holy Spirit

In later traditions, such as the Aramaic Targum to Ruth, the characters in the book of Ruth, including Ruth herself, interact with angels and the holy spirit (רוח הקדש). Unlike in the watchers tradition, however, the interaction between celestial beings and this woman is only righteous. The divine messenger or spirit gives warning, blessing, and instruction in Ruth. The term by which the messenger is known differs according to the location of the recipient. When the recipient of the celestial message is in a holy location (i.e., in Bethlehem), the message is delivered by the holy spirit (2:11; 3:15, 18). However, when the revelation is given on "unclean soil" (i.e., in the land of Moab), it is an angel who is the messenger (1:6).[164]

Echoes of Giants in the Family

In addition to connections mentioned above between the gigantic illegitimate offspring of the watchers and the women and the Moabites, there are two others as well, one from Hebrew biblical tradition and one from later Jewish traditions about Ruth's family background. According

4Q511 35.7; 48, 49, 51.2–3. In 4Q510 1.5 reference is made to "the spirits of the ravaging angels and the bastard spirits." See Martínez and Tigchelaar, *Dead Sea Scrolls*, II:792/93; 796/97; 798/99; I:352/53; II:1032/33; 1034/35; 1028/29.

163. *1 Enoch: A New Translation*, 39.

164. Levine, *Aramaic Version of Ruth*, 11.

to Deut 2:10–11, the land inhabited by the Moabites was formerly occupied by the Emim, also known as Rephaim, giants. That these were not friendly giants can be seen in the fact that the name "Emim" has as its root "terror" (אמה). So the Moabites, who exercise the sinful legacy of the watchers also come from the land formerly inhabited by a gigantic race of people.

In later Jewish tradition, Orpah, Ruth's sister-in-law is held to be the mother of the giant Goliath, as well as three other gigantic offspring:

> It is written: "And Orpah kissed her mother-in-law but Ruth clave unto her." Let the sons of the kiss (the one who kissed) fall into the hands of the one who clave unto, as it is written; "These four were born to the giant (ha-ra-fah) in Gath, and fell by the hand of David." Rabba taught, because of the four tears Orpah shed on her mother-in-law she was worthy that four mighty men would come forth out of her as her offspring.[165]

Clearly the giants born to Orpah are not the monstrous offspring of an illicit relationship with an angel. They are, rather, the rewards of Orpah's appropriate grief at leaving Naomi even if one of them was the enemy of David and the Israelites. However, perhaps again, there is an echo of a tradition linking Moabites with the gigantic offspring that come from illicit unions.

A Vision of Eschatological Hope

The story of Ruth, for all its transgression, deception, and the presence of Moabite risk to the well-being of Israel, does have a very happy ending. The ending is happy, in part, because Ruth's transgressions lead to a good and fruitful union, and even a Moabite woman becomes the source of the most praiseworthy king of Israel. Even in this genealogical outcome there is a happy surprise. The people and elders gather around Boaz after he has acquired the right to redeem Ruth and "maintain the dead man's name on his inheritance, in order that the name of the dead may not be cut off from his kindred" (Ruth 4:11). However, the blessing they pronounce upon Boaz has nothing to do with the dead man. Rather, the blessing is this: "through the children that the Lord will give you by

---

165. *b. Sotah* 42b (trans. Cohen, 42). The status of Boaz, and Ruth as well, as 'giants' is recorded in *Ruth Rab.* 4:3: "R. Abbahu said: If a giant marries a giantess, what do they produce? Mighty men. Boaz married Ruth. Whom did they produce? David."

this young woman, may your house be like the house of Perez, whom Tamar bore to Judah" (Ruth 4:12 NRSV). Tamar's union with Judah was made in order to maintain the name of her dead husband. However, the union is remembered as raising up a child to Judah, technically the child's grandfather. Just so, in the genealogy at the conclusion of Ruth, the dead husbands are not remembered, only the husbands who actually sired the children. The genealogy goes through Boaz, not through the dead husband: "Salmon of Boaz, Boaz of Obed, Obed of Jesse, and Jesse of David" (Ruth 4:21–22 NRSV). A law meant to preserve a former family gives way to a new family. Rather than as a way to maintain a name for the dead, the levirate law by which Boaz obtains Ruth leads to the joining of Moabite and Israelite in the child Obed, resulting in a bright future for Israel.

In this way, the story of Ruth also foreshadows the Matthean community in which family is radically reconfigured. In Matthew alone of the synoptic gospels, Jesus gives the admonition, "And call no one your father on earth, for you have one Father—the one in heaven" (Matt 23:9 NRSV). When his mother and brothers are outside the place where Jesus is meeting with his disciples and want to speak to him, Jesus says, "Who is my mother, and who are my brothers?" (Matt 12:48 NRSV). He answers his question by pointing to his disciples and saying, "Here are my mother and my brothers! For whoever does the will of my Father in heaven is my brother and sister and mother" (Matt 12:49–50 NRSV). Ruth, as in Matthew's Gospel, shows a family that does not abide by the expected configuration of an earthly father whose decisions direct family activities; nor does the family remain within the same ethnic group. One's conduct shows one's allegiance and the high standard of חסד, ("goodness," "kindness," "lovingkindness,"[166] a word which occurs three times in the brief book of Ruth[167]) or "the will of my Father in heaven" is what brings the family together and gives it existence and meaning.

Katherine Doob Sakenfeld remarks that the book of Ruth presents a picture of the ideal eschatological community and functions as "an extended metaphor for God's New Creation." [168] With its picture of a community in which old and young alike are cared for, where there

---

166. *New Brown, Driver, Briggs, Gesenius*, 338b–39a.

167. Ruth 1:8, 2:20, and 3:10.

168. Sakenfeld, "Ruth 4," 63.

is physical sustenance for all, where ethnic identities cease to divide, and people participate in the divine חסד, Ruth shows an "eschatological vision of future hope."[169] Sakenfeld notes that the hopefulness of the text stands out especially since the story of Ruth is set in the days of the judges, a time marked by Israelite warfare against enemy nations as well as internecine carnage in which women especially suffer (see, for example, Judg 19–21).[170] So, into the midst of a time of warfare and struggle comes a picture of peace, righteousness, and plenty. God gives blessing and God's name is blessed, and human fruitfulness is shown not only in the birth of Obed, but also in an entire genealogy of descendants. Does this "ideal eschatological community" bear any resemblance to an Enochic picture of the eschatological hope, to a time when the consequences of the watchers' transgressions will no longer hold sway over humanity?

The ideal eschatological community presented in Ruth does share elements in common with the renewed creation envisioned in *1 Enoch*. In particular, Ruth and *1 Enoch* share a fruitful humanity, a plentiful earth, righteousness, the blessing of God, and worship of the divine. In *1 Enoch*, after the four archangels make intercession to God on behalf of humanity and the earth because of the destruction, violence and godlessness which has resulted from the watchers' transgression, God responds by commissioning the archangels to do various tasks. Michael's task is to imprison the watchers (*1 En.* 10:11), and set in motion the destruction of the giants (*1 En.*10:12). He is also charged with the renovation of the earth and its earthly inhabitants (*1 En.* 10:16—11:2). That the renewal of the earth and humankind is a future event is indicated in *1 En.* 10:13, "in that day," which marks the time of final judgment,[171] the final destruction of the bound watchers, and the time of renewal. In the new creation, human fertility will abound: "they will live until they beget thousands" (*1 En.*10:17).[172] Earth will yield plentiful harvests: "every vine that will be planted on it will yield a thousand jugs of wine; and of every seed that is sown on it, each measure will yield a thousand measures; and each measure of olives will yield ten baths of oil" (*1 En.*

---

169. Ibid.

170. Ibid., 65.

171. Pomykala, "Scripture Profile," 269.

172. *1 Enoch: A New Translation*, 30.

10:19).[173] Righteousness will abound: "let the plant of righteousness (and truth) appear . . . and the deeds of righteousness (and truth) will be planted forever with joy" (*1 En.* 10:16).[174] God's blessing will be given to humanity: "I shall open the storehouses of blessing that are in heaven; and make them descend upon the earth" (*1 En.* 11:1).[175] Worship of God will be offered by all humanity: "all the peoples will worship (me): and all will bless me and prostrate themselves" (*1 En.*10:21).[176] In fact, the universal nature of the eschatological righteousness ("all the sons of men will become righteous," *1 En.* 10:21)[177] and worship is also similar to Ruth's picture of ethnic inclusiveness in the people of God where Moabite and Israelite are both virtuous, share in חסד, and become ancestors of the future great king of Israel. In *1 Enoch* 91, where the eschatological vision is again described, the universal nature of righteousness is shown once more: "all humankind will look to the path of everlasting righteousness . . . And the first heaven will pass away in it, and a new heaven will appear . . . After this there will be many weeks without number forever, in which they will do piety and righteousness (*1 En.* 91: 14, 16, 17)."[178]

The vision in *1 En.* 10:16–11:2 uses language from Genesis 8 and 9, following the flood. The vision of the renewal of the earth connected with חסד is also seen in the language and imagery of Psalm 85:10–13:

> Steadfast love (חסד) and faithfulness will meet;
> righteousness and peace will kiss each other.
> Faithfulness will spring up from the ground,
> and righteousness will look down from the sky.
> The Lord will give what is good,
> and our land will yield its increase.
> Righteousness will go before him,
> and will make a path for his steps. (NRSV)

173. Ibid.
174. Ibid.
175. Ibid., 31.
176. Ibid., 30.
177. Ibid.
178. Ibid., 142–43. The universal nature of the worship of God and righteousness reflects the language of Isa 65:20–25, and Isa 66:18–23. Pomykala, "Scripture Profile," 270; and Nickelsburg, *1 Enoch 1*, 227, 228.

The mention of חסד in verse 10 (and earlier in verse 7) brings to mind the story of Ruth as well, in which חסד, righteousness and plenty abound. The vision of universal righteousness, plentiful fertility on the earth and among humans, and worship of God is a vision shared by Ruth and by *1 Enoch*.

Summary

The Book of Ruth is the story of a woman who transgressed ethnic and social barriers in order to bring about good for herself, her family, and the Israelite people. Because of Ruth's Moabite heritage, with its attendant reputation for illicit sexual activity, idolatry, and bloodshed, her story contains concerns similar to those of the Enochic template. Also, in Qumranic literature, Moabites and the illegitimate offspring of the watchers and women were described using the same term, ממזר. In addition, the term גבור, used for the offspring of the watchers and women in *1 Enoch* appears in Ruth. Not only did Ruth marry a גבור, but also according to much later texts, Ruth was the aunt of giants. Ruth's story has a very happy ending, an ending which shows a glimpse of the eschatological future, containing elements of the Enochic eschatological hope as well. Ruth's family, configured by חסד, composed of various ethnic groups, and brought together by the man who chooses Ruth, rather than the man with primary legal right to Ruth, foreshadow Matthew's concern for a new family of Jesus. In the Matthean family configuration, patrimony belongs to God alone. Those who belong to Jesus' family are those who do the will of God, not those of blood relation (Matt 12:50), and in this family, children are given prominence and cared for (Matt 18:2–6).

The Wife of Uriah

The fourth of the women of the Hebrew Bible to be named in Matthew's genealogy is the wife of Uriah (Matt 1:6), also known as Bathsheba.[179] The part of her story that most directly involves Uriah is told in 2 Sam 11:1–27. The narration of the birth of the son of David and Bathsheba

---

179. In Greek, the absence of her name is even more striking. There is no word for "wife." The Greek reads simply, τῆς τοῦ Οὐρίου.

named in the genealogy, Solomon, is found in 2 Sam 12:24–25. Bathsheba also figures prominently in the story of Solomon's accession to the throne in 1 Kgs 1:11–40 and in the downfall of Adonijah in 1 Kgs 2:13–26.

As it is with the stories of the other women named in Matthew's genealogy, transgression is involved in Bathsheba's story, and this fact may be behind Matthew's unusual appellation for her in his genealogy, "the wife of Uriah." David commits adultery with Bathsheba, and when she becomes pregnant, David takes steps to deceive Uriah[180] so that Uriah will not know that the baby is not his own (2 Sam 11:6–13). When Uriah does not act according to David's plan, David arranges to have Uriah, who is a soldier, killed in battle (2 Sam 11:14–25). David's attempts to deceive Uriah and his illicit relationship with Bathsheba are brought to the fore by Matthew's referring to her through her relationship with Uriah. This is, in fact, the reason given by some scholars for Matthew's designation of Bathsheba in this way.[181] Calling Bathsheba "the wife of Uriah" does draw attention since the evangelist includes the other three women by name and Bathsheba's name is used in the story in 2 Samuel. In fact, when David first inquires about her identity, it is reported to him, "This is Bathsheba, daughter of Eliam, the wife of Uriah the Hittite" (2 Sam 11:3). That is, her own name, and not the name of her husband, is used first. Calling her "the wife of Uriah" is also startling since it is not the son of Uriah who ends up in the genealogy, but rather the child of Bathsheba by David, and not the child conceived while Uriah was still alive. The child conceived while Uriah was still alive did not live. The child named in the genealogy, Solomon, then, has no connection with Uriah—except for the fact that his mother was actually the wife of Uriah, and would have remained so had not David

180. But was Uriah actually deceived? Meir Sternberg presents a discussion of the story in which the gaps of the story are explored with the effect that the reader considers both possibilities: Uriah knew about his wife's infidelity with David; Uriah did not know about his wife's infidelity with David. See Sternberg, "Gaps," 186–229. Sternberg notes that "Biblical narratives are notorious for their sparsity of detail." However, this story "is frugal to excess even relative to the biblical norm" (ibid., 191). Sternberg says that to the question of Uriah's knowledge of what was going on, "the text does not permit any univocal answer: both affirmative and negative hypotheses arise with a legitimate claim to gap-filling" (ibid., 201).

181. For example, Davies and Allison, *Matthew 1–7*, 174–75; Weren, "Five Women," 300.

intervened with illicit sexual relations, deception, and bloodshed. David's sin with Bathsheba was even remembered as his one downfall, e.g., in 1 Kgs 15:5, "David did what was right in the sight of the Lord, and did not turn aside from anything that he commanded him all the days of his life, except in the matter of Uriah the Hittite" (NRSV).[182] So does Matthew name her in this way solely in order to highlight David's crime? Does Matthew wish only to make the point that Bathsheba was the wife of Uriah the Hittite and remained so even though David took her for his own sexual pleasure?[183]

While this explanation is valid, and does address the presence of transgression in Bathsheba's story, I will look at another possible reason for highlighting the role of Uriah in the story: remembering Bathsheba as the wife of Uriah brings to mind the role of the paired set of illicit arts taught by Asael, the arts of beautification and the arts of war. That is, while the story of Bathsheba, Uriah, and David concerns transgression by means of the illicit arts of beautification that lead to illicit sexual relations, it also concerns the arts of war in a very pointed way. Were it not for war, the story of Bathsheba's encounter with David would not have happened in the first place and David would not have Uriah's blood on his conscience, if not his hands.

To explore this connection, I will first examine the theme of the illicit arts taught by the watchers as they are involved in this story. I will next examine the story in light of the story of the watchers and the women in order to identify parallels between the two narratives. I will conclude with an examination of other themes related to the Enochic paradigm as they appear to be present in the Bathsheba story.

---

182. In the Damascus Document as well, David's crime against Uriah is remembered as his one fault, even while he is excused for having more than one wife: "and the ones who went into the ark Gen 7:9 'went in two by two into the ark' and about the prince it is written: 2 Deut 17:17 'He should not multiply wives to himself'. However, David had not read the sealed book of the law which was in the ark, for it had not been opened in Israel since the day of the death of Eleazar and of Jehoshua, and Joshua and the elders who worshipped Ashtaroth had hidden the public (copy) until Zadok's entry into office. And David's deeds were praised, except for Uriah's blood" (CD-A v.1–5; Martínez and Tigchelaar, *Dead Sea Scrolls*, I:557.

183. It seems safe to expect that Matthew would view Bathsheba as remaining the wife of Uriah given Jesus' teaching on remarriage in Matt 19:4–9, even though there is no discussion of the circumstance of remarriage after one's spouse is killed by one's new spouse.

Connections with the Enochic Template

USE OF THE ILLICIT ARTS

Calling Bathsheba "the wife of Uriah" connects her story with both illicit sexual relations and war, two areas of illicit pedagogy taught by the watchers. In fact, in Bathsheba's story they are connected in a particularly poignant way: were it not for battle, the adultery and subsequent murder may not have happened.

Recall that in *1 Enoch* Asael teaches human beings how to make weapons of war and materials for the beautification of women.[184] The story of Bathsheba, David, and Uriah is a story that combines these elements: skills of war and a desirable woman. In fact, the story is narrated so the reader has the sense that it is the practice of war itself that makes possible the adulterous behavior. The story begins, "In the spring of the year, the time when kings go out to battle" (2 Sam 11:1 NRSV). A piece of information that gives the story a context (it is spring, therefore it is time kings go to war) also shows how deeply people are entrenched in using the arts of war. Spring is associated with battle. War is now a predictable event with its own appropriate season. Accordingly, "David sent Joab with his officers and all Israel with him; they ravaged the Ammonites, and besieged Rabbah" (2 Sam 11:1 NRSV). What piques our curiosity, however, is the narrator's note: "But David remained at Jerusalem" (2 Sam 11:1 NRSV). "Kings go out to battle," but not this one. David has sent others, who presumably act on his behalf. The war appears to be going well. The Ammonites are ravaged and Rabbah is besieged. But David remains at Jerusalem, and that is where the trouble begins.

The scene of David on his rooftop shares some elements with the Enochic scene of the watchers about to transgress and leave their appointed heavenly station. David looks down from his roof and sees a very beautiful woman (2 Sam 11:2) just as the watchers look down from

---

184. *1 En.* 8:1, "Asael taught men to make swords of iron and weapons and shields and breastplates and every instrument of war. He showed them metals of the earth and how they should work gold to fashion it suitably, and concerning silver, to fashion it for bracelets and ornaments for women. And he showed them concerning antimony and eye paint and all manner of precious stones and dyes. And the sons of men made for themselves and for their daughters, and they transgressed and led the holy ones astray" (*1 Enoch: A New Translation*, 25).

lofty places and spy "the beautiful and comely daughters of men" (*1 En.* 6:1).[185] The fact that David is up on his roof is mentioned twice in the verse. The woman's beauty is emphasized ("the woman was very beautiful," 2 Sam 11:2 NRSV). David inquires about the woman and is told, "This is Bathsheba daughter of Eliam, the wife of Uriah the Hittite" (2 Sam 11:3 NRSV). David sends "messengers [מלאכים] to get her, and she came to him, and he lay with her" (2 Sam 11:4 NRSV). In *1 Enoch,* after seeing the comely women the watchers decide to "choose for ourselves wives from the daughters of men" (*1 En.* 6:1).[186] David decides to choose for himself someone who is already the wife of a man. Shemihazah, the watcher, and David, the voyeur, share in knowing that what they do is wrong. Shemihazah knows that if he takes a human wife he "shall be guilty of a great sin" (*1 En.* 6:3).[187] David knows that Bathsheba is already the wife of another man. Shemihazah does not want to be alone in his crime, and when he expresses his fear that the other watchers will not join him in this unlawful action, they swear an oath that they will join him. David's crime is solitary in that he alone instigates adultery. However he has messengers who presumably know it is another man's wife they are bringing to the king's house. It is part of the watchers' plan to beget children by the women (*1 En.* 6:1). It does not appear to be part of David's aforethought that a child may come of his illicit meeting with Bathsheba, but Bathsheba does become pregnant. When she apprises David of the pregnancy, he plans how not to be held accountable for his crime.

David calls Uriah home from the battle and tries twice to persuade Uriah to go to his own home and have sexual relations with his wife so that no one, or most especially, Uriah, will not know that the child has been conceived with David. Uriah will not go. The first time Uriah refuses on the grounds that he is a soldier and his compatriots are in-volved in a war: "The ark and Israel and Judah remain in booths; and my lord Joab and the servants of my lord are camping in the open field; shall I then go to my house, to eat and to drink, and to lie with my wife?" (2 Sam 11:11 NRSV). In other words, Uriah will be loyal to his fellow soldiers even though, and only at the king's behest, he is away from them. The luxuries the king is granting himself—to eat, to drink,

185. Ibid., 23.
186. Ibid.
187. Ibid.

to lie with, ironically, Uriah's wife—Uriah refuses to enjoy. The next day, David gets Uriah drunk, but Uriah still does not go home.

David decides then to have Uriah killed in war by positioning him in an area of intense fighting (2 Sam 11:15). Joab follows David's command and puts Uriah in the place "where he knew there were valiant warriors"[188] (2 Sam 11:16 NRSV). David's plan works: Uriah is killed (2 Sam 11:17). Using the arts of war, David kills a soldier, in order to be able to obtain the woman he got by illicit means. When Joab sends David reassuring word of Uriah's death (2 Sam 11:21), David sends reassuring word of his own to Joab, "Do not let this matter be evil in your eyes for the sword consumes at will—now one and now another" (2 Sam 11:25).[189] The Lord, however, takes another view of the situation. As the next section begins the narrator says, "And the thing that David did was evil in the eyes of the Lord"[190] (2 Sam 11:27). The sword had consumed at the will of David, and the Lord does not like it.

In the story of the wife of Uriah and David, there is a melding of two sets of skills taught by the watchers, the arts of war, and the beautification of women. These skills result in two of the sins humans commit due to the watchers' transgression: illicit sexual intercourse and the shedding of blood. But while battle provides the context for the story as well as a means for David, or so he thinks, to get out of trouble, is it really fair to say that "the beautification of women" is actually also at play in the story? To answer, I first briefly revisit the narrative of the giving of the skills of beautification by Asael in *1 Enoch* 8.

I addressed above the subject of the tradition that through this piece of instruction Asael set things in motion for the introduction of evil into the world. Asael taught skills for the beautification of women, the women used them, and made themselves irresistible to angels. Two aspects are present then in this strand of the tradition: the women learned skills for making their physical appearance irresistible, and angels fell for it. Once the watchers saw how beautiful the women were,

---

188. The Hebrew phrase here is אנשי־חיל, not גברים. Uriah will die because of the plans of one called גבור חיל, David (in 1 Sam 16:18), even if he dies literally at the hands of אנשי־חיל.

189. My translation. The NRSV translation, "Do not let this matter trouble you" and the NASB's, "Do not let this thing displease you," do not show the parallel set up with the next section.

190. My translation.

they could not help themselves and were "led astray" (*1 En.* 8:1).[191] In this telling, then, the women bear some responsibility for the angels' misdeeds. In fact, it is they, not the angels, who "transgress" (*1 En.* 8:1).[192]

According to later interpretations of the Bathsheba and David story, David finds himself in a similar predicament: he is simply unable to resist the beauty of Bathsheba, regardless of how she came to have that kind of power. Josephus thus places onto Bathsheba both the guilt for David's powerlessness to resist and the sin itself:

> For when later in the evening he took a view round him from the roof of his royal palace, where he use to walk at that hour, he saw a woman washing herself in her own house; she was one of extraordinary beauty, and therein surpassed all other women; her name was Bathsheba. So he was overcome by that woman's beauty and was not able to restrain his desire, but he sent for her, and lay with her. Hereupon she conceived with child, and sent to the king, that he should contrive some way for concealing her sin (Josephus, *Ant.* 7,7,1).[193]

While cosmetics as such aren't described, Bathsheba's beauty is central to the story. When David sees that she is beautiful, he sets in motion the actions that will lead to dire consequences for Bathsheba's life with Uriah. The subject of her bathing is an issue for some. Was she trying to get David's attention?[194] The reader is not told specifically. The

191. *1 Enoch: A New Translation*, 25.

192. Ibid.

193. Later Christian writers continued the theme of David's virtue and Bathsheba's sin. For example, Cassiodorus writes, "Jerome, citing others, points out that Bathsheba manifested a type of the Church or of the human flesh, and says that David bore the mark of Christ. . . Just as Bathsheba when washing herself unclothed in the brook of Cedron delighted David and deserved to attain the royal embrace, and her husband was slain at the prince's command, so too the Church, the assembly of sins by the bath of sacred baptisms, is known to be joined to Christ the Lord. The sin of adultery is shown to have been foreign and uncharacteristic, since it was lamented with such concentration of mind. The sudden confession of the thief attracts us. We rejoice that Peter's tears were quickly in evidence . . . But David with his more prolonged attempt to wipe away his sins afforded all men a chance to absolve themselves. He ensured that his tears, running down the faces of the people who came after him, are dried with no lapse of time" (Cassiodorus, *Explanation of the Psalms* I, 492–93).

194. Weren mentions "Some exegetes presume that she took a bath in order to attract the king's attention, but this conclusion goes far beyond what the story tells us" (Weren, "Five Women," 300). The lure of a woman bathing is behind Reuben's il-

reader is told that Bathsheba was bathing and that she was a very beautiful woman. The reader is not told that David cannot resist, just that he does not, even though he knows that she really is "the wife of Uriah."

QUESTIONABLE PARENTAGE

Following Uriah's death, David marries Bathsheba.[195] The child whom they had conceived during their illicit affair dies, but they conceive a second child who lives, Solomon. Solomon's father is David, but his mother is not (really, licitly) David's wife. While Solomon's paternity *per se* is never in question—he is the son of David and Bathsheba—the licit nature of his parents' relationship is in question, due to the nature of its beginning and the necessity of Uriah's death to clear the way for David to take Bathsheba as his wife. As the episode between David and the prophet Nathan (2 Sam 12:1–15) indicates, David's actions toward Bathsheba and her husband are "evil in [the Lord's] sight" (2 Sam 12:9 NRSV). That the child of this first union between David and Bathsheba dies in effect cleans the slate for a new beginning, a relationship that results in the birth of Solomon. However, as mentioned above, the question arises for the reader of Matthew: would Matthew have seen the situation this way? Or would there remain, in the evangelist's eyes at

---

licit action in having sexual relations with his father's concubine Bilhah (see *T. Reu.* 3:11–14). Reuben sees Bilhah bathing and is unable to sleep. When Reuben then finds the not only naked but also drunken Bilhah asleep he has sexual intercourse with her. Although she is unaware of Reuben's actions, an angel reveals Reuben's sin to Jacob. In Gen 35:22 one reads only that Reuben slept with Bilhah and that Jacob heard of it. It is Reuben's encounter with Bilhah and his ruminations on the power of promiscuity that lead Reuben to his pronouncement, cited in the previous chapter also: "Evil are women, my children, because, having no power or strength over man, they use wiles trying to draw him to them by gestures; and whom she cannot overcome by strength, him she overcomes by craft" (*T. Reu.* 5:1–2) and Reuben's statement that the women "bewitched the Watchers before the Flood" (*T. Reu.* 5:6). That Bathsheba was bathing and attracted David's attention could, as in *T. Reu.*, become not the story of David's looking where he ought not to look, but the story of a woman's scheming to attract a man by her looks, as women did with the watchers. Another version of the encounter between Reuben and Bilhah is told in *Jub.* 33:1–9. In Jubilees, no alcohol is involved. Reuben sees Bilhah bathing, goes to her house at night, and lies with her when she is asleep. His "laying with her" awakens her; she cries out; Reuben flees. Later, Bilhah informs Jacob of what has happened (VanderKam, *Jubilees: A Critical Text*, 357).

195. As noted above, David is called a גבור, and thereby Bathsheba is another ancestor of Jesus associated with a גבור.

least, the taint of an illicit beginning? Others did not turn a blind eye to David's mistreatment of Uriah: David's actions toward Uriah do remain a part of David's record according to 1 Kgs 15:5.

BATHSHEBA, QUEEN MOTHER, גבירה

Another potential connection with the Enochic template is Bathsheba's role as Queen Mother. It is, after all, her son Solomon, rather than the child she conceived while Uriah was still living, who is the next ancestor named in the genealogy of Jesus. As mentioned at the beginning of this section, Bathsheba figures prominently in the story of Solomon's accession to the throne in 1 Kgs 1:11–40 and in the downfall of Adonijah in 1 Kgs 2:13–26. The Hebrew word for queen mother is גבירה, from the root, גבר, also the root of גבור, described in detail above. Z. Ben-Barak has argued that there was no official institutionalized position for the גבירה in ancient Israel.[196] However, she notes that some גברות rose to prominence and exerted influence over their sons' reigns by virtue of their own power and personalities. These influential queen mothers include Ma'acah, the queen mother of Abijam/Abijah (2 Chr 36:9–11); Hamutal, queen mother of Jehoahaz (2 Kgs 23:31, 36); and Nehusta, queen mother of Jehoiachin (2 Chr 36:9–11). Each of these kings were younger sons, with the exception that, according to 2 Kgs 24:17, Jehoiachin was the nephew rather than younger brother, of Zedekiah. According to Susan Ackerman, "Bathsheba, in advocating Solomon's kingship over that of Adonijah, is the paradigmatic exemplar of the גבירה who schemed for succession on behalf of her younger son."[197]

The role of the גבירה, whether official and institutionalized or not, has been the subject of some discussion of interest to this book on connections with the Enochic template. Two questions in the discussion are worth noting here because of their possible connections. The first is whether or not the גבירה had any responsibilities within the cultic life of Israelite society. The second is, if the answer to the first is yes, what was the nature of that cultic role?

In regard to the first question, as mentioned above, Ben-Barak answers in the negative: there was no institutionalized role for the

196. Ben-Barak, "The Status and Right of the Gĕbîrâ," 23–34. See also Ben-Barak, "The Queen Consort," 33–40.

197. Ackerman, "Queen Mother," 179–94.

queen mother. However, Neils-Erik Andreasen believes that the גבירה officially functioned as a "lady counselor," who gave counsel especially in regard to succession, and in the case of Bathsheba in particular, in judicial matters and mediation between political factions.[198] Andreasen draws on earlier research that shows the possibility that the official duties of the queen mother in Israel have their roots in the role of the queen mother, or *tawananna*, in Hittite culture, who had not only social and political responsibilities, but cultic duties as well. Following H. Donner, Andreason argues that, although there is no possibility that Hittite political structures directly affected those of the united kingdom in Jerusalem, Hittite structures were preserved in Syria "well into the first millennium B.C."[199] In turn, the political structures of the united kingdom were influenced by those of Syria.[200] The office of queen mother was an important part of the Hittite structure that may have been passed along into the southern kingdom in particular. As the office of queen mother eventually took root and took its particular form in Israelite society, the cultic functions of the גבירה were eliminated.[201] There is, in fact, no biblical evidence for a cultic function for anyone identified as a queen mother in Israel or Judea within Israelite religion, or at least within biblically sanctioned Israelite religion.

It seems, however, that at least one גבירה may have been connected with cultic activity related to Asherah. Ma'acah, queen mother of Asa, according to 1 Kgs 15:13 (2 Chr 15:16) is removed as גבירה because she made "an abominable thing to the Asherah"[202] (לאשרה מפלצת) which Asa cut down and burned in the Kidron Valley. Susan Ackerman argues that Ma'acah was fulfilling her duties as גבירה by making an image, pole, or cult statue for the goddess Asherah.[203] According to Ackerman, in so doing Ma'acah was not introducing a foreign element into Judean worship; the worship of both YHWH and Asherah was "the norm in the southern kingdom in the ninth century, the eighth century, and the sev-

198. Andreasen, "The Role of Queen Mother," 188–89.

199. Ibid., 181.

200. Ibid.

201. Ibid., 187.

202. My translation.

203. Ackerman, "Queen Mother," 182.

enth century."[204] Whether or not worship of Asherah alongside YHWH was actually considered "the norm," or in what way it would be considered "the norm" is beyond the scope of the present study. However, that the queen mother held some sort of official duty in regard to the cult of Asherah is a rudimentary answer to the question, if there were cultic duties assigned to the גבירה, what were they?

Another response, more directly related to our present study of the Enochic template, comes from G. W. Ahlström, who maintained that the role of the גבירה was to play the role of the king's consort during the sacred marriage rite.[205] To Ahlström the interaction of Bathsheba and David on the roof was a narrative that originally was about a sacred marriage ritual between the king (David) and his consort (Bathsheba) on the roof where such rituals were to take place.[206] As I commented above in the section on Tamar, the subject of the sacred marriage ritual is complex and hardly agreed upon by scholars. There is no evidence in the biblical text of David and Bathsheba's meeting on the roof that clearly indicates that they were involved in a *hieros gamos* ritual. In the case of Tamar at least, her designation as קדשה may indicate the possibility of a vestigial story linking her with a ritual in which a woman has sexual relations with a man who is identified as a divine being. However, it is interesting that the possibility has been raised again, in regard to another of the women ancestors named in Matthew's genealogy, of some tradition in which earthly and heavenly boundaries are crossed and sexual relations are involved between beings associated with each of those realms. In the case of Bathsheba, her role as גבירה involving sacred marriage is best mentioned as a possibility only, but an interesting one that would once again link a woman in Matthew's genealogy with the Enochic template.

Summary

Bathsheba is involved in transgression in her relations with David. Given the power differential between them, she may be seen as the victim in the story, even if Israelite law finds both parties in adultery

204. Ibid.

205. Ahlström, *Aspects of Syncretism*, 79.

206. Ibid.

accountable.[207] This story parallels the Enochic story of the celestial watchers who look down from heaven and desire the daughters of men. When these rebellious angels see the beautiful women, they transgress their heavenly station, and take the women as wives for themselves. In the story of Bathsheba, David also looks down, literally, from his rooftop, and sees the beautiful daughter of Eliam, the wife of Uriah. King David transgresses his powerful station and takes another man's wife who is desirable to him. The transgression combines two areas of the illicit pedagogy of the watchers, the arts of seduction and the arts of war. When Asael first teaches them, the combination may seem puzzling—what has metallurgy to do with cosmetics? Scholars have tried to explain the connection.[208] In this story, they are combined in a particularly powerful way. During a time of war, a king takes the beautiful object of his affection and uses the arts of war to keep his acquisition. As in *1 Enoch*, there are גברים in this story: Bathsheba not only married a גבור, she was herself a גבירה, and an effective one at that, securing the throne for her son Solomon. Whether the גבירה had a designated cultic role and the nature of that cultic role remain open questions, but I note that others assert the possibility that her cultic role would have included playing the female consort in a sacred marriage ritual.

The Four Women and the Enochic Template

Table II summarizes ways in which the four women from the Hebrew Bible have connections with the Enochic template.

207. For more on legal and other attitudes toward adultery in Israel, see Marsman, *Women in Ugarit and Israel*, 180–86; Pressler, *The View of Women*, 21–43; Matthews, Levinson, and Frymer-Kensky (eds.), *Gender and Law*; Westbrook, "Adultery in Ancient Near Eastern Law," 542–80.

208. For example, Nickelsburg points out the similarities between the Asael material and the Prometheus myth, especially as told by Aeschylus. Fire is required for these arts which Asael teaches: metallurgy, mining and the making of dyes (Nickelsburg, *1 Enoch 1*, 193). However, in the preparation of eye paint, fire appears not to have been necessary (ibid., 193 n. 15). Nickelsburg also believes that it is possible that the references to silver, gold, gems, cosmetics, and dyes are an expansion of the myth of Asael's teaching about metallurgy for the purposes of war (ibid., 193).

Table II: Connections between the Four Women and the Enochic Template

	Transgression	Interaction between Angels and Women	Issues with Offspring	Outcome
Enochic Template	Watchers leave heavenly station, have sexual relations with women, teach illicit skills and arts	Sexual relations, teach illicit skills and arts, beget children	Offspring are giants; called illegitimate; ravenous and violent	Death, destruction by giants; illicit sexual relations, bloodshed, and idolatry by humans. Evil spirits that result from the transgression of the watchers still cause problems for humanity.
Tamar	Acts as prostitute in order to have sexual intercourse with father-in-law	In the role of prostitute, use of illicit arts relating to seduction; Tamar is called a קדשה. As such she would enact rituals involving sexual relations with celestial beings; Later rabbinic traditions involve angelic guidance of Tamar and Judah.	When she is first found to be pregnant, Judah assumes Tamar has acted as a prostitute and orders her burned to death. The children are revealed to be Judah's.	Tamar is called "righteous." Despite Judah's not enacting the law, his own line is continued.

	Transgression	Interaction between Angels and Women	Issues with Offspring	Outcome
Rahab	Is a Canaanite prostitute; crosses ethnic boundaries by announcing her allegiance to the God of Israel and aiding Israelite spies to conquer her land.	As a prostitute, makes use of the illicit arts relating to seduction. The spies she helps are also called מלאכים messengers/angels. In later traditions they are interpreted to be angels along the same lines as the messengers/angels who visited Abraham and Lot. Rahab assists them in ways similar to the ways angels hide Noah and Enoch and assist Lot, the magi, and Joseph.	No offspring are named in the story. Matthew names Rahab as mother of Boaz, a גבור, the same word translated as giant in the LXX.	Rahab helps the Israelites enter Canaan and conquer the Canaanities. She and her family remain in the land. Later she is praised for her hospitality and for receiving angels.

	Transgression	Interaction between Angels and Women	Issues with Offspring	Outcome
Ruth	Is a Moabite woman who crosses ethnic boundaries by moving to Judah and swearing allegiance to the God and people of Naomi; transgresses social boundaries through her encounter with Boaz on the threshing floor, and interaction he advises she conceal by leaving before daylight.	In preparation for her encounter with Boaz, makes use of the illicit arts relating to seduction. In later traditions, Ruth is said to be aided by angels who guide and direct her action.	Ruth is wife of Boaz, a גבור; Her sister-in-law Orpah is the mother of four גברים according to later tradition; as a Moabite, her ancestral home is the former residence of a race of giants. The marriage of Ruth and Boaz, which results in the birth of Obed, can take place only after legal issues are resolved.	A community which provides a glimpse of eschatological hope. Also Ruth and Boaz are the grandparents of King David.

	Transgression	Interaction between Angels and Women	Issues with Offspring	Outcome
Bathsheba	King David has sexual relations with her while she is yet "the wife of Uriah," making her an adulteress. The adultery leads to David's decision to have Uriah killed and marry Bathsheba.	Use of illicit arts of beautification and arts of war	First child dies, second child, Solomon, has one parent known as the wife of another man. After the death of Uriah, Bathsheba marries David, who is called a גבור and associates with גברים.	Immediate outcome is sad: sin, death, and grief. Longer term outcome is the birth of Solomon and Bathsheba's role as גבירה in securing Solomon's reign as king and eliminating rivals. The possibility is noted that the role of the גבירה could have included taking part in a sacred marriage rite.

Just as the watchers transgress the boundary between the heavenly and earthly realms and transgress the sanction against the sharing of heavenly secrets, each of the four women transgresses at least one kind of boundary, whether ethnic, social, or legal.

Further, each of the women makes use of the very skills that the watchers teach humans, particularly skills related to beautification and seduction. In the stories of Rahab and Bathsheba war-making, another of the illicit arts, is also involved in the plot. Within traditions about all but Bathsheba, the women have interactions with celestial beings. In the cases of Tamar and Rahab, the women are perceived (wrongly in the case of Tamar, and rightly in the case of Rahab) to be prostitutes; both women are connected with traditions involving celestial beings.

Tamar's story specifically contains references to a role for women associated with sexuality involving celestial beings, the קדשה. Rahab, the prostitute, hosts men who are in later tradition called "angels," although within the story no explicit reference is made to sexual relations between her and the men.

Illegitimate and gigantic offspring are the outcome in the unions between the watchers and the women. In the case of three of the four women (not in the case of Rahab) there are legal issues to deal with in order to determine the legitimacy of their human offspring. In Rahab's case, however, her offspring—not known directly from any canonical tradition—would be the child of a reformed prostitute. Rahab and Ruth both give birth to children who are called גברים, one of the words designated as "giants" in the LXX.[209] Bathsheba's child Solomon is not called a גבור. However, her (second) husband David is identified by that term (1 Sam 16:18); he gathers גברים around him (2 Sam 23:8; 1 Kgs 1:8). When David dies, Solomon assumes the throne (thanks to Bathsheba's actions), גברים submit to Solomon (1 Chr 29:24). Bathsheba is a גבירה, a queen mother, a title with the same root as גבור, and possibly some connection with a sacred marriage ritual.

The results of the watchers' transgressions are disastrous: unrighteousness, death, destruction, and idolatry. Evil spirits who came into being because of the watchers' transgression still cause suffering for humanity. However, despite the fact that the women's stories involve many of the very same elements as the watchers' stories do, the women's transgressions, use of illicit arts, and offspring result, not in disaster, but in righteousness and hope.

The evangelist Matthew, in naming these four women as ancestors to Jesus, makes use of the Enochic template, but subverts its elements so that the descendent of these transgressive women will be the cause of Matthew's hope and the subject of his Gospel. It is time to look at how Matthew uses the elements of the Enochic template as Matthew addresses the fifth woman named in his genealogy, Mary, and the birth and identity of her child Jesus.

---

209. Stuckenbruck, "Origins," 89.

4

Transgression Redressed

With the fifth woman named in Matthew's genealogy and the Matthean birth narrative, the evangelist asserts that the birth of Jesus overturns the effects of the Enochic watchers' template by using the very elements of that template. The birth of Jesus, according to Matthew, redresses the watchers' transgression. That the watchers' template helps to shape the Matthean birth narrative becomes evident through an examination of the following details: the structure of the genealogy and infancy narrative, Joseph's suspicion of Mary's pregnancy, and the resolution to his suspicion, namely his discovery that the child has been conceived by the Holy Spirit. Importantly, the child is the product of the heavenly (Holy Spirit) and earthly (Mary), but without sexual union between the heavenly Holy Spirit and earthly Mary. With the possibility that the Holy Spirit was identified as an angelomorphic celestial being at the time the evangelist wrote the Gospel further parallels may be seen between the two stories. In the dreams that direct human agents in divine plans, there are parallels with Enoch's role in addressing the watchers' fall. The advent of the magi who follow a star in order to show homage to the king whose star it is, an element unique to the Matthean infancy narrative, shows that from the beginning of Jesus' life, the watchers' transgressions have been overcome through the events surrounding Jesus' birth. In the birth of Jesus, then—from the presence of Mary in the final words of the genealogy, to Joseph's suspicions about Jesus' birth and the angelic resolution of Joseph's worries through the birth of a human and divine being without sexual union between human and divinity, to the dreams which guide human agents to carry out divine plans, to the appearance of magi who, although they are astrologers and stargazers, worship appropriately—the elements of the Enochic watchers' template are overturned and used for good, not evil.

As I move from the subject of transgression reassessed, addressed in the previous chapter of this book, to the subject of the redression of the watchers' transgression through the narrative of Jesus' infancy, I will address these subjects: (1) the conclusion of the genealogy; (2) Joseph's suspicions and their affinities with the suspicions attached to Noah's birth in *1 Enoch* and *Genesis Apocryphon*; (3) the conception of Jesus by the angelomorphic Holy Spirit; (4) dreams as revelatory about the purpose of the Deity for human agents and for the future of human well-being in both Matthew 2 and *1 Enoch*; and (5) the magi who use illicit arts taught by the watchers to locate Jesus and worship him.

The Fifth Woman

Matthew's Gospel begins with a genealogy in which women are named whose stories recall elements of the watchers' transgression narrative, beginning with the illicit mating of heavenly beings with earthly women. Immediately following the genealogy, Matthew tells the birth story of Jesus, a birth in which a heavenly being brings about a birth with a woman. However, in the case of Jesus, this birth, through the interaction of a heavenly being and an earthly woman, does not bring disaster; it brings salvation.

The fifth woman named in Matthew's genealogy is Mary (Matt 1:16). Scholars have noted that with the mention of Joseph, Mary, and Jesus, the pattern of the genealogy changes.[1] All of the other men named in the genealogy become the subject of the next use of the aorist active of ἐγέννησεν (from γεννάω, "fathered," "begot"). For example, Matt 1:2 says, "Ἀβραὰμ ἐγέννησεν τὸν Ἰσαακ, Ἰσαὰκ δὲ ἐγέννησεν τὸν Ἰακωβ." With the mention of Joseph, Mary, and Jesus in Matt 1:16, the pat-

---

1. See, for example, Davies and Allison, *Matthew 1–7*, 184–85; and Harrington, *Matthew*, 32. Parambi notes that this is actually a "double pattern break," a single "pattern break" having been seen already in each of the first four women mentioned in the genealogy with the addition of ἐκ plus the genitive of the mother's name. With the mention of Mary a structure is seen that is different from that used for the men and the one used for the women in the genealogy (Parambi, *Discipleship of Women*, 65).

tern of repeated uses of ἐγέννησεν between fathers and sons is broken.[2] Joseph is the object of the verb ἐγέννησεν of which his father, Jacob, is the subject. But, for the next male in the sequence, Jesus, ἐγεννήθη (aorist passive) is used. Called the "divine passive,"[3] the form is used again in Matt 1:20, 2:1, and 2:4, and means "was conceived" or "was born."[4] The use of the divine passive separates Joseph, named in the genealogy as the husband of Mary, from the child Jesus. It is actually Mary "from whom was born Jesus, who is called Messiah" (ἐξ ἧς ἐγεννήθη Ἰησοῦς ὁ λεγόμενος Χριστός, Matt 1:16). Joseph is called "husband of Mary," and the son named in connection with him he does not father. A yet-to-be-named divine progenitor behind the birth is hinted at by the presence of the passive voice.

Matthew moves directly from his genealogy to the birth narrative of Jesus, forging a closer link between the people mentioned in the genealogy and the events which follow. This is in marked contrast with the position of the genealogy in Luke's Gospel, which follows the baptism of the adult Jesus (Luke 3:23–38). In Luke, the placement emphasizes the title "Son of God," which appears in both the genealogy and the narrative of the baptism of Jesus; the genealogy serves as an elaboration of the title "Son of God" which Jesus receives at his baptism.[5] Matthew, it seems, wants to continue the theme of undoing the watchers' transgression, foreshadowed in the stories of the four women of the Hebrew Bible, which will be completed in the story of the fifth woman, Mary, her unusual entry into motherhood, and her suspicious husband Joseph. By following the genealogy immediately with the

2. I noted the pattern break when women are mentioned in the preceding chapter.

3. Davis and Allison, *Matthew 1–7*, 184.

4. Ibid.

5. Johnson, *Purpose*, 238. Johnson also thinks that an important reason for the differences between the details within the Matthean genealogy and the Lukan genealogy is that Luke emphasizes the prophetic role of Jesus. The names given for the monarchic period in each genealogy are entirely different after David, with Luke following a Nathanic line for Jesus, rather than the Solomonic line offered by Matthew. Johnson proposes that Luke is aware of traditions that identify Nathan, the third son of David (2 Sam 5:14; 1 Chron 3:5; 14:4), as the prophet of the same name (see Johnson, *Purpose*, 240–52). Also on the comparison between the Matthean and Lukan genealogies, see Brown, *Birth*, 84–94. Of course, by including Solomon and his mother in his version of the genealogy, Matthew also includes an important example of the watchers' illicit arts at work through the reference to the events involving David, Uriah, and Bathsheba, mentioned in chapter 3 above.

birth narrative, the redressing of the watchers' transgression continues to unfold. The genealogy that contains women whose stories use the watchers' illicit arts and motifs from the Enochic watchers' narrative to good ends and not evil ones leads ultimately to Mary whose child will completely undo the results of the watchers' rebellion and fall.

Whose Child is This?

While Joseph may not share with his forefathers the right to the verb γεννάω in the active mood, he does share with some of those who came before him a mood about a pregnancy in his family, namely suspicion. Joseph finds out that Mary, to whom he is engaged, but with whom he has not had sexual relations, is pregnant (Matt 1:18). Because Joseph is a righteous man and does not wish to disgrace Mary publicly, he makes plans to divorce her quietly (Matt 1:19). So far, then, Joseph has done two things: he has noticed the pregnancy of Mary, his betrothed, and made a reasonable assumption about how she got that way, that is, by another man. But the reader knows what Joseph does not yet know: Mary is pregnant by the Holy Spirit (ἐν γαστρὶ ἔχουσα ἐκ πνεύματος ἁγίου, Matt 1:18). This is the first of Matthew's assertions about the actor behind the divine passive in the genealogy. At this point in the story, though, Joseph believes that his betrothed has been unfaithful to him.

Joseph shares this suspicion of unfaithfulness—or better, this certainty, since he knows the child is not his—with some of his forebears, notably with Lamech, father of Noah, in *1 Enoch*. As noted in the previous chapter, Joseph's family tree includes suspicious sexual behavior (Rahab), efforts to avoid suspicions of illicit sexual behavior (Ruth), and suspicions of illicit paternity (Tamar and Bathsheba). Concerns about married women engaging in sexual relations with strangers also figure in the narratives of Abram and Sarai (when Pharaoh takes an interest in Sarai, whom Abram has introduced as his sister rather than wife, Gen 12:10–20; and again, as Abraham and Sarah, with Abimelech, Gen 20:1–18); as well as in the story of Isaac and Rebekah (same issue, with Abimelech, Gen 26:6–16). Joseph's story, however, points us to yet another ancestor who suspects his wife of infidelity. This time the concern is not just paternity, but also the birth of a savior figure. I look now at story of Lamech and his wife and note the similarities and differences between their story and the story of Mary and Joseph.[6]

The story of the birth of Noah is presented in *1 Enoch* 106—107. Although Gen 5:28–29 mentions the birth of Noah, the Enochic version is an expansion on the brief passage in Genesis.[7] In *1 Enoch* Lamech has married and his wife gives birth to a son (Noah). However, the child is born with an unusual appearance and atypical abilities. His body appears "whiter than snow and redder than a rose, his hair was all white and like white wool and curly" (*1 En.* 106:2).[8] He has a glorious countenance and his eyes emit light like the light of the sun. Although a newborn, he is able to stand and praise God (*1 En.* 106:2–3). After seeing the infant Noah, Lamech fears that the child is not his; he suspects that the child is the product of one of the watchers (*1 En.* 106:5–6) who must have impregnated his wife. What else could explain the child's odd appearance and proclivities? Knowing the watchers' earlier-noted sexual interaction with women and the strange offspring produced by those unions, Lamech believes his wife has been unfaithful with a watcher. But, as in the Matthean narrative of the birth of Jesus, the reader knows what the man involved does not: "she conceived from him [Lamech] and bore a child" (*1 En.* 106:1). Still ignorant of the truth of the situation, Lamech goes to Methuselah to ask him to ask Enoch to discover the truth of the unusual child's paternity (*1 En.* 106:4–7).[9]

6. Similarities and differences between the Matthean infancy narrative and the story of Noah's birth in *1 Enoch* have been noted by George Nickelsburg in "Patriarchs Who Worry," 137–58.

7. Ibid., 177. *1 Enoch* is not the only expanded version of the story. The story is also told in the *Genesis Apocryphon* (1Qap Gen), which is, as Nickelsburg describes, "a massive expansion of a brief notice in Gen 5:28–29" (ibid., 180). For more on the *Genesis Apocryphon*, see Avigad and Yadin, *A Genesis Apocryphon*; Bernstein, "Divine Titles," 291–310; Fitzmyer, *Genesis Apocryphon*; Greenfield and Qimron, "The *Genesis Apocryphon*," 70–77; Qimron, "Toward a New Edition," 106–9.

8. *1 Enoch: A New Translation,* 164.

9. The version in *1 Enoch* does not include the episode included in 1Qap Gen in which Lamech first goes to his wife, here named Bitenosh, confronting her about the unusual nature of the child and his suspicions about the child's origins. Bitenosh swears an oath that Noah is Lamech's child, and begs him to recall their pleasure in the sexual relations through which Noah was conceived (1Qap Gen 2:3–18). The "heat" and "pleasure" to which Bitenosh refers are evidence of conception according to Greek medical thought of the fourth century BCE. See Peters, *Noah Traditions,* 117.

Enoch provides Methuselah with much information about his grandchild's origin and destiny. Enoch affirms that Noah is the child of Lamech and not of any watcher (*1 En.* 106:18). Further, Enoch informs Methusaleh about the flood (*1 En.* 106:15), and how Noah will play a role in the judgment against the watchers and "will cleanse the earth from the corruption that is on it" (*1 En.* 106: 17).[10] Enoch also tells Methuselah, "this child will be righteous and blameless" (*1 En.* 106:18).[11] Enoch reveals that the child should be named Noah. He also reveals the name's significance: because of Noah's role in the incipient flood, "he will be your remnant, from whom you will find rest" (*1 En.* 106:18).[12] Another etymology for "Noah" is given in 107:3, "he who gladdens the earth from destruction."[13] Methuselah takes the information back to Lamech (*1 En.* 107:3). In *1 Enoch*, then, there is a chain of messengers who inform Lamech of what heavenly beings know. However, Lamech cannot know the situation for certain without revelation from the heavenly sphere to the earthly. Enoch, who has been given privileged access to heavenly secrets, tells Methuselah, who tells Lamech what is really going on. The child, Noah, does have unusual attributes, but these are not due to his progenitor. Noah, as Enoch assures Methusaleh, is the child of mere mortals, and Lamech is his father. Noah's unusual appearance denotes, not unfaithfulness on the part of Bitenosh, but rather Noah's "divine beauty" and is fitting for one with a divinely appointed function.[14]

In the case of Joseph, he too harbors suspicions, but not that Mary's child is of supernatural origins. There is nothing to indicate that the child Mary carries has a celestial being as a father. Joseph likely

10. *1 Enoch: A New Translation*, 166.

11. Ibid.

12. Ibid.

13. Ibid., 167. How does "he who gladdens" ("gladden," εὐφραίνω, = חדי) "the earth from destruction" relate to "Noah" [נח, or נחם,]? Nickelsburg suggests that the ח found in both חדי and נח is alliterative and that joy is related to rest or consolation. Another possibility is that the Greek reflects an Aramaic textual corruption from חדת ("to renew") to חדי ("to gladden"). Noah will "renew the earth from destruction" because he will repopulate the earth following the flood. Noah's renewing of the earth would provide an *inclusio* to the beginning of Enoch's speech to Methuselah, "The Lord will renew his commandment upon the earth" (*1 En.* 106:13). See Nickelsburg, *1 Enoch 1*, 549–50.

14. Nickelsburg, "Patriarchs Who Worry," 143.

suspects infidelity of the pedestrian, human kind. However, as in the case of Lamech, heavenly revelation sets the paternal record straight. An angel comes to Joseph in a dream and informs him that the child is of the Holy Spirit (Matt 1:20). As in the case of Noah, this child too has a divinely appointed purpose: "he will save his people from their sins" (Matt 1:21 NRSV). As in the case of Lamech, Joseph is to give the child the name indicated by the heavenly messenger, which signifies the child's salvific function (Matt 1:21). Both Lamech and Joseph had suspicions about the children carried by their wives; both received information from a heavenly messenger about the reality of the infants' origins and purpose.

The Matthean birth narrative, therefore, bears some similarity to the story of Noah's birth in *1 Enoch*, but with one important difference. Lamech suspects that his child is of celestial origin—but Noah is not; Joseph does not suspect that Jesus is the product of a union between the human Mary and a celestial being—but Jesus actually is. The other important difference is that in the Matthean narrative there is no indication that sexual relations play any role in the conception of Jesus. Mary has not had sexual relations with a celestial being in order to become "with child by the Holy Spirit." Neither has she had sexual relations with the man to whom she is betrothed. In fact, effort is made to expunge the possibility of any sexual relations whatsoever between Mary and Joseph while Mary is pregnant. Joseph "did as the angel of the Lord commanded him; he took her as his wife, but had no marital relations with her" (οὐκ ἐγίνωσκεν αὐτὴν) until after the child is born (Matt 1:25 NRSV). Mary's virginal status is further reflected in the fulfillment formula quotation in Matt 1:23. Matthew's statement is the same as the LXX text of Isa 7:14, "Look, the virgin (ἡ παρθένος) shall conceive and bear a son," rather than reflecting the Hebrew עלמה which would be better translated as νεᾶνις, "young girl." The child Jesus is in fact the product of the union of earthly and heavenly beings. Jesus is one who crosses the boundaries between earthly and heavenly, but without sexual relations taking place between beings of the two realms. Jesus' existence as a mix between the earthly and heavenly and one who crosses the boundaries between the two is reflected in his name, "Emmanuel, which means 'God is with us'" (Matt 1:23 NRSV).

Matthew makes a point of showing Jesus as Emmanuel, God is with us, as an eschatological reality later in his narrative of events in the life of the adult Jesus. Matthew specifically refers to this identity of Jesus as Emmanuel, God is with us, through his inclusion of the stories of the healing of the hemorrhaging woman who touches the fringe of his garment (τοῦ κρασπέδου τοῦ ἱματίου αὐτοῦ; Matt 9:20–22) [15] and the healing of those in the crowd who touch the fringe of his garment (Matt 14:36). [16] The fringe, κρασπέδον, is the equivalent in the LXX of the tassels the Israelites are commanded to wear on their garments in Num 15:38–39 and Deut 22:12 (ציצת in Num 15:38; גדלים in Deut 22:12). The tassels are to remind the people of the commandments of God and their identity as a holy people (Num 15:40). In Zech 8:23, however, the tassels take on an eschatological significance, pointing to the time when the nations will come to Jerusalem to worship God: "In those days ten men from all languages and nations will take hold of the tassels of a Jew (καὶ ἐπιλάβωνται τοῦ κρασπέδου ἀνδρὸς Ἰουδαίου; LXX) for we have heard that God is with you" (ὁ θεὸς μεθ' ὑμῶν ἐστιν; LXX[17]). In Zechariah, the grasping of the tassels signifies the eschatological realization of the nations that God is present with the Jews. Matthew interprets Zechariah's singular Jewish man, ἀνδρὸς Ἰουδαίου, quite literally in both Matt 9:20–22 and 14:36.

Matthew draws attention to the eschatological significance of the woman's touching the tassel on his garment, as may be seen in the differences between his telling of the incident and the way it appears in Mark and Luke. In Mark's version, the woman touches not the fringe, κρασπέδον, but Jesus' garment, ἱματίων. In Luke's version, as in Matthew's, the woman touches the κρασπέδον itself. Thus Luke's version also appeals to the eschatological significance of the woman's action. However, Matthew retains Mark's detail that "the woman was saying, 'If I may touch even his garments (τῶν ἱματίων αὐτοῦ), I will be healed' (Mark 5:28), albeit characteristically clearing up the detail of the audience of the woman's speech by adding that she was saying these words "to herself" (Matt 9:21). The woman's statement, whether

---

15. The healing of the hemorrhaging woman also appears in Mark 5:25–34 and Luke 8:43–49. As in Matthew, the healing of the woman appears within the context of the raising from the dead of the daughter of a man (called ἄρχων, ruler or leader in Matthew; named Jairus and identified as a leader of the synagogue; in Mark 5:22 and Luke 8:41).

16. The healing of all who touch Jesus' κρασπέδον occurs also in Mark 6:56.

17. My translation.

to herself or aloud, is not included in Luke's version. Matthew has taken over the woman's musing that if she touches Jesus' garment she will be healed, as in Mark, but Matthew adds the eschatological detail that it is the fringe that she actually touches, as in Luke. In Matthew's version, the woman herself may not even realize the full implication of her action: she, perhaps even unwittingly, shows Jesus to be Zechariah's Jew whose tassel is grasped because his presence mediates God's presence. Whether the woman fully perceives the significance of her action or not, Jesus, in Matthew's version of the story, is fully aware of her actions. Unlike in Mark and Luke's accounts in which Jesus asks, "Who touched my garments?" (Mark 5:30 NRSV) and "Who touched me?" (Luke 8:45 NRSV), in Matthew's version, Jesus turns and sees her and speaks directly to her, knowing that she has touched his tassels because of her faith (Matt 9:22). More will be said about Jesus' healing methods in the next chapter, but here note that Matthew, by having Jesus address the woman directly rather than having to ask about the identity of the one who touched him, shows that Jesus perceives the significance of the woman's actions, even if she does not. In Luke's version, it is Jesus who appears not to grasp the entirety of the situation: if he understands the symbolism, he does not appear to know who is responsible for the action. In Matthew, through his statement that the woman touches the tassel of Jesus' garment, rather than the garment alone, and Jesus' knowing who it is who touched him, Jesus appears fully cognizant of all aspects of the situation: he is Emmanuel, God is with us, foretold in Zechariah and witnessed to by the hemorrhaging woman.

Later in the narrative Matthew reports that many people touch the fringe of Jesus' garments in order to receive healing (Matt 14:36). Even though Luke includes the detail of the fringe in the story of the woman, it is Mark, rather than Luke, who includes the story of the crowds being healed by touching the fringe of Jesus' garment (Mark 6:56). Matthew includes the grasping of the κρασπέδον in both the story of the woman and the crowd. For Matthew, Jesus is the Jew whose tassels are grasped—first by a hemorrhaging woman, then by many people; in Jesus the presence of "God with us" is made real not in some future time ("in those days"), but now.[18] Jesus' identity as Emmanuel, which begins in Matthew's infancy narrative, means that eschatological righteousness has become a present reality in Jesus.

18. Deines, "Not the Law," 59–60. See also Cummings, "The Tassel of His Cloak," 47–61.

Crispin H. T. Fletcher-Louis makes use of a tradition attested in Ezekiel to make sense of the tassels incident; he argues that Jesus saw himself as the eschatological high priest, "the physical, human, embodiment of the divine Glory."[19] Fletcher-Louis's comments also highlight the eschatological nature and the manifestation of divine holiness in Jesus' interaction with the woman who touches the fringes of his garment and those in the crowds who are healed when they touch Jesus' fringes. Although Fletcher-Louis focuses on Mark's version in his explication, his point would be made even more strongly if he looked at Matthew's version instead. The Ezekiel passage to which Fletcher-Louis refers gives the information that the priests must not wear their sacred garments when they interact with people in the outer court of the temple. The passage says, "When they go out into the outer court to the people, they shall remove the vestments in which they have been ministering, and lay them in the holy chambers; and they shall put on other garments, so that they may not communicate holiness to the people with their vestments" (Ezek 44:19 NRSV). In other words, the holiness of the priestly garments is in a tangible sense contagious. The idea that one may "catch" holiness by means of touching garments is also communicated in Exod 30:29, in which Moses is informed that "everything that is anointed with the oil of consecration—and that includes the priestly garments—is supercharged with holiness,"[20] so that "whatever touches them will become holy" (Exod 30:29 NRSV). The woman and the crowds who follow Jesus evidently believe his garments, even just the fringes of them, have the same sort of "contagious" holiness. Fletcher-Louis also thinks that the fringes Jesus wears are the *tsitsit* of Num 15:38, but points out that those "*tsitsit* are the ordinary Israelites' equivalent of the *tsits*, the rosette that bears the Name of God on the high priest's forehead."[21] Because all Israelite males wear the tassels, the entire nation is "a kingdom of priests" (Exod 19:6).[22] Fletcher-Louis continues, "perhaps in mediating contagious holiness through that symbol of the whole nation's priesthood [Jesus] was not so much interested in his own, singular, high priesthood as the fulfillment of the call that the whole of Israel be a 'kingdom of priests,' sharing the

19. Fletcher-Louis, "Jesus as the High Priestly Messiah: Part 2," 76.

20. Ibid., 67.

21. Ibid., 69–70.

22. Ibid., 70.

contagious, restorative, ontology of the high priest."[23] This emphasis on
the "kingdom of priests" fits well with Matthew's emphasis on the participation of Jesus' followers in all aspects of his ministry, in particular
at the conclusion of Matthew's Gospel when even teaching is included
in what Jesus' followers are to do (Matt 28:19–20).[24]

In the episodes connected with the touching of the fringes on
Jesus' garments, Matthew's narrative of the adult Jesus builds upon his
claim that Jesus, as announced to Joseph, is Emmanuel, God is with us.
However, unlike in Matthew's Gospel, in *1 Enoch*, the ultimate presence
of righteousness and an end to postdiluvial evil is still a future event.
Enoch informs Methuselah that despite Noah's role in cleansing the
earth of the current unrighteousness, still more unrighteousness, and
worse, is in store. The postdiluvial evil will continue until a final period
when there will

> arise generations of righteousness.
> And evil and wickedness will end,
> and violence will cease from the earth;
> and good things will come upon the earth to them.
> (*1 En.* 107:1)[25]

Noah will bring comfort, but the flood will not bring the final eradica-
tion of unrighteousness from the earth, as the community for whom
1Enoch was written would have known from their own experience. In
the case of Jesus, however, no further period of unrighteousness is in
store for people and the earth. Enoch informs Methuselah that more
unrighteousness will follow Noah. The angel who informs Joseph has
only good news about Jesus.

Table III shows the similarities and differences between the stories
of the birth of Noah and the birth of Jesus. The stories of Joseph and
Lamech share several similarities and have some important differences.
Each man is upset because of the birth or conception of a child he has
reasons to think is not his own. Each receives an angelic message to put
his mind at ease. The content of the message indicates that the child will
play a significant role for the people of the earth, a role reflected in the
name each is instructed to give the child. Each child is named according

23. Ibid.
24. Jesus' pedagogy and its difference from that of the watchers is addressed below.
25. *1 Enoch: A New Translation*, 167.

to the angelic messenger's instructions. In the case of Lamech, the child is truly his, and truly the product of human sexual interaction. In the case of Joseph, however, the child is from the Holy Spirit, and not the product of any sexual interaction. Lamech's child, Noah, will be righteous and will bring cleansing to the earth. The cleansing, however, will be temporary and more evil will prevail on the earth. Jesus, is superior to Noah in the sense that his name indicates that "he will save people from their sins," that in him, "God is with us," and that his presence means that eschatological righteousness is made a present reality.

Table III: Comparison of the Birth Stories of Noah and Jesus

	Husband's Suspicion	Informant	Reality	Child's Identity and Purpose	Husband's Response
Lamech	The child is the product of a union between his wife and a watcher.	Methusaleh (Lamech's father) goes to Enoch on Lamech's behalf. Enoch has taken on angelomorphic qualities and has been granted access to heavenly revelation.	Noah is truly the son of Lamech and his wife, a human child—the product of human sexual interaction.	His name will be Noah. He will be righteous and blameless and participate in the cleansing of the earth from corruption. Two etymologies of his name are given: "from whom you will find rest" (1 En. 106:18); "he who gladdens the earth" (1 En. 107:3).	The child's name is called Noah (1 En. 107:3).

Joseph	The child (unborn) is the product of Mary and another man.	An angel of the Lord comes to Joseph.	The child is the product of Mary and the Holy Spirit—but no sexual interaction has taken place.	The child's name will be Jesus, "for he will save his people from their sins" (Matt 1:21); another name is given in Matt 1:23, Emmanuel, "God is with us."	Joseph does everything the angel says, including naming the baby Jesus.

I look next at a possibility that would bring us even closer to the repair of the Enochic watchers' template. Rather than being simply the product of the non-sexual union between a heavenly being (Holy Spirit) and a human woman (Mary), it may be that Matthew had in mind a tradition that conceived of the Holy Spirit as angelomorphic when the evangelist told his story of the child Jesus being "from the Holy Spirit" and having a human mother.

The Child is from the (Angelomorphic) Holy Spirit

An additional link between the Enochic watchers' template with its watchers who impregnate women and Matthew's transgression-repairing narrative is found in the angel's statement to Joseph, "The child conceived in her is from the Holy Spirit" (Matt 1:20 NRSV). The possibility exists that at the time of Matthew's writing, the Holy Spirit was thought of as an angelomorphic[26] figure. If this is the case, then Matthew draws

26. Bogdan Bucur, in his arguments for an early Christian "angelomorphic" pneumatology, makes use of this definition of "angelomorphic" proposed by Crispin Fletcher-Louis: "Though it has been used in different ways by various scholars, without clear definition, we propose its use wherever there are signs that an individual or community possesses specifically angelic characteristics or status, though for whom identity cannot be reduced to that of an angel" (Fletcher-Louis, *Luke-Acts*, 14–15). According to Bucur, "The virtue of this definition is that it signals the use of angelic *characteristics* in descriptions of God or humans, while not necessarily implying that the latter are angels *stricto sensu*" (Bucur, "Hierarchy," 175). See also Bucur, "The Son of God," 125; Bucur, "Revisiting Christian Oeyen," 409; Bucur, "The Angelic Spirit in Early Christianity," 193.

out the parallels and the distinctions between the Enochic template and the genesis of the Christ. According to the Enochic watchers' template, angels have sexual relations with women: beings from heavenly and earthly realms mix. Heavenly and earthly boundaries are transgressed, and the results are evil, unrighteousness, and death. According to Matthew's narrative, the angelomorphic Holy Spirit conceives a child by a woman, but without sexual contact. Angelic and human mix, heavenly and earthly boundaries are transgressed, but the result is salvation. Scholars, most notably John Levison, have noted that the use of "spirit" (πνεῦμα) to denote an angelic being is recognizable in Second Temple Judaism and frequent at Qumran;[27] Bogdan Bucur has established that speaking of the Spirit in angelomorphic terms remained an option in Christianity as late as the fourth century.[28] I will summarize some of Levison's and Bucur's evidence before returning to the subject of the Spirit by whom Mary is pregnant with the Christ child.

Levison identifies at least five sources in Jewish tradition in which the Holy Spirit is described as an angelic being, one of which is in the Balaam story. That Balaam's story contains a reference to the divine spirit as an angelomorphic being is significant because, as I will show in the next section of this chapter, both 1 Enoch and Matthew have significant overlaps with the Balaam story. First, Levison points out that within the Hebrew Bible the Holy Spirit is described in diverse terms, including as the angel that led Israel through the wilderness. Isaiah 63:9–10 states,

> In all their distress he was distressed;
> the angel of his presence saved them.
> In his love and in his pity he redeemed them;
> He lifted them up and carried them all the days of old
> But they rebelled and grieved his holy spirit . . . [29]

The "angel of his presence" was the angel sent to accompany Israel through the wilderness in Exod 23:20–23.[30] Israel was commanded not

27. Levison, "The Angelic Spirit," 464–93; Levison, The Spirit in First Century Judaism. See also Gieschen, Angelomorphic Christology.

28. Bucur, "Revisiting Christian Oeyen," 413.

29. This is the alternative rendering in The New Oxford Annotated Bible with the Apocrypha: An Ecumenical Study Bible NRSV, OT: 953, which follows the reading indicated in the BHS.

30. Levison, "The Pluriform Foundation," 67. Also Levison, "The Angelic Spirit," 471, although here Levison cites Isa 63:9–14, rather than 7–14. Verse 9 is where מלאך actually appears, but verse 7 is the beginning of the section.

to rebel against this angel. Here, however, the prophet says that they did rebel and grieved YHWH's "holy spirit." The "holy spirit" appears to be synonymous with the "angel." Second, Levison also points out the tendency to show the spirit as angelic within the LXX, for example in LXX Judg 13:24–25; LXX 1 Kgs 22:19–24; LXX Isa 63:7–14; LXX Mic 2:7 and 11; 3:8; and LXX Hag 2:5.[31] Third, in the Dead Sea Scrolls, Levison counts approximately fifty times when angelic beings are identified as spirits.[32] Levison's fourth and fifth sources are Philo and Josephus who both identify the spirit as an angelic being in their interpretations of the story of Balaam from Numbers 23–24. In Philo's interpretation, when Balaam was inspired, Balaam's rational faculties were displaced by an angelic spirit who used his vocal organs to create a prophetic utterance.[33] Philo argues that he himself is inspired by an angelic spirit when he interprets Torah,[34] and that the beings called "demons" (δαίμονας) "by the other philosophers"[35] would be better called "angels."[36] In Josephus's version of the episode in Numbers, when an angel approaches Balaam and his ass, it is the divine spirit who approaches. In his description of the event, Josephus seems to use angel and spirit interchangeably: "But on the road an angel of God (ἀγγέλου θείου) confronted him in a narrow place . . . and the ass whereon Balaam rode, conscious of the divine spirit approaching her (τοῦ θείου πνεύματος) . . ."[37] In Josephus's interpretation of the Balaam story the angel and the divine spirit are the same. As will be addressed below, Balaam provides background for Matthew's infancy narrative and has connections with *1 Enoch* as well. Here, note that Josephus's understanding that Balaam encountered the angelomorphic divine spirit may provide a further link between the

31. Levison, *The Spirit in First Century Judaism*, 46 n. 44.

32. Ibid. Geischen also notes that "angels" and "spirits" are used interchangeably in some Qumran texts. For example, in the War Scroll, "angels" and "spirits" are used as parallel terms in 1QM 12.8–9: "The heroes of the army of his angels [צבא מלאכים]are listed with us;/ the war hero is in our congregation;/ the army of his spirits [צבא רוחיו] with our infantry and our cavalry" (Geischen, *Angelomorphic Christology*, 115).

33. Levison, "The Prophetic Spirit," 192, referring to Philo's *Vit. Mos.* 1.274 and 1.277.

34. Levison, "The Prophetic Spirit," 200.

35. Philo, *Som.* 1.141 on Gen 28:12 in Levison, "The Prophetic Spirit," 194.

36. Ibid.

37. Josephus, *Ant.* 4.108. Greek cited 1 July 2009. Online: http://pace.mcmaster.ca/York/york/showText?text=anti.

Matthean Holy Spirit from whom the child Jesus is born through the participation of Mary but without sexual interaction and the angels of the Enochic watchers' template who impregnate women. Using the examples of the Balaam episode and others, Levison, then, makes the case that within Jewish tradition there are sources that describe the holy spirit as an angelic being.

Bucur examines what he calls the "angelomorphic Holy Spirit" in a number of early Christian writings and argues that various authors spoke of the Holy Spirit in angelomorphic terms, at least until the fourth century. In the fourth century, descriptions of the Holy Spirit in angelomorphic terms would have been abandoned because of the Arian and Pneumatomachian controversies.[38] For example, the words spirit and angel were sometimes used interchangeably or in parallel ways, such as in the Shepherd of Hermas where *Mandate* 5, 2, 7 speaks of "the spirit of righteousness," and *Mandate* 6, 2 has "the angel of righteousness."[39] Within the New Testament writings, in Acts 8:26, 29, and 39, the being who guides Philip is called "angel of the Lord," "spirit," and "spirit of the Lord."[40] In the Shepherd, πνεῦμα is used to designate a variety of angelic beings,[41] as part of an early Christian tradition that used the Second Temple tradition of the seven principal angels "in the service of Pneumatology." For example, Shepherd describes a group of seven angelic spirits, the "first created ones" (πρῶτοι κτισθέντες), one of whom is the Son of God.[42] The description of the presence of the Holy Spirit within the Christian ascetic "is conveyed in angelomorphic terms, with a penchant for the metaphors of clothing, renewal, purification, rejuvenation, strengthening, and vision."[43] Clement brings together angels, spirits, and the Holy Spirit, when he describes the seven first-born princes of the angels (*Strom.* 6.16.142–43)[44] as the "heptad of the Spirit" (*Paed.* 3.12.87).[45] Clement also connects angels and the Spirit in

38. Bucur, "Son of God," 142.

39. Ibid.,122–23.

40. Ibid.

41. Ibid., 122.

42. In *Vision* 3.4.1 and *Similitude* 5.5.3. See Bucur, "Revelation's *Wirkungsgeschichte*," 179.

43. Ibid., 142.

44. Ibid., 181.

45. Ibid., 182.

Adumbrationes in 1 Pet 2:3 and 4:14, where he writes, "the Lord works through archangels and through angels that are close, who are called 'the Spirit of Christ' . . . He says, 'Blessed are you, because there rests upon you that which is of his glory, and of God's honor and power, and who is His Spirit.' This 'his' is possessive, and designates the angelic spirit."[46] With these and other examples,[47] Bucur makes a case for an understanding of the Holy Spirit in angelomorphic terms within early Christian thought.

It is not established that the evangelist Matthew had such an angelomorphic conception of the Holy Spirit. Clearly he distinguishes between the ἄγγελος κυρίου (angel of the Lord), who appears to Joseph to inform him that he should take Mary as his wife and the πνεύματός ἁγίου (Holy Spirit) who is responsible for the conception of the child (Matt 1:20); they are not the same being. But might they both have been understood as having angelic characteristics? If so, then it would be even more important for Matthew to distinguish between them: the angelomorphic being who is responsible for Mary's pregnancy is a particular holy being, rather than merely one of a company of angels who crosses the boundary between the realms of heaven and earth. If angelomorphic, the Holy Spirit who impregnates Mary, but without sexual interaction and for good purpose (the child "will save his people from their sins," Matt 1:21), provides great contrast with the angelic watchers who impregnate women through sexual interaction for their own purposes ("to beget children for ourselves," *1 En.* 6:2[48]). Even if not angelomorphic, the Holy Spirit still provides the contrast between a heavenly being who impregnates a woman and causes a child to be born for good purposes, and heavenly beings whose impregnating women results in monstrous creatures and destruction in the world.

In this section Balaam was introduced, whose dream visions led to his encounter with the angelomorphic divine spirit. In Matthew, information about the action of the Holy Spirit and the identity of the child is conveyed through dreams. Dreams are an important mode of revelation in both Matthew and *1 Enoch*. I look next at dreams and

46. Bucur, "Revisiting Christian Oeyen," 402.

47. On Justin Martyr's angelomorphic pneumatology, see Bucur, "The Angelic Spirit."

48. *1 Enoch: A New Translation*, 23.

dreamers in Matthew and *1 Enoch* to see yet another point of commonality between the two.

I Had a Dream: Dreams as Revelatory in Matthew 1–2 and 1 Enoch

Dreams are important in both Matthew's infancy narratives and *1 Enoch*. In Matthew, dreams contain the revelation of God that moves the narrative forward according to God's purposes. A faithful recipient of divinely inspired dreams, Joseph acts in accordance with the divine instruction he receives in his dreams. The magi also receive a dream and act in accordance with its directions. In *1 Enoch*, Enoch's dream visions help establish him as a faithful recipient of God's revelation. His faithful execution of God's commands received in his dreams also helps move the story and divine purposes forward. Through their faithful carrying out of commands received in dreams, both Joseph and Enoch act as protector of an important person sent to bring salvation.

A third noteworthy dreamer may be added to Joseph and Enoch as important to understanding the role of dreams in both *1 Enoch* and Matthew: Balaam receives messages from God in dreams that he is to bless rather than curse Israel. The Balaam tradition helped to shape Matthew's infancy narrative and the dream visions of *1 Enoch*. This is the same Balaam whose encounter with the angelomorphic divine spirit figured in Josephus's interpretation of the event.

This section proceeds as follows: first, I look at dreams in the Matthean text, and note the distinction between auditory message dreams and visual symbolic dreams. Second, I look at dream visions in *1Enoch* and identify them according to their dream type. Third, after noting points of comparison between Enoch the dreamer and the Matthean dreamer Joseph, I look at Balaam whose dreams put him at odds with the Moabite king but in concord with divine purpose. Through this examination, I will show that all three—Joseph, Enoch, and Balaam—are established as trustworthy recipients of divine dream messages; and that Matthew and *1 Enoch* have a cosmic and eschatological concern that is beyond the interests of the Balaam of the Numbers tradition, but is a concern of a non-biblical account of Balaam.

Dreams in Matthew

No fewer than five dreams are mentioned in Matthew's infancy narrative, in Matt 1:20–25; 2:12; 2:13–15; 2:19–21; and 2:22. This means that of the thirty-one verses that follow Matthew's genealogy in 1:1–17 and lead to the conclusion of the infancy section at 2:23, thirteen verses—almost half—give full accounts of dreams or report the outcome of dreams. Four of the dreams provide instructions for Joseph (Matt 1:20–25, Joseph is told not to be afraid to take Mary as his wife; 2:13–15, Joseph is told to take the child and his mother to Egypt; 2:19–21, Joseph is told to take the child and his mother to Israel; and 2:22, Joseph is warned against living in Judea and goes to Galilee instead). One of the dreams provides instructions for the magi (Matt 2:13, the magi are warned to return home by another way). Later in the Gospel, Matthew also includes mention of the dream of Pilate's wife, in Matt 27:19, another instance of instruction: Pilate's wife tells her husband, sitting in judgment of Jesus, "Have nothing to do with that innocent man, for today I have suffered a great deal because of a dream (ὄναρ) about him" (NRSV). Other than these six references to dreams in Matthew's Gospel, five in the infancy narrative, there are no other instances of dreams in the synoptic gospels. The Acts of the Apostles contains some appearances of angels and visions,[49] but no dreams. Clearly, dreams are significant to Matthew and to his infancy narrative in particular. The importance of revelatory dreams also provides another point of intersection between Matthew and *1 Enoch*. I look first at the structure and significance of dreams in Matthew's infancy narrative.

Matthean Auditory Message Dreams

The dreams in Matthew's infancy narrative fit the category of the auditory message dream found in ancient Near Eastern texts, including texts in the Hebrew Bible, and in apocalyptic texts.[50] According to Robert Gnuse, the dreams in Matthew chapters 1–2 follow the form

49. Acts 10:1–8, Cornelius sees the angel of the Lord; Acts 10:9–20, Peter hears a voice and has a vision; Acts 16:9, Paul has a vision of a man of Macedon; Acts 18:9, 23:11, 27:23, Paul is encouraged by an angel.

50. See Gnuse, "Dreams," ch. 2 of *Dreams and Dream Reports*, 34–128; Gnuse, "Dream Genre," 97–120; Prabhu, *Formula Quotations*, 1–300.

of the auditory message dream as described by A. Leo Oppenheim,[51] a form also identifiable in the Hebrew Bible narratives about Abram (Gen 15:12–21)/Abraham (Gen 21:12–14), Abimelech (Gen 20:1–8), Hagar (Gen 21:16–20), Isaac (Gen 26:2–6, 24–25), Jacob (Gen 28:10–22; Gen 31:10–17; Gen 46:1–7), Laban (Gen 31:24), Balaam (Num 22:8–13, 19–21; Num 24:2), Samuel (1 Sam 3:1–18), and Solomon (1 Kgs 3:4–15/2 Chron 1:6–12; 1 Kgs 9:1–10).[52] According to Oppenheim's study of Sumerian, Akkadian, Hittite, Assyrian, Chaldean, Babylonian, and Egyptian dream reports, auditory message dreams follow this structure:

1. context of the auditory message dream—who received it; when, where, and under what conditions;

2. spoken message, or content, of the dream;

3. termination of the dream, indicated by the dreamer's awaking and realizing that he was dreaming;

4. fulfillment of the dream, often through the dreamer's undertaking the deity's command.[53]

In Gnuse's analysis of the five dreams in Matthew 1–2, he shows that each dream report has this basic structure.[54] Gnuse, however, supplements Oppenheim's structure by adding grammatical details and a recognition of a theophany, which occurs in three of the dream reports (Matt 1:20; 2:13; and 2:19).[55] In each of these three, the theophany is an appearance of an angel to Joseph. In all five dream reports, the fulfillment of the dream is the human agent's obedience to the Deity's command to undertake some action. In three of the Matthean dream reports, the obedient action is physical relocation (ἀνεχώρησαν; Matt 2:12, they [the magi] departed; εἰσῆλθεν; Matt 2:21, he [Joseph] went; ἀνεχώρησεν; Matt 2:22, he [Joseph] departed). In three dream reports, the obedient action is Joseph's "taking" (in all three, παρέλαβεν) of ei-

51. Gnuse, "Dream Genre," 98. See also Oppenheim, *Interpretation of Dreams*, 179–255. On dreams in early Christianity, see Bovon, "These Christians Who Dream," 144–62. On dreams in early Jewish Apocalyptic see Flannery-Dailey, "Lessons," 231–47; and Lange, "Dream Visions," 27–34.

52. Gnuse, "Dreams," 78–85.

53. Gnuse, "Dream Genre," 99.

54. See ibid., 106–9 for his outline of how the five dream reports adhere to Oppenheim's structure.

55. Ibid., 108.

ther "his wife" (Matt 1:24) or "the child and his mother" (Matt 2:14–15; Matt 2:21). The literary purpose of all five dreams is divine guidance in order to move the narrative forward. The dreams provide deliverance and protection for the characters involved.

Gnuse undertook his study of the Matthean dreams in order to show that as auditory message dreams, they are more like the dreams of the Elohist material in Genesis than they are like the symbolic and predictive dreams of Joseph's namesake in Genesis or of Daniel.[56] Previously, George Soares Prabhu[57] had noted similarities between the dreaming of Mary's husband and the dreaming of his patriarchal namesake in Genesis, and also with the dream reports in the book of Daniel. Gnuse, however, argues that the Matthean infancy narratives show the dream events surrounding the birth of Jesus in a similar pattern to the dream events occurring to the patriarchs in Genesis listed above, such as Abram/Abraham, Isaac, and Jacob. According to Gnuse, the Matthean dreams are not the stuff of people identified primarily as dreamers or dream interpreters like the Genesis Joseph and Daniel. By including auditory message dreams in the infancy narrative, the evangelist situates Jesus' birth and infancy in an environment familiar to a long line of leaders of God's people, including figures such as Abraham, Isaac, and Jacob.

Gnuse and others have shown how the dreams and the obedient actions connected with them also parallel events in the life of Moses.[58] For example, both Moses and Jesus are hidden as infants to protect them from a leader who desires their deaths (Exod 2:2–3 and Matt 2:16–18); after the death of the rulers who seek to harm Moses and Jesus, Moses and Joseph each receive a message from a divine figure to return home (Exod 4:19, God commands Moses to return to Egypt; and Matt 2:19–20, an angel commands Joseph to bring Jesus and his mother back to Israel).

However, might it be that Matthew wishes not to choose some of the great figures in Israelite history (such as Abraham, Isaac, and Jacob) over others (such as Joseph and Daniel) for characters in Jesus' birth

56. Ibid., 119.

57. Prabhu, *Formula Quotations*, 223–25.

58. For example, Allison, *New Moses*. See especially pages 140–65 for Allison's review of the Moses typology in Matthew's birth and infancy narratives; Brown, *Birth*, 110–19; Brown, "The Meaning of the Magi," 577.

narrative to emulate, but rather to evoke as many names and events as possible by using the dream form? It seems that for the evangelist who begins his Gospel with a genealogy which evokes a span of history, a multitude of stories, and literally names dozens of ancestors he sees forming Jesus' lineage, using the dream genre would provide the evangelist yet one more way to bring to mind a connection between Jesus and his forebears in Israelite history. Gnuse's study shows that the auditory message dream form connects the Matthean dreams not only with patriarchs, but with a wide range of characters, including Abimelech, Hagar, Laban, Balaam, Samuel, and Solomon as well. I will show, for instance, the importance of Balaam for both Matthew and *1 Enoch* below. In the biblical material, as Gnuse shows, auditory message dreams are received and obeyed by a diverse group which includes a foreign king (Abimelech), a woman who is a matriarch of a(nother) "great nation" (Gen 20:18; Hagar), a man who was an enemy of Jacob/Israel (Laban), a foreign prophet who was hired by foreign king Balak to curse Israel, but could not (Balaam), an Israelite prophet (Samuel), and a king of Israel (Solomon). Matthew does not seem interested in limiting the number of evocations he makes in the infancy narratives to only a few. Perhaps, although the form of the Matthean Joseph's dream is the auditory message dream, his dreaming is also meant to make connections with his namesake in Genesis as well.

Visual Symbolic Dreams

The dreams of those who dream auditory message dreams do stand apart from the type of dreams that the Joseph of Genesis has and he and Daniel interpret. The dreams in the Joseph story (Genesis 37, 40, and 41), in Daniel (Daniel 2, 4), and also a dream of an unnamed Midianite (Judges 7) are of the type identified by Oppenheim as visual symbolic dreams. Briefly stated, visual symbolic dreams usually need interpretation by someone other than the dreamer and often are predictive.[59] The form of visual symbolic dreams is similar to that of auditory message dreams, although they are often more complex and contain more details.[60] According to Wolfgang Richter, visual symbolic dreams have the following pattern:

59. Gnuse, "Dreams in the Ancient World," 45.
60. Ibid., 75.

1. announcement of the dream;

2. introductory dream formula;

3. the dream itself, which contains an image or images and a description of their activity;

4. interpretation of the dream;

5. dream fulfillment.[61]

In the instances of the Hebrew Bible's symbolic dreams, the dreams reveal the moving forward of God's plans for Israel through a human person who acts in accordance with the divine will. In each of the three examples in the Hebrew Bible, the faithful agent of the divine becomes a ruler over others and the God of Israel is glorified. In the case of Joseph in Genesis, Joseph is both a dreamer and a dream interpreter. The significance of Joseph's own dreams (Gen 37:5–11) and the results of his dream interpretation for the Pharaoh (Gen 41:1–32)[62] lead to Joseph's being put in charge of Egypt and saving not only the Egyptians, but also the sons of Israel and their families. Daniel, a righteous man who refuses to defile himself with Babylonian food and wine (Dan 1:8), is an interpreter of dreams and visions ("Daniel could understand visions and dreams of all kinds"; Dan 1:17) through the visions he receives ("During the night the mystery was revealed to Daniel in a vision"; Dan 2:19). The result of his interpretation of King Nebuchadnezzar's dreams (Dan 2:1–45; Dan 4:4–27) is that Daniel is appointed to a high position, made ruler over Babylon, and is put in charge of all the wise men (חכימין) of Babylon (Dan 2:48). In addition, King Nebuchadnezzar acknowledges the superiority of Daniel's God (Dan 2:47; 4:1–3, 34–37). Daniel advises the king to repent (Dan 4:27) and the king acknowledges that the ways of God are right and just (Dan 4:37). In Judges 7, Gideon is instructed by God to go eavesdrop on conversations in the Midianite camp. Just as Gideon arrives, he overhears an anonymous Midianite telling his dream to another Midianite who interprets it for him. The interpretation of the dream reveals that God is giving the Midianites into the hands of Gideon and the Israelites. In all three examples, Joseph,

61. Wolfgang Richter, in Gnuse, "Dreams in the Ancient World," 75.

62. Joseph receives the commission to interpret Pharaoh's dreams because Joseph had earlier interpreted the dreams of the chief cupbearer and the chief baker in Gen 40:8–22.

Daniel, and Gideon, symbolic dreams are interpreted in such a way as to show the divine plan moving forward through the cooperation of a human agent who, in reward for his ability to interpret dreams or his faithfulness to God, receives a position of rulership that aids the people of God.

Although the specific form of the dream—the visual symbolic dream—is different in these three cases, of Joseph, Daniel, and Gideon, from the auditory message dreams of the Matthean birth narratives, the result of each dream and dream interpretation is very much in keeping with themes from Matthew's first two chapters. The Matthean dreams and those of the Joseph, Daniel, and Gideon stories show these themes: protection, righteousness, correct worship, repentance and salvation, and theophany. Like the Matthean dreamer Joseph, Joseph the dreamer of Genesis is a protector of people. Mary's husband takes Mary and Jesus to Egypt in order to protect them; Joseph becomes governor of Egypt and protects Hebrews and Egyptians. Just as the Matthean Joseph is motivated by righteousness and receives dreams, Daniel's righteousness brings him the opportunity to interpret the dreams of Nebuchadnezzar through the visions he receives. Daniel's interaction with Nebuchadnezzar and the Babylonians results in Gentiles' acknowledgment of the superiority of the God of Israel; Joseph's attention to dreams brings about the birth of Jesus who will be acknowledged as savior and worthy of worship by both Jews and Gentiles. Daniel's dream interpretation includes a call to repentance for Nebuchadnezzar; Joseph is informed that the child Jesus will save his people from their sins. In the case of Gideon, the dream that Gideon overhears indicates victory over his people's enemies and the furtherance of God's plan to move the people into the land of Canaan. Gideon had earlier seen a vision of the Lord/the angel of the Lord (Judg 6:11–24). He exclaims, "I have seen the angel of the Lord face to face!" (Judg 6:22). Gideon also fights against improper worship of Baal and Asherah (Judg 6:25–32). The Matthean Joseph also acts as a deliverer of Jesus who will be the ultimate deliverer of people. Just as Gideon is granted a theophany, Joseph is the protector of Jesus, called "Emmanuel," God is with us. Gideon fights against improper worship. Jesus will be the object of, and promote correct worship. Looking at the three examples of those who receive, interpret, and overhear visual symbolic dreams, it is clear that themes in each of these stories are themes that Matthew also takes up in his story of the dreamer Joseph and the baby Jesus whom his dreams are meant to protect.

People and events connected with both kinds of dreams—auditory message dreams and visual symbolic dreams—may be useful to Matthew as references behind his portrayal of Jesus and the dreams that surround his birth and infancy. That is, Matthew may want the readers of his Gospel not to think only of Moses, and Joseph, or even only the three oft-named patriarchs Abraham, Isaac, and Jacob, for example, as figures behind the infancy narratives; Matthew may have a larger number of dreamers and those who understand the significance of dreams in mind when he places dreams prominently into his story of Jesus' birth and infancy.[63] With this possibility in mind, I look next at dreams in *1 Enoch* and find another point of connection between themes in Matthew and the Enochic template. Perhaps Matthew desires his readers to think not only of dreamers in what became the canonical Hebrew scriptures when his readers encounter the Matthean dreams, but also the dreams and interpretations of Enoch as well.

Dreams in 1 Enoch

Both types of dreams, visual symbolic dreams and auditory message dreams, are found in *1 Enoch*. Two large blocks of dream material appear in *1 Enoch* 13–16, part of the *Book of the Watchers*, and *1 Enoch* 83–90, known as the *Book of Dream Visions*. I look at each, beginning with the visual symbolic dreams of the latter section, and then proceeding to the auditory message dream of *1 Enoch* 13–16, the dream that shares the form that the Matthean dreams take.

DREAMS OF THE BOOK OF DREAM VISIONS

The so-called *Book of Dream Visions* is two dream visions which may be classified as visual symbolic dreams. The first of the dreams is in *1 Enoch* 83–84, and takes place when Enoch is "lying down in the

---

63. For example, J. Duncan M. Derrett seeks to show that narratives about Alexander, in addition to narratives about Moses' infancy are "woven together in Matthew's nativity in order to produce an impression that Jesus is greater than Moses, Abraham, and Alexander all together" (Derrett, "Further Light," 101).

house of Mahalalel" (*1 En.* 83:3).[64] Mahalalel is Enoch's grandfather and also serves as the interpreter of Enoch's dream. Enoch sees a vision of terrible destruction of the earth, which Mahalalel interprets as the judgment that will come upon the earth through its utter destruction and sinking into the abyss. This destruction will be the great flood. Mahalalel instructs Enoch to pray that a remnant may be saved upon the earth. Enoch does so. His prayer contains a reference to the watchers' transgression: "And now the angels of your heavens are doing wrong" (*1 En.* 84:4).[65] In chapters 85–90, Enoch reports a second dream vision, known as the *Animal Apocalypse*.[66] Enoch reports that he saw this vision "on my bed" (*1 En.* 85:3). This dream reviews eras in human history and is predictive, but does not seem to need an interpreter. This dream also makes reference to the fall of the watchers and its aftermath in *1 En.* 86:1–3, as noted in chapter 2, above. These dreams in *1 Enoch* have been likened to the dream visions in the Joseph story in Genesis and in the Book of Daniel.[67] The Enochic dreams, like the dreams of the Joseph and Daniel stories, do contain images that need interpretation, either within the text or by readers of the text, rather than the command and command fulfillment of the auditory message dream. Here I summarize how Enoch's dream visions exhibit the pattern of the visual symbolic dream.

Enoch's First Dream Vision (*1 Enoch* 83–84)

1. announcement of the dream: *1 En.* 83:1–2, "I will show you the visions that I saw . . . Two visions I saw."[68]

2. introductory dream formula: *1 En.* 83:3, "I was lying down in the house of Mahalalel, my grandfather, (when) I saw in a vision."[69]

---

64. *1 Enoch: A New Translation*, 117.

65. Ibid., 119.

66. Ibid., 120. For more on the *Animal Apocalypse*, see VanderKam, *Enoch: A Man*, 72–89. VanderKam dates the *Animal Apocalypse* to "perhaps a couple of years" after the writing of Daniel's visions in about 165 BCE, the time of the Maccabean revolt (ibid., 63). See chapter 2.

67. For example, by Nickelsburg, *1 Enoch 1*, 32. See Gen 37:5–10; 40:1—41:49 and Daniel 2, 4, and 7.

68. *1 Enoch: A New Translation*, 117.

69. Ibid.

3. the dream itself, which contains an image or images and a description of their activity: *1 En.* 83:3–5, Enoch's vision of destruction of natural features on the earth.

4. interpretation of the dream: *1 En.* 83:7–9, Mahalalel interprets the dream as indicating judgment on the earth through its utter destruction.

5. dream fulfillment: The dream is fulfilled outside of the immediate narrative context, when the flood happens. Obeying Mahalalel's instructions, Enoch has prayed for the salvation of a remnant, and this comes to pass through Noah.

Enoch's Second Dream Vision (*1 Enoch* 85–90)

1. announcement of the dream: *1 En.* 85:1–2, "After this I saw a second dream . . . incline your ear to the dream vision of your father."[70]

2. introductory dream formula: *1 En.* 85:3, "I saw in a vision on my bed, and behold[71]. . ."

3. the dream itself, which contains an image or images and a description of their activity: *1 En.* 85:3–90:38. Enoch sees images recounting history from the creation of Adam and Eve through the final judgment and the birth of an eschatological, probably messianic figure,[72] imagined as a white bull with great horns.

4. interpretation of the dream: No interpretation of the dream is provided within the text. The reader must understand the correlation between the various fauna, astral, human and heavenly beings mentioned and their historical counterparts.

5. dream fulfillment: The author assumes the reader will recognize that the events leading up to the present time have been fulfilled. Nickelsburg believes that the events of *1 En.* 90:6–19 describe events taking place from 265/255 BCE to 181/171 BCE,

70. Ibid., 20.

71. Ibid. "Behold," is the introductory dream formula in the dreams in Gen 37:7, 9; 40:9,16; 41:1, 5; Dan 2:31; Judg 7:13).

72. Nickelsburg, *1 Enoch 1*, 406, writes that this is the general opinion. Whether the figure is modeled after Adam, Seth, Noah, Abraham, or some or all of them is uncertain.

plus some events of the wars of Judas Maccabeus (166–161
BCE). Events described in *1 En.* 90:20–38 are Enoch's vision of
the final judgment, the coming of the eschatological figure, and
the rejoicing of the Lord. The Lord rejoices, presumably because
the advent of this figure means the end of unrighteousness and
no more catastrophes on the earth. It seems that the readers are
to presume that the accuracy of Enoch's vision of past events
ensures the ultimate fulfillment of the parts of Enoch's vision
that are predictive of the future.

Both dream visions in the *Book of Dream Visions* exhibit the pattern
suggested by Richter for symbolic dream visions, with the qualification
that due to the eschatological nature of the second dream, the fulfillment of its last details lie outside of the narrative context of *1 Enoch.*
The reader is to trust that the accuracy of the parts of Enoch's dream
that have already been fulfilled in history guarantees the accuracy of
the eschatological sections as well. I look next at the dream report in
the *Book of the Watchers.*

THE DREAM VISION IN THE BOOK OF THE WATCHERS

Enoch has a dream recorded in the *Book of the Watchers* in which he
is commissioned to reprimand the watchers and in which he ascends
to heaven and receives a vision of the divine throne room, *1 En.* 13:7–
16:4. This section corresponds with the auditory message dream form.
However, within the context of the auditory message is a much larger
section of visual dream material. The whole section may be divided in
this way:

1. *1 En.* 13:7–10: a summary statement that Enoch had a dream
in which he was commissioned to reprimand the watchers and that he
received visions.

2. *1 En.* 14:1–16:4: a more detailed account of his commissioning and reprimand, including a restatement of the commissioning of
Enoch (*1 En.* 14:1–3); the judgment against the watchers (*1 En.* 14:4–7);
an account of Enoch's ascent into heaven (*1 En.* 14:8); his vision of his
entrance into throne room of God (*1 En.* 14:9–23); his entrance into the
presence of God (*1 En.* 14:24); God's commissioning of Enoch (*1 En.*
15:1–2); the content of the reprimand of the watchers (*1 En.* 15:2–16:4).

The last section contains a summary of the watchers' fall (*1 En.* 15:3); a statement about why the watchers' transgression is problematic and how watchers and humans were meant to differ: the watchers were meant to be eternal spirits and had no need of procreation; men were given women in order that they might beget children (*1 En.* 15:4–7); and a summary of the consequences of the watchers' transgression, namely the presence of giants and their evil spirits and all the havoc they wreak upon earth (*1 En.* 15:8–11). The section concludes with a statement about the final judgment and consummation of the great age (*1 En.* 16:1) and one more statement by God telling Enoch what to announce to the watchers (*1 En.* 16:2–4).

The dream of Enoch in *1 En.* 13:8–16:4 has elements of the visual symbolic dream, but positions them within the auditory message dream. The purpose of the dream is twofold: it identifies Enoch as one commissioned (three times!) to speak on behalf of the Deity; it conveys information about the Deity and divine purposes, and the current situation, that is, the spirits of the giants presently cause problems on earth and for humankind, but there will ultimately be a day of judgment. Enoch's dream follows the pattern of the auditory dream form, again using Oppenheim's outline:

1. context of the auditory message dream—who received it; when, where, and under what conditions: "I went and sat by the waters of Dan in the land of Dan, which is south of Hermon, to the west. I [Enoch] recited (to God) the memorandum of their [the watchers'] petition until I fell asleep" (*1 En.*13:7)[73]

2. spoken message, or content, of the dream: see above. The dream has both a spoken message (which includes the commissioning of Enoch) and visual content (vision of the throne room, description of the Deity, et al.)

3. termination of the dream, indicated by the dreamer's awaking and realizing that he was dreaming: "and when I had awakened" (*1 En.* 13:9);[74] at the end of the second block of vision material, Enoch is taken on a journey. Enoch describes the visions he receives on this extensive journey, but there is no statement

73. *1 Enoch: A New Translation*, 32.
74. Ibid., 33.

that he woke up at the conclusion of this section. The mention of awaking at the conclusion of the brief summary section in *1 En.* 13:7–10 serves to conclude the larger visionary material as well.

4. fulfillment of the dream, often through the dreamer's undertaking the Deity's command: the fulfillment to the entire block of dream material in *1 En.* 13:7–16:4 is again mentioned in the summary section of *1 En.* 13:7–10. The watchers assemble and Enoch "recited in their presence all the visions that I had seen in the dream, and I began to speak the words of truth and the vision and reprimand to the watchers of heaven" (*1 En.* 13:10).[75]

In this dream Enoch is commissioned to communicate the response of the Deity to the watchers and the petition they make to the Deity through Enoch. Enoch describes his ascent to heaven and his vision of the heavenly throne room, and, although he is careful to avert his eyes ("I had my face bowed down," *1 En.* 14:24[76]), Enoch is able to describe the splendor and wondrous appearance of the "Great Glory" seated upon the throne (*1 En.* 14:20) and to report the words that God spoke directly to him. The vision establishes Enoch as a reputable agent of the Deity and Enoch faithfully carries out his commission.

The obvious similarities of the visual elements of Enoch's dream with material from Daniel and Ezekiel have been noted,[77] as has the similarity between Enoch's commissioning and the commissioning of prophets in the canonical biblical material.[78] However, except for the large amount of visual material, the basic form of Enoch's dream in the *Book of the Watchers,* is not visual symbolic imagery that needs interpreting (as in Daniel), but rather, auditory message material that identifies Enoch as a chosen and suitable agent and sends him to do a task, which Enoch faithfully does. In this way, Enoch's dream in the *Book of the Watchers* parallels the biblical auditory message dreams mentioned above, including the auditory message dreams in the Gospel of Matthew. So, although visual elements within Enoch's dream show

75. Ibid.

76. Ibid., 36.

77. Nickelsburg, *1 Enoch 1*, 32; VanderKam, *Enoch: A Man*, 47; VanderKam adds Isaiah and Micaiah ben Imlah to the list of comparable descriptions, although he notes that they do not ascend, as Enoch is granted to do.

78. Nickelsburg, *1 Enoch 1*, 248.

similarities with the visions of other dream recipients and interpreters, such as Daniel, the form that Enoch's dream takes also has similarities with the auditory message dreams received by the Matthean Joseph and his biblical predecessors. Like the examples Gnuse supplies from the Hebrew scriptures of the dreams of Abraham, Balaam, and others, and like Joseph in the Matthean material, Enoch receives a message from the Deity; the message contains information and a command; Enoch fulfills his divinely appointed task.

Further, Enoch is not simply obedient. He is righteous. Like the Matthean Joseph who is identified as a righteous man (δίκαιος in Matt 1:19) shortly before he receives his first auditory message dream, Enoch is called a "righteous man" (*1 En.* 15:1; also in 1:2) and "scribe of righteousness" in *1 En.* 12:4 and 15:1.[79] Enoch's righteousness, like Joseph's, is part of the reason he is given the dream he receives. Also, according to *1 En.* 1:1, righteous Enoch receives his dream visions as part of the salvation of the righteous: "The words of the blessing with which Enoch blessed the righteous chosen who will be present on the day of tribulation, to remove all the enemies; and the righteous will be saved."[80] Enoch, like Joseph, is righteous and acts on behalf of the righteous. Enoch's concern is with the salvation of the righteous. Joseph's concern is to protect his charge, Jesus, from his enemies. Enoch and Joseph have righteousness and concern for the righteous in common.

Like Enoch and Joseph, Jesus himself will grow up to be identified as one who is "righteous." Significantly, this is the message of the other dream in Matthew's Gospel. Pilate's wife has a dream and sends a message to her husband even as he is sitting in judgment of Jesus, "Have nothing to do with that righteous man, for today I have suffered a great deal because of a dream about him" (Matt 27:19 NRSV). Like Enoch, Jesus also is concerned with the salvation of the righteous. But, in a way that shows him to be superior to Enoch, Jesus is not merely the messenger of salvation, he causes it. Joseph is told that Jesus will "save his people from their sins" (Matt 1:21 NRSV). Righteous Enoch delivers the message that God will bring peace, protection, and mercy upon God's people, who are called "the righteous" ("With the righteous he will make peace, and over the chosen there will be protection, and

79. Andrei Orlov describes the significance and development of this honorific in *Enoch-Metatron Tradition*, 54–56.

80. *1 Enoch: A New Translation*, 19.

upon them will be mercy. They will all be God's," (*1 En.* 1:8).[81] Enoch's message also gives the image of light shining on the people as a sign of God's favor towards them: "Light will shine upon them, and he [God] will make peace with them" (*1 En.* 1:8).[82] Matthew gives a similar message about the blessed fate of the righteous: "the righteous will shine like the sun in the kingdom of their Father" (Matt 13:43 NRSV), and "the righteous [will go away] into eternal life" (Matt 26:46 NRSV).

In both *1 Enoch* and Matthew, the destiny of the righteous is in marked contrast to that of the unrighteous. Enoch has this message about what is in store for the wicked: "Look, he comes with the myriads of his holy ones, to execute judgment on all, and to destroy all the wicked, and to convict all humanity for all the wicked deed that they have done, and the proud and hard words that wicked sinners spoke against him" (*1 En.* 1:9).[83] Similarly Jesus announces, "The Son of Man will send his angels, and they will collect out of his kingdom all causes of sin and all evildoers, and they will throw them into the furnace of fire, where there will be weeping and gnashing of teeth" (Matt 13:41–42 NRSV).

Enoch and Joseph are not only obedient respondents to the messages received in their respective auditory message dreams. More than merely obedient, Enoch and Joseph are also righteous. Jesus, the one Joseph's dreams instruct him to protect, is also righteous. Like Enoch, Jesus is concerned with the righteousness of others. However, unlike Enoch, Jesus does not merely act as a messenger to the righteous; Jesus actually brings about the salvation of his people.

It is necessary to examine one more dreamer whose dreams show connections with both Enoch and the Matthean Joseph in order to complete this examination of dreams as a point of connection between Matthew's infancy narratives and *1 Enoch*. It may be that the dream visions of Balaam influenced both *1 Enoch* and Matthew. It may also be that Matthew's particular approach to using the Balaam material exhibits an Enochic influence.

81. Ibid., 20.
82. Ibid.
83. Ibid.

Balaam's Dreams

In Numbers 22, the Moabite king Balak summons Balaam son of Beor to curse his adversaries the Israelites. Balaam, a professional diviner who, under normal circumstances, is able to put curses on people, sometimes uses sorcery (נחשים, Num 24:1), and receives revelations from God. In addition to receiving dreams from the Deity, Balaam also functions as an exorcist, performing a ritual intended to "exorcise ('drive out'), via the appropriate apotropaic rituals, the foreign people with its foreign god(s)/daimon(s) threatening to violate" Balak and his people.[84] Despite Balak's willingness to pay Balaam for his expert abilities, and despite many attempts by Balaam to curse the Israelites, Balaam receives messages from God indicating that Balaam must not curse those whom God has blessed (Num 22:12; 23:8, 20). Following God's instructions, Balaam utters four oracles in which he blesses Israel, much to the displeasure of his would-be patron, King Balak. As Gnuse points out, at least two episodes within the Balaam-Balak story fit the auditory dream format. A look at each shows how they follow the auditory message dream pattern.

In the first episode, Num 22:8–13, Balak's messengers have just approached Balaam, fee in hand, and told Balaam what his customer Balak seeks. Balaam tells them to spend the night in the location where they are, by a river (Num 22:5).[85] In the morning, Balaam will tell them the response he receives from the Lord. As Balaam has promised, God comes to Balaam during the night. However, God instructs Balaam not to curse the Israelites. In the morning, Balaam delivers the message of the dream to Balak's messengers (in Num 22:13 called "princes of Balak," שרי בלק).[86] Balaam tells the princes to go back to their own country.

---

84. Moore, *Balaam Traditions*, 98.

85. Enoch also has his dream vision in *1 Enoch* 13–16 by a river.

86. שׂר can mean "chieftain," "chief," "ruler," "official," "captain," or "prince." *The New Brown Driver Briggs Gesenius*, 978. The NRSV translates the plural form of the word in Num 22:13 as "princes." Since Balaam provides background for Matthew's Gospel, might the later association of the magi who appear in Matthew's Gospel with kings have to do with the princes who appear in Balaam's story? Balaam tells the princes to go back to their own country after his dream. In Matthew, the magi (who are in later tradition called kings) have a dream in which they are directed to return to their own country, but by another way (Matt 2:12). Luz credit Caesarius of Arles (d. 543) with the first mention that the magi were kings (see Luz, *Matthew 1–7*, 111).

This episode has all of the elements of the auditory message dream: a context which indicates that it is night when the interaction with the Deity takes place (Num 22:8); the spoken message from God indicating that Balaam must not curse the Israelites (Num 22:12); an indication of the termination of the dream, when it is morning and Balaam arises (Num 22:13); and the fulfillment of the dream, when Balaam delivers the message that he will not do as Balak desires (Num 22:13).

In the second episode, Num 22:19–21, the events of the first episode are largely repeated, although this time Balak sends more princes, even more distinguished ones (Num 22:15) than he sent the first time. Again, Balaam tells his visitors to spend the night and await the message that Balaam will receive from the Lord (Num 22:19). During the night God comes to Balaam (the context of the dream; Num 22:20), but this time tells Balaam to go with the men, but to do only what God tells Balaam to do (the message of the dream; Num 22:20). Balaam gets up in the morning and goes with the princes of Moab (the termination and fulfillment of the dream; Num 22:21). As Gnuse notes, the word "dream" is not used in either episode,[87] but the nocturnal context and the adherence to the auditory message dream format indicates that Balaam receives communication from the Deity in dreams.

Like Enoch and the Matthean Joseph, Balaam is an obedient respondent[88] to the instructions he receives from God during dreams. It is interesting to note that in all three of their cases, Enoch, Joseph, and Balaam, each receives a dream response that is contrary to what their petitioners, or the usual way of conducting affairs, would direct them to do. Enoch receives his dream after being asked by the watchers to take their petition to God; he receives notice that the watchers' petition is denied and Enoch must rebuke them. Joseph, following the usual expectations of righteous behavior prepares to dismiss Mary; he receives notice that he should take Mary as his wife. Balaam is commissioned by Balak to curse Israel; he receives notice that he must not because God has blessed them. All three are given the message via a dream to do the opposite of what is expected or requested of them.

---

87. Gnuse, "Dreams in the Ancient World," 83.

88. Balaam, however, is not called righteous. He does, however, do what God instructs him to do.

Balaam and Enoch

Two other points of comparison between Enoch and Balaam should be noted here before proceeding to other connections between the dreams of the Enochic, Matthean, and Balaam stories. The first has to do with the language found in Numbers and *1 Enoch*. The second has to do with a non-biblical story of Balaam. First, scholars have noted that the opening verses of *1 Enoch* are very similar to the language and form of the Balaam oracles, especially Num 24:15–17,[89] but also in Num 23:7, 18; 24:3, 20, 21, and 23. In particular, the formula, "took up his discourse and said," is used in the passages in Numbers and in *1 En.* 1:2. Numbers 24:15 and *1 En.* 1:2 both speak of the visionary having his "eyes opened by God." Numbers 24:16 and *1 En.* 1:2 both speak of the vision coming to the one who hears words from divine beings and seeing "the vision of the Almighty" (Numbers) or the "Holy One" (*1 Enoch*). As Nickelsburg notes, there is no way to tell if the author of *1 Enoch* intends an allusion to Balaam or not, but similarities exist between the two dreamers and their reports.[90] Not only is the form of their reports similar, but they both claim to have received words from the heavenly realm and a vision of the Deity in their dream visions.

With the *Book of the Dream Visions* and the dream in *1 Enoch* 83–84, once again there may be evidence of the influence of Balaam. This time the comparison may be made with a non-biblical text, an inscription from Deir 'Allā, dated 750 to 700 BCE.[91] In this text the seer[92]

89. Nickelsburg, for example, notes, "The parallels to the Balaam oracles have been recognized by all commentators who have had access to the full and more accurate Greek text of this section" (Nickelsburg, *1 Enoch 1*, 137 n. 1). Nickelsburg provides a table showing the similarities between Num 24:15–17 and *1 En.* 1:2–3 and *1 En.* 93:1–3 (ibid., 138).

90. Ibid., 137.

91. Naveh, "Date of the Deir," 256–58. A detailed analysis of this text is beyond the scope of this book. For more information on the Deir 'Allā Inscription, see Hackett, *Balaam Text*; Levine, "Deir 'Allā Plaster Inscriptions," 195–205; McCarter, "The Balaam Texts," 49–60; Moore, *Balaam Traditions*, 66–96; Sasson, "Book of Oracular Visions," 283–309. Unfortunately, the text is very fragmentary, so much of what has been reconstructed cannot be considered to be conclusive (Nickelsburg, *1 Enoch 1*, 348).

92. Moore identifies Balaam as enacting the following roles in the Deir 'Allā text: as diviner/seer, he functions as an ornithomantic (practicing augury by watching and interpreting the behavior of birds), a rhabdomantic (using a rod to effect some outcome, perhaps in the way that Jacob did when he outwitted Laban by increasing the strength

named Balaam, son of Beor, has a dream vision that he interprets as predicting a disaster about to be inflicted upon people because of a disruption of cosmic order. That is, the incipient destruction is not due to moral corruption, but rather that the natural order of the cosmos has been turned upside down.[93] According to McCarter's reconstruction of the text, the reversal of the natural order is described through occurrences such as a poor woman "'has mixed myrrh,' the fragrance of noble ladies and royalty";[94] "'the stork,' whose kindness to its young is a subject of world-wide folklore and whose name itself, *hasid*, seems to mean 'the Kindly One'" has mistreated its young,[95] and some beings that do not ordinarily consume wine "have drunk wine."[96] McCarter wonders if "Nazarites" (*nzrn*) should be restored at this point in the text.[97] Even something as unnatural as "the dead have heard from far away" has occurred.[98] These, and other examples in the world of human and animal behavior, indicate that the created order has become inverted. The gods have noticed the chaos and have "declared a cosmic catastrophe."[99] To put an end to the disaster, they plan to unleash a "final cosmic disaster in which the world will lapse into an all-encompassing gloom."[100] The description of the disaster is similar to the darkness prophesied in Isa 13:10, "The stars of heaven and their constellations will not show their light. The rising sun will be darkened and the moon will not give its light." Other Hebrew Bible passages threatening similar darkness and destruction include Ezek 32:7–8, "When I blot you out, I will cover the heavens and make their stars dark; I will cover the sun with a cloud, and the moon will not give its light. All the shining lights in the heavens

---

of his own herd and weakening Laban's in Gen 30:27–43), and an oneiromantic (receiving and interpreting dreams). As exorcist, Balaam makes homeopathic images and recites incantations (Moore, *Balaam Traditions*, 66–96).

93. McCarter, "Balaam Texts," 58.

94. Ibid.

95. Ibid.

96. Ibid.

97. Ibid. All three of these elements are referred to in Matthew's first two chapters: myrrh, one of the magi's gifts; *ḥasīd*, related to חסד, a central theme in the book of Ruth; and *nzrn*, related to Ναζωραῖος (*Nazōraios*), what Jesus is called in Matt 2:23.

98. McCarter, "Balaam Texts," 58.

99. Ibid., 57.

100. Ibid., 57–58.

I will darken above you and put darkness on your land, says the Lord God" (NRSV); Joel 2:10, "The earth quakes before them, the heavens tremble. The sun and the moon are darkened, and the stars withdraw their shining" (NRSV); and others.[101]

In order to avert the disaster, Balaam engages in magical rituals and succeeds in preventing destruction.[102] The exact nature of the rituals is uncertain, due to the fragmentary nature of the inscription. However, it appears that Balaam performs an exorcistic ritual, perhaps involving burning an image[103] and some action involving moaning.[104] Regardless of the details of Balaam's actions, they work. Disaster is averted. The inscription at Deir 'Allā was created to commemorate Balaam's successful prevention of eschatological devastation.[105]

Balaam's dream in this inscription "is both an auditory message dream and a visual symbolic dream."[106] It contains an auditory message to Balaam as well as images that Balaam must interpret. In form and content, Balaam's dream has similarities with Enoch's dream visions. Although Nickelsburg mentions the Deir 'Allā inscription with reference to *1 Enoch* 83–84, in its dual form of both auditory message dream and visual symbolic dream, it is also similar in form to *1 En.* 13:7–16:4, in which Enoch receives clear auditory commands from the Deity, but also receives a vision. In terms of the contents of Balaam's dream vision, predicting cosmic disaster that will wipe out all creation, the subject matter is more similar to Enoch's dream vision in *1 Enoch* 83–84, in which the entire "earth is swallowed up in the great abyss" (*1 En.* 83:4).[107] However, even in *1 En.* 13:7–16:4, the subject of the dream vision is the disruption of cosmic order caused by the watchers. The boundaries established by the Deity between heaven and earth have been transgressed. The watchers have "forsaken the high heaven" (*1 En.* 15:3) and "will have no peace" (*1 En.* 16:4).[108] Because of their actions, evil spirits "will make desolate until the day of the consummation of the

---

101. Joel 3:3–4; 4:15; Isa 34:4.

102. Gnuse, "Dreams in the Ancient World," 58.

103. Moore, *Balaam Traditions*, 91.

104. Ibid., 93.

105. Gnuse, "Dreams in the Ancient World," 58.

106. Ibid.

107. *1 Enoch: A New Translation*, 117.

108. Ibid., 38.

great judgment" (*1 En.* 16:1).[109] Enoch's vision foretells the eschatological judgment when the evil spirits will no longer afflict the creation, but until then, they have free reign on the earth. In Enoch's prayer following his dream vision and its interpretation in *1 Enoch* 83, Enoch prays that utter devastation of the world may be averted through the saving of a remnant (*1 En.* 84:5). But Enoch notes that until the eschatological judgment, the watchers are doing wrong and humans suffer the wrath of God (*1 En.* 84:4). Both Enoch and Balaam's concerns in the Deir 'Allā inscription are cosmic in scope and nature. Although Balaam's oracles in Numbers concern more than just the Midianites,[110] in Numbers, the presenting problem is Balak's worry about the strength of Israel and Balak's desire to keep the Israelites from conquering his people. However, in *1 Enoch* and in the Deir 'Allā inscription, the presenting problem is that the divinely intended order of the cosmos has been upset. The seer's job in these cases is to prevent the total annihilation of creation and humanity, rather than, as in Numbers, simply either to curse one group of people, or report that the cursing cannot be done. In this way, the Deir 'Allā inscription version of Balaam's oracles and efforts have some similarity with Enoch's function in his dream visions in the *Book of Dream Visions* and the *Book of the Watchers*.

Here again there is another point of comparison shared by Enoch, the Deir 'Allā inscription's version of Balaam, and the Gospel of Matthew. In all three, the purpose of the actions undertaken is of cosmic import and not the concern of one people or ethnic group in particular. In all three, there are eschatological implications for the dreams and those on whose behalf the dreamers receive their divinely-inspired messages. I have noted the cosmic scope of the Enoch's and Balaam's dream visions above. In the Matthean dream visions, it is clear that Matthew's intention is to identify the child who is protected by the dreamer Joseph as someone with cosmic and eschatological significance. Within the infancy narrative itself, Matthew provides the dream message that the child will be called "Emmanuel, which means, 'God is with us'" (Matt 1:23 NRSV). The presence of the star that the magi follow (Matt 2:2) connects the infancy narrative with the Gospel's later references to astronomical phenomena, specifically the eschatological

109. Ibid., 37.

110. Balaam's oracles are predictive for Moab, Edom, Seir, Amalek, the Kenites, Asshur, Kittim, and Eber as well. See Num 24:17–24.

discourse of Matt 24:29–31 in which the *parousia* of the Son of Man is described. The description includes what appears to be a combination of LXX Isa 13:10[111] and 34:4,[112] "the sun will be darkened, and the moon will not give its light; the stars will fall from heaven, and the powers of heaven will be shaken" (Matt 24:29 NRSV). When Jesus is crucified, the sun is darkened for three hours (Matt 27:45), a description that may be based on Amos 8:9, "I will make the sun go down at noon, and darken the earth in broad daylight" (NRSV). The astronomical sign that appears at Jesus' birth also portends the astronomical signs marking the crucifixion of Jesus and the eschatological judgment of the world.

The gifts the magi bring to Jesus and the fact that magi bring them also indicate that Jesus is of cosmic and eschatological importance.[113] Isa 60:1–9, describing the glory of the restored Zion, includes these references, "Nations will come to your light, and kings to the brightness of your dawn" (Isa 60:3 NRSV), "the abundance of the sea shall be brought to you, the wealth of the nations shall come to you" (Isa 60:5 NRSV), "to bring your children from far away, their silver and gold with them, for the name of the Lord your God, and for the Holy One of Israel, because he has glorified you." (Isa 60:9 NRSV). In Isaiah's vision the glory of the Lord shines on Zion, and Zion itself becomes radiant (Isa 60:5). In Matthew, the star attracts the gift-bearing magi who bring their wealth to honor the child called Emmanuel. Davies and Allison point out the similar theme of *Ps. Sol.* 17:31 in which all the nations of the earth come bringing gifts to see the glory of the Lord.[114] The eschatological

111. For the stars of the heavens and their constellations
will not give their light;
the sun will be dark at its rising,
and the moon will not shed its light.

112. Heaven shall roll up like a scroll,
and all the stars will fall
like leaves from a vine
and as leaves fall from a fig tree.

113. The magi and their gifts will be addressed in more detail below.

114. Davies and Allison, *Matthew*, 27. See Wright (ed.), *Psalms of Solomon*, 193. Wright's translation of *Ps. Sol.* 17:31 reads,

He will have nations come from the ends of the earth
to see his glory,
giving back her scattered children
and to see the glory of the Lord
with which God has glorified her.

and cosmic implications of Jesus according to Matthew also are shown outside of the infancy narrative, for example, during the crucifixion of Jesus when an earthquake takes place and holy ones are raised, go "into the holy city and appeared to many" (Matt 27:51–53 NRSV),[115] and in Jesus' statement in Matt 28:18 that "all authority in heaven and on earth has been given to me," and that "I am with you always, to the end of the age" (Matt 28:20 NRSV). The child whom Joseph's dreams direct him to protect is a child whose birth is marked by an astrological phenomenon. This child will grow into an adult who will speak of astrological phenomena as marking significant events and whose own life events will be marked by astrological events with eschatological and cosmic significance.

I look now at one more point of comparison between the Matthean infancy narrative, Enoch's dream visions, and Balaam's dream visions.

THE STAR THAT WILL RISE AND THE PLANT THAT WILL SPRING UP IN A LATER GENERATION

Above I noted some similarities between Balaam's oracles and the announcement of Enoch's identity as "a righteous man whose eyes were opened by God, who had the vision of the Holy One and of heaven, which he showed me" (*1 En.* 1:2),[116] particularly in terms of the formula with which Enoch announces his vision ("he took up his discourse and said;"[117] *1 En.* 1:2, 3; 93:1, 3; cf. Num 24:15). Balaam and Enoch share another aspect in common regarding their oracles: both receive visions concerning a future generation. Balaam says, "I see him, but not now; I behold him, but not near" (Num 24:17 NRSV) in reference to the star that will rise out of Jacob. Enoch remarks, "Not for this generation do I expound, but concerning one that is distant I speak" (*1 En.* 1:2).[118] Both Balaam and Enoch receive visions whose outcome will be fulfilled at a

---

However, Wright notes that what he has translated as "giving back," is in the Greek, "bearing as gifts" (φέροντες δῶρα).

115. Allison, *End of the Ages*, 40–46, explains how Matthew draws especially on LXX Ezek 37:7 and LXX Zech 14:4–5 in order to emphasize the eschatological significance of Jesus' crucifixion.

116. *1 Enoch: A New Translation*, 19.

117. Ibid., 19, 140.

118. Ibid., 19.

later time. At this point there is a contrast between Balaam and Enoch, the dream visionaries whose visions concern a future generation on the one hand, and the Matthean infancy narrative on the other, in which dreams indicate, not a future promise, but the arrival of the awaited one. For Matthew and his dreamers, Joseph and the magi, the future is now.

Balaam's oracle in Num 24:17 has long been seen as a possible backdrop to the appearance of the star that the magi follow in Matthew 2.[119] Balaam's oracle is, "I see him, but not now; I behold him, but not near—a star shall come out of Jacob; a scepter shall rise out of Israel" (NRSV). Raymond Brown links this passage with a verse from the prior oracle which in the LXX reads, "There shall come a man out of Israel's seed, and he shall rule many nations," (Num 24:7).[120] The LXX also translates the "scepter" of MT Num 24:17 as "a man," so, "a man (ἄνθρωπος) will rise out of Israel." The LXX version makes Balaam's oracles point even more clearly toward an expected person who will come in the future. Balaam's oracle of the star rising out of Jacob, a man who will rule many nations, seems to have fueled expectations for the advent of some eschatological personage or personages. For example, the *Damascus Document*, CD-A VII 18–20 refers to Balaam's oracle as promising an

119. See, for example, Brown, "The Meaning of the Magi," 577–78; Derrett, "Further Light," 102; Hull, *Hellenistic Magic*, 124–25; Instone-Brewer, "Balaam-Laban," 207–27; McNamara, "Were the Magi Essenes?" 317. Of these sources, Instone-Brewer's article is the one with the greatest focus on the Balaam traditions. Instone-Brewer links the four scripture quotations in Matthew 2 with biblical, Targumic, and pseudepigraphical sources about Balaam. In the extrabiblical sources, Balaam becomes identified with Laban and is also "transformed" into "a super-enemy who lived for hundreds of years and who tried to kill the baby ancestor of the Messiah" (209). According to these traditions, Balaam was first called Laban. As Laban he tried to kill Rachel's children. When the Israelites settled in Egypt, Balaam's two sons, Jannes and Jambres were magicians who worked in the court of Pharaoh. It was these two sons of Balaam who suggested to Pharaoh that he kill the Israelite children. Later, after the exodus, while the Israelites were in the wilderness, Balaam again tried to kill the Israelites. Balaam was finally himself killed, but not before he made his prophecy about the star rising out of Jacob and the scepter of the Messiah. Instone-Brewer shows how the post-biblical texts embellish the biblical account in such a way as to weave together traditions about Balaam, Moses, Pharaoh, and dangers to the children of Israel. It is plausible that these traditions, although written later, would have been known at the time of Matthew and served as material for the evangelist's story.

120. Brown, "The Meaning of the Magi," 577. The MT version of Num 24:7 reads, "Waters will flow from his buckets; his seed will have abundant water."

eschatological figure called, "The Interpreter of the Law," (the Star) and another called "The Prince" (the Scepter).[121] In *4QTestamonia*, the passage seems to refer to the coming of a Davidic Messiah.[122] It seems likely that at the time of Matthew, Balaam's oracle could still have been seen as referring to the advent of a promised messianic figure. Balaam had a vision of a star rising out of Jacob, although for Balaam the star would not be manifest immediately. He said, "I see him, but not now; I behold him, but not near." Balaam's oracle describes a future event. The future nature of Balaam's oracle makes it fit nicely with Matthew's aims. For Matthew, now many years after Balaam's dreams, magi appear on the scene claiming to have seen "a star at its rising" (Matt 2:2). The magi interpret the star to indicate that the king of the Jews has been born (Matt 2:2). Herod knows that this event can indicate no less than that the Messiah has come, as is evident by his inquiring of the chief priest and scribes "where the Messiah was to be born" (Matt 2:4 NRSV). When the magi find Jesus, they fulfill both Balaam's oracle and Enoch's description of speaking to a future generation. The magi see Jesus "now" and behold him "near." They worship the one awaited for generations, now, here, and named at the end of Matthew's recounting of the generations.

But it is not just a star for which the magi's dreaming predecessors are looking. It is also a "plant" that grows from a seed: a seed and plants are mentioned in Numbers 23–24 and *1 Enoch* 10. This plant may also help explain the explanation that follows the last of Joseph's dreams in Matthew, Matt 2:23, "There he made his home in a town called Nazareth, so that what had been spoken through the prophets might be fulfilled, 'He will be called a Nazorean'" (NRSV). I address the meaning of "Nazorean" first and then the seeds and plants in Balaam's oracles and *1 Enoch*.

The meaning of "Nazorean" has been the subject of much debate amongst scholars, most of which is beyond the scope of this book.[123] However, one possibility connects the word with some of the themes discussed here. David Instone-Brewer suggests that the word behind

---

121. McNamara, "Were the Magi Essenes?" 314; Martínez and Tigchelaar, *Dead Sea Scrolls*, I: 560/61.

122. McNamara, "Were the Magi Essenes?" 314; Martínez and Tigchelaar, *Dead Sea Scrolls*, I: 356/57.

123. See Davies and Allison, *Matthew 1–7*, 275–81; Hagner, *Matthew 1–13*, 40–42; Luz, *Matthew 1–7*, 122–24.

Matthew's Ναζωραῖος (Matt 2:23) is *Natziri*, from a spelling of Nazareth with a *ṣādê* rather than a *zayin*, as it was spelled in a synagogue inscription in Caesarea found in 1962.[124] If Matthew was thinking of Natziri, then Matthew could have been thinking of Jesus as a fulfillment of Isa 11:1, "A shoot will come forth from the stem of Jesse, and a branch (נצר) from his roots will bear fruit."[125] Passages using similar images, although not the word נצר, which occurs in this context only in Isa 11:1, include Isa 53:2, "He grew up before him like a tender shoot (יונק)"; Jer 23:5 and 33:15, "a righteous branch (צמח) from David"; and Zech 3:8 and 6:12, "my servant, the branch (צמח)."[126] If calling Jesus a Ναζωραῖος comes from a reference to "branch," then it is possible that Matthew sees Jesus as the fulfillment of Balaam's oracle which contains plant imagery as well. Balaam's vision shows that "his seed shall have abundant water" (Num 23:7) and Israel's tents and encampments are described as various plants: "palm groves," "gardens," "aloes," and cedar trees" (Num 23:6). In *1 Enoch*, following the watchers' transgression and its aftermath, the archangels are commissioned to various tasks to respond to the disaster. Sariel is sent to Noah to hide himself so that he might survive the coming flood (*1 En.* 10:1–3). Of Noah it is said, "From him a plant will be planted, and his seed will endure for all the generations of eternity" (*1 En.* 10:3).[127] As part of Michael's commission to renovate the earth, he is instructed to "let the plant of righteousness and truth appear, and it will become a blessing, (and) the deeds of righteousness and truth will be planted forever with joy" (*1 En.* 10:16).[128] In referring to Jesus as a branch, Matthew may be describing him as the fulfillment of the visions of Balaam and Enoch. Jesus, according to Matthew, is the long-awaited seed of Noah, a plant of righteousness and truth.

---

124. Instone-Brewer, "Balaam-Laban," 224.

125. Ibid., 225. The link between Matt 2:23 and Isa 11:1 has been made by others as well, for example, Davies and Allison, *Matthew 1–7*, 277, and those they cite. The appeal of Isa 11:1 is its reference to the Davidic line, which fits with Matthew's concerns about Jesus' identity.

126. Instone-Brewer, "Balaam-Laban," 224; Davies and Allison, *Matthew 1–7*, 278.

127. *1 Enoch: A New Translation*, 28.

128. Ibid., 30.

Summary of Dreams and Dreamers

Without yet having explored fully the Matthean infancy narrative, I pause to summarize my findings thus far in terms of the commonalities and differences amongst the dreams of Enoch, Balaam, and Matthew. Reviewing their similarities and differences helps to explore the possibility that Matthew has in mind traditions connected with both Balaam and Enoch as he crafts his story of Jesus' infancy and the dreams that occur while Jesus is in Joseph's care.

When reviewing the dreamers Enoch, Balaam, and Joseph and the magi from the Matthean birth narrative, I note the following similarities: the form of dreams, the response to dreams, and the scope of dreams. In terms of the form of dreams, Enoch, Balaam, and the Matthean dreamers[129] all receive auditory message dreams, although Balaam of the Deir 'Allā inscription and Enoch also receive symbolic vision dreams. In terms of the response to dreams, Enoch, Balaam of the Numbers account, and the Matthean dreamers are all faithful respondents to the divine instructions they receive during their dreams. In each case, their faithful response, that is, their carrying out of the directions given to them, puts them at odds with their regular *modus operandi* or the desires of those who seek their visionary capacities. Enoch will disappoint the watchers on whose behalf he petitions God when he must deliver the message that they will be punished. Balaam frustrates Balak when he refuses to curse Israel. Joseph will marry, rather than put aside, the pregnant Mary. The magi will both go home by another way and disregard Herod's instructions to report back to him about their findings.

In terms of the scope of dreams, in the case of Enoch, the Deir 'Allā inscription's version of Balaam, and the dreams that help protect the infant Jesus in Matthew's Gospel, the purpose of the actions undertaken by the dreamers is of cosmic import and the dreams have eschatological implications. Enoch and Balaam avert total eschatological catastrophe. In the case of Balaam at Deir 'Allā, due to the fragmentary condition of the inscription, it is impossible to be certain about what the author might have said about what happens after the cosmic disaster is averted. In the case of Enoch, the reader is told that although a remnant will

---

129. In this discussion I leave aside Pilate's wife who appears much later in the Gospel, focusing on the five dreams of Matthew's infancy narrative. Technically speaking, she also would be included in a category called, "Matthean dreamers."

survive the great destruction, there is yet to come a final eschatological judgment. In the case of the child the Matthean dreams serve to protect, Jesus is identified as someone with cosmic and eschatological significance. Enoch, Balaam in both sources, and the Matthean dreamers all share similar forms of dreams, faithful responses to dreams, even if the response is different from regular expectations, and the cosmic and eschatological scope of their dreams.

The dreams and dreaming of Enoch and Balaam are different from those of Joseph and the magi in two important ways: dream fulfillment and the identity of the dreamers themselves as heroes of the narrative. In terms of dream fulfillment, Enoch receives his visions for a future "generation" (*1 En.* 1:2); Balaam's vision of a star rising out of Jacob is something he can "see" but not "now" (Num 24:17). Both visionaries have had their eyes opened by God and both have heard the words of God in their dream visions. But neither will see the ultimate fulfillment of their visions. In the case of the Matthean dreams, the dreams themselves are part of the fulfillment of Balaam's and Enoch's visions. Through the Matthean dreams, the one arising out of Jacob who is now visible is brought to birth and protected. In the birth of Emmanuel, God is not only near, but "with us" (Matt 1:23). Matthew recounts generation after generation to have his genealogy culminate in the birth of Jesus, "who is called the Messiah" (Matt 1:16 NRSV).

The other important difference between the stories of Enoch and Balaam and the story Matthew tells is that Jesus is not a dreamer. In the case of *1 Enoch* and Numbers 22–24, the main characters of the story[130] are the dreamers. In the case of Matthew's Gospel, the fulfiller of the angel's words in the dream to Joseph, the one whom Joseph must move to protect, the one on whom the magi do not inform, is Jesus. Jesus does not dream. He is not, in this sense, merely another Enoch or another Balaam, or even another Joseph or magus. He is the subject of dreams, not the dreamer of dreams; he is the revealed presence of God, rather than the one to whom God grants revelation through dreams.

---

130. Although one could certainly make the case for both that the main actor is the Deity who directs the main characters. Both Enoch and Balaam are responding to God, not technically driving the action forward on their own.

Dreamers in the Background of Matthew's Infancy Narrative

I will again mention the subject of dreams when I investigate the magi more thoroughly below. However, before departing from a focus on the trio of Balaam, Enoch, and the Matthean dreams, I briefly revisit the subject of weighing the possibility of Enochic traditions as one more source from which Matthew drew as he composed his infancy narrative. Once more I exercise caution and repeat that there is no evidence in the text of Matthew's infancy narrative for a direct quotation from *1 Enoch*. Nor is Enoch mentioned by name as a parallel figure to any of the characters in Matthew's text. However, I suggest that there is yet one more location where Matthew's knowledge of the Enochic traditions would strengthen the story Matthew tells through the associations the Enochic traditions bring with them to the story of Jesus. So, what can be claimed about the influence of dream traditions from *1 Enoch* on Matthew's infancy narrative, especially if Balaam is a logical dreamer to have influenced Matthew's Gospel?

First, it is a false choice to choose only one tradition as the backdrop for Matthew. After all, Matthew may have Joseph's namesake from Genesis in mind, as well as several other dreamers from the Hebrew Bible in addition to Balaam as he writes, even as Matthew evidently has non-dreamers such as Moses in mind as he composes his narrative. Matthew evidently has combined many traditions, including traditions about the Joseph of Genesis, Moses, and Balaam, in his narrative. But does adding Enoch to the list of influences actually add anything to our understanding of Matthew's intent as he writes his opening chapters?

What Enoch provides that Balaam, for one, does not, are the following three aspects, mentioned above, but summarized here, which have a clearer connection with Matthew's infancy narratives than does Balaam the dreamer alone. Enoch is a dreamer who is righteous, not merely obedient; whose message concerns not just a future fulfillment, but actually a fulfillment for a future generation; and whose dreams have large-scale salvific import. First, Enoch is identified as righteous and is commissioned to deliver a message to God's righteous people. Like Enoch and Joseph, Balaam is obedient to the messages he receives in dreams, but he is not identified as righteous. In fact, according to traditions recorded later, Balaam is actually an enemy of God's people.[131] Second, having witnessed Matthew's concern with generations, to the extent of beginning his Gospel with a genealogy, Enoch poses his message in terms of having a message, not just for the future, but for a future "generation" (*1 En.* 1:2).[132] Third, Joseph's dreams instruct him to protect Jesus whose life will have large-scale salvific import. Enoch's dreams also concern cosmic and eschatological affairs. In *1 En.* 13:7–16:4, Enoch's dream concerns the transgression of the watchers, their upsetting of cosmic order, and its aftermath. In *1 Enoch* 83–84, which may show some connections with the Deir 'Allā inscription's version of the Balaam oracles, Enoch's dream reveals the coming disastrous flood. Enoch's prayer helps save a remnant so that all creation is not destroyed, although Enoch acknowledges that a future great day of judgment still lies in the future. In the rest of the *Book of Dream Visions, 1 Enoch* 85–90, Enoch's symbolic vision dreams reveal the entire history of humanity leading up to and including the final judgment acknowledged by Enoch in *1 Enoch* 84. In summary, what Enoch contributes to the background of dreams and dreamers in the Matthean infancy narrative is an emphasis on righteousness, dreams for a future generation—entirely fitting for Matthew's emphasis on Jesus as the one whose birth is the culmination of the genealogy Matthew lays out—and dreams with eschatological, heavenly, and earthly connotations.[133] In addition, the Enochic watchers' template provides the link between two aspects relevant to Matthew's infancy narrative: (1) the Balaam story as a source for Matthew, and (2) the fact that in Matthew's time, the Balaam story was one of the *loci* for traditions about the angelomorphic divine spirit. The Enochic watchers' template brings to the fore why Balaam and the angelomorphic divine spirit are important pieces of Matthew's background: the child born to an angelomorphic Holy Spirit and a woman, but without sexual contact is the appropriate one to repair the transgressions of the rebel angels who had illicit sexual contact with women.

131. See Instone-Brewer, "Balaam-Laban."

132. In fact, although the numbers are dissimilar from Matthew's accounting of generations in terms of groups of fourteen (Matt 1:17), Enoch gives his own accounting of ages in the so-called *Apocalypse of Weeks* (*1 En.* 93:1–10; 91:11–17) in terms of ten weeks.

133. It is possible that Matthew could be aware of the Deir 'Allā version of the Balaam story, just as it is possible that Enoch is aware of it. However, it seems more likely that if Matthew is aware of Enochic traditions, then his association, if there is one, with the Deir 'Allā Balaam would come through *1 Enoch*.

The birth of Jesus—foretold, according to Matthew, in Balaam's dream vision and Enoch's visions for a future generation—redresses the watchers' transgression.

I look next at the first visitors to the child Jesus in Matthew's story, the magi who use one of the forbidden arts, astrology, to locate the infant in order to pay him homage. These astrologers are associated with others of the illicit arts as well.

Magi

An examination of the story of the magi and their visit to the infant Jesus as told in Matthew 2 shows another instance of the themes from the Enochic watchers' template being used, not for the destruction of creation and humankind, but for righteous purposes and to set a pattern for those who will be Jesus' righteous followers. Specifically I examine the subject of the magi[134] as practitioners of astrology and other magical arts mentioned in the catalogue of the Enochic watchers' illicit arts. In this section I look at elements of the Enochic watchers' template as they related to the arts associated with the magi.

When the magi make their way to visit and honor the child Jesus in Matthew 2, once again in Matthew's opening chapters, characters in the story use the illicit skills that were taught by the watchers to their wives in *1 Enoch*. In Matthew's genealogy the illicit skills are brought to mind by the narratives alluded to by Matthew's inclusion of the women. In Matthew 2, however, the use of one illicit art is actually identified within the narrative itself. The very first event Matthew narrates following the birth and naming of Jesus (Matt 1:25) is the advent of the magi who come because they have been following the movements of a star: "In the time of King Herod, after Jesus was born in Bethlehem of Judea, magi from the East came to Jerusalem, asking, 'Where is the one who has been born king of the Jews? For we saw his star at its rising and we came to worship him'" (Matt 2:1–2).[135] The surprise visit by the magi

---

134. On the magi, see Beare, *Matthew*, 73–81; Brown, *Birth*, 165–201; Bruns, "Magi Episode," 51–54; Davies and Allison, *Matthew 1–7*, 224–56; Derrett, "Further Light," 81–108; Hagner, *Matthew 1–13*, 22–32; Harrington, *Matthew*, 40–50; Luz, *Matthew 1–7*, 101–16; Nock, "Paul and the Magus"; Nolland, "The Sources for Matthew 2:1–12," 283–300.

135. My translation.

with their request to find the one whose title Herod already bears does not engender excitement, but fear: Herod "and all Jerusalem with him" was afraid (or, "troubled," ἐταράχθη; Matt 2:3). Herod gathers together the chief priests and the scribes of the people to launch an investigation into the magi's quest. While the magi have used astrology, Herod and Jerusalem's religious experts use scripture. Their sources direct them toward Bethlehem. Herod sends the magi on their way, telling them to return to inform him where they find the child for the subterfuge that Herod also wants to worship the child. The magi leave the city and once again see the star. Their reunion with the star causes them to "be over-whelmed with joy" (Matt 2:10; NRSV) and the star directs them to the child. When they find the child they worship him as had been their aim. They also offer their now famous gifts of gold, frankincense, and myrrh. As Joseph had received divine direction regarding the identity of the child, the magi now receive the second dream in the Matthean narrative and the first of the dreams intended to protect the child from harm: the magi are warned not to return to Herod, so instead they return to their home by another way (Matt 2:13). The first human reactions to the birth of the child are joy and worship (magi) and fear and decep-tion (Herod). An astral body has directed the magi to Jesus. Heavenly intervention in the form of a dream and the obedience of the magi who receive the dream guarantee the child's safety, for now. Who are these first seekers and worshippers of the child, who take their direction from dreams and stars, two heavenly sources?

The Skills of the Magi

The word "magi" has a broad range of meanings and practices asso-ciated with the people called by that name. Some of these practices include the skills taught by the fallen angels to their wives. The word μάγος was used as an official title to identify an esteemed Persian class of religious experts,[136] a meaning found since the sixth century BCE.[137] Nock writes, "Their functions are ritual, and they are also credited with

---

136. Hull, *Hellenistic Magic*, 126. See also Bickerman, "Darius I, Pseudo Smerdis, and the Magi," on the history of the magi.

137. Nock, "Paul and the Magus," 309.

skill in interpreting dreams."[138] However, by the fifth century BCE,[139] the word seems also to have taken on a broader meaning of "magician" in general and does not necessarily indicate a specialist of Persian ethnicity.[140] The word μάγοι also appears with the derogatory connotation of "quack" or someone merely seeking profit.[141] The derivative noun de-

138. Ibid.

139. Ibid.

140. For example, in Euripides' *Orestes*, μάγοι is used of magicians generally. Ibid. Nock thinks that the transition of magi from denoting a particular Persian priestly class to a more general meaning of "magician" associated with a variety of skills and practices, honest and dishonest, may be explained by the fact that the with the conquests of Alexander, many magi most likely would have had to live in Greek cities in which they could not keep up their Persian traditions. Change was inevitable and their numbers would have decreased. They may even have added new magi not of Persian extraction "by some sort of adoption." Magi without their former status and cultural support and "perhaps stripped of former revenues may well have used their prestige and their reputation as magicians and have become more or less professional magicians" (ibid., 319–20). By the time of Pausanius, it seems acceptable to him to be unspecific about the deity or deities served by the magi's actions: "Entering the chamber a magician (*anêr magos*) piles dry wood upon the altar; he first places a tiara upon his head and then sings to some god or other an invocation in a foreign tongue unintelligible to Greeks, reciting the invocation from a book. So it is without fire that the wood must catch, and bright flames dart from it." Which "god" or which "foreign tongue" seems unimportant (Pausanius, *Description of Greece* 5.27.6).

141. Hippocrates, for instance, speaks disdainfully of the views of some people, characterizing the people as "of the type of our present-day magi and purifiers and mendicants and humbugs," in *On the Sacred Disease* 2.4. In Sophocles' *Oedipus Tyrannus*, 385, Oedipus laments, "[Creon] sets this wizard on me, this scheming quack (μάγον τοιόνδε μηχανορράφον), this fortune teller peddling lies" (Sophocles, *Three Theban Plays*, 440). It is difficult to say with any certainty whether or not Matthew had in mind magi in the original sense of Persian priests or in the more general sense of magician-magi who could count a Persian origin as only a small and distant part of their heritage. The question may also be asked of whether or not Matthew intended to use "magi" in the sense of "quack" and practitioners who were in the same general category as charlatans. Was Matthew paying a compliment by including the magi amongst the child's first visitors, acknowledging that honorable, albeit possibly non-Jewish, dignitaries from "the East" had recognized the significance of the birth of Jesus; or was the evangelist's compliment more of a back-handed nature: even snake oil salesman who aren't from around here can recognize what Herod and his high society cronies from the big city cannot? It is apparent that Matthew wants to contrast the joyful, worshipping magi with the fearful, scheming Herod. However, one may not need to parse exactly what Matthew thinks of the magi in order for the evangelist to make his point. Matthew need not be calling the characters who get it right "quacks" in order to make the contrast. The contrast between the behavior of the magi and Herod and his religious co-conspirators is enough. The magi do not need to be either esteemed

scribing what the magi practice appears first, according to Nock, in the *Helena* of Gorgias: μαγεία, which includes the use of ἐπῳδαί, "charms."[142] In Euripides' *Orestes*, various possible explanations for Helen's disappearance are put forth, including, "the power of drugs" (φαρμάκοισιν), or "magicians" (μάγων τέχναισιν), or "thieving gods" (θεῶν κλοπαῖς).[143] According to Herodotus, μάγοι are dream interpreters,[144] and had as part of their duties chanting a narrative of the birth of the gods.[145] Herodotus also records that μάγοι used φαρμακεύσαντες, "spells," to calm a river.[146] That φαρμάκον and related terms come in a variety of forms can be seen in Euripides' *Hippolytus*, when the Nurse offers Phaedra "charms to soothe thy love," a φίλτρον. Phaedra asks of the φίλτρον, "Is thy drug (φαρμάκον) a salve (χρίστον, "rubbed on") or a potion (πότον, "drunk")?"[147] Xenophon reports that it was during the

---

for being magi or denigrated as charlatans in order for the reader to get the message that the magi do correctly what Herod does not. The magi may be what other characters in Matthew's Gospel are: judged by their actions. See, for example, Matt 10:40–42: "Whoever welcomes you welcomes me, and whoever welcomes me welcomes the one who sent me. Whoever welcomes a prophet in the name of a prophet will receive a prophet's reward; and whoever welcomes a righteous person in the name of a righteous person will receive the reward of the righteous; and whoever gives even a cup of cold water to one of these little ones in the name of a disciple—truly I tell you, none of these will lose their reward" (NRSV); and Matt 28:31–46, in which those who fed, gave drink to, welcomed, clothed, took care of, and visited one of the least, did these things to the Son of Man and are welcomed into the kingdom. Those who did not do them to the least, and therefore to the Son of Man, are sent into eternal punishment.

142. Nock, "Paul and the Magus," 309.

143. Euripides, *Orestes* (trans. Peck and Nisetich), 79. In the idea of "thieving gods" who would take a woman, Helen, is there an echo of the watchers' template as well, in which angels take women who are not of their kind?

144. Herodotus, *The Histories* 1.119.

145. Herodotus, *The Histories* 1.132.

146. Herodotus, *The Histories* 7.114. That Herodotus is not merely enchanted by what the magi do is shown by another piece of information he gives which never seems to be quoted when scholars ponder the magi in Matthew's Gospel. Herodotus says, "The magi are a peculiar caste . . . the Magi not only kill anything, except dogs and men, with their own hands but make a special point of doing so; ants, snakes, animals, birds—no matter what, they kill them indiscriminately. Well, it is an ancient custom, so let them keep it" (1.140.2–3).

147. Euripides, *Dramas of Euripides*, 318; Euripides, *Children of Heracles*. Josephus also says that a φαρμάκον identified as a "love potion" (φιλτρον) was involved in King Herod's sister Salome's bringing down of Herod's first wife, Mariamne (Josephus, *Ant.* 15.224–25, in *Complete Works*, 412).

time of Cyrus that the college of magi was instituted; the magi directed Cyrus in how to sacrifice to the gods.[148] In the book of Daniel, μάγοι appear in the court of Nebuchadnezzar in LXX Dan 1:2; 2:2, 10, 27; 4:4 (7); 5:7, 11, 15, where μάγος is used to translate אשף. The אשפין in Daniel are part of a cadre of practitioners of oracular skills who attempt to interpret the king's dreams. These other practitioners include חרטמין (miracle performers or dream interpreters),[149] מכשפין (diviner who uses herbs),[150] and כשדאין.[151] This last term seems to be a comprehensive term including the other three terms and identifying them all as dream interpreters, but not giving detail about what methods they use in their trade. Their methods may include soothsaying, exorcism, and astrology.[152] Ann Jeffers notes the difficulty of identifying the skills that the אשפין practice. However, the word seems to be "a Babylonian loanword āšipu, meaning 'exorcist', with the more subtle meaning of 'diagnostician', someone who 'recites prayers and incantations.'"[153] It may be that the אשפין as exorcists cast out the demons responsible for disquieting dreams, or that they ask demons for the meanings of dreams.[154] In this sampling of texts, there are a host of functions ascribed to people called μάγοι. These functions include dream interpretation, perhaps in ways related to exorcism or consulting with demons, the use of charms, spells, and pharmacological substances, giving directions about making

148. Xenophon, *Cryopaedia* 8.1.23.

149. Jeffers, *Magic and Divination*, 44.

150. Ibid., 66.

151. Ibid., 57.

152. Ibid. Another word that appears to be a comprehensive term in Daniel is חכמין or "wise men," which appears in Dan 2:24, 27, 48; 4:15[18]; and 5:7. The word is used as a category, one word that includes the אשפין, חרטמין, מכשפין, and כשדאין. Jeffers describes the חכמין as a "professional class of wise magicians" (ibid., 40). The LXX translates חכם as σοφός. Magicians of this sort also appear in the court of Pharaoh in Gen 41:8; Exod 7:11. They are condemned in Isa 3:3 along with the counselor and the expert in charms. They are also mentioned in a negative light in Isa 19:11–12; 44:25; and 47:10. In all cases they seem to be involved in dream interpretation or oracular divination of some kind.

153. Ibid., 28.

154. Ibid., 30. Jeffers also offers the intriguing possibility that the etymology of "Joseph," usually יסף "to add," is more likely עסף "to take away," possibly referring to exorcism (ibid., 29). Joseph, like Daniel is able to interpret the disturbing dreams of the ruler, although Daniel's skills are better than those of all the other dream interpreters, including the אשפין in Nebuchadnezzar's court.

sacrifices to gods, and narrating the story of the birth of the gods. The word originated in association with Persian practices but came in time to have a broader meaning of magicians in general.

Some of the skills of the μάγοι are the same as those the watchers teach in their illicit pedagogy, namely the use of φαρμακείας and ἐπαοιδάς. The watchers teach their wives both φαρμακείας and ἐπαοιδάς in *1 En.* 7:1,[155] which Nickelsburg translates as "sorcery and charms." Shemihazah is credited with teaching ἐπαοιδάς, "spells," in *1 En.* 8:3.[156] The watcher Hermani is said to have taught φαρμακείας and ἐπαοιδάς / *ḥrṭmw* as well as ἐπαοιδῶν λυτήρια, "the loosing of spells," according to *1 En* 8:4.[157] The associates of those called μάγοι (אשפין) in Daniel, the חרטמין (translated ἐπαοιδοίς in the LXX, miracle performers or dream interpreters), מכשפין ("φαρμάκος" in the LXX, "diviners who uses herbs"), and כשדאין ("Χαλδαίοις," in the LXX, "Chaldeans," "dream interpreters"), also have knowledge of the illicit arts. Clearly, the magi, according to Greek interpretations, have as part of their heritage knowledge of skills identified as illicit in the Enochic watchers' template.

When they show up in Matthew's narrative, however, it is not their skills of enchantment or sorcery that come to the fore, but their behavior as people who watch the movement of the stars and interpret their meaning. The magi arrive in Jerusalem looking for the king because "we saw his star at its rising" (Matt 2:2 NRSV). Matthew gives two references to their prior watching of this particular star, in Matt 2:2, just mentioned, and in 2:7 when Herod learns from them when the star had appeared. But the reader also gets to watch these star observers in action: in Matt 2:9, when the magi see the star again and verify that it is the same star they had previously watched, and in 2:10 when they observe that the star has come to a stop. No specific information is given about how the magi practice, what in particular they look for, or how they interpret what they see. What Matthew wants the reader to know is that these men watch stars, correctly interpret them, and respond appropriately.

155. Nickelsburg, *1 Enoch 1*, 197.
156. Ibid., 189.
157. Ibid., 198.

In their practice of astrology,[158] the wise men engage in another of the illicit skills taught by the watchers in the Enochic template, observing the astronomical bodies, the stars in particular. According to *1 En.* 8:3, "Kokabel taught the signs of the stars. Ziquel taught the signs of the shooting stars."[159] Other watchers also teach the signs of lightning flashes, the earth, the sun, and the moon.[160] The magi know and use what the watchers were not supposed to teach but taught anyway.

The subject of astrology in Enochic literature is more complex than that of the other skills the watchers teach, in part because there are parts of the Enochic tradition that show Enoch as the founder of astrology[161] and as someone to whom the secrets of astronomical phenomena are revealed. Knowledge of the stars is not condemned altogether in *1 Enoch.* In chapters 17–36, Enoch is given a tour of the cosmos and is shown the workings of the sun, moon, and stars. He sees, for example, "the place of the luminaries and the treasuries of the stars" (*1 En.* 17:3).[162] He sees the gates of heaven, including the small gates through which "pass the stars of heaven, and they proceed westward on the path that is shown them" (*1 En.* 36:3). In the *Book of the Luminaries,* also called the *Astronomical Book, 1 Enoch* 72–82,[163] the angel Uriel shows Enoch laws that govern the sun, moon, and stars. In *1 En.* 80:1, Uriel says to Enoch, "I have revealed everything to you so that you may see

---

158. According to Kocku von Stuckrad, astrology has "the doctrine of correspondences" as an important characteristic: "astrologers try to establish analogies and symmetric correspndences between the planetary zone and the earth." Astrology is "a concept of interpretation describing the *quality* of a given time, i.e. the essence of simultaneously and synchronocially occurring events which are connected to inherent symbols and meaning. The measuring instruments for this purpose are the zodiac and the stars' movements" (von Stuckrad, "Jewish and Christian Astrology," 5–6). See also Charlesworth, "Jewish Astrology," 183–200.

159. *1 Enoch: A New Translation,* 25.

160. Also in *1 En.* 8:3.

161. For example, according to Pseudo-Eupoloemus, writing 150–100 BCE, Enoch was the first to discover astrology. See VanderKam, *Enoch,* 109; and Böttrich, "Astrologie in der Henochtradition," 224–45. On astrology, including information on Enoch's role, see also Charlesworth, "Jewish Astrology," 183–200; and von Stuckrad, "Jewish and Christian Astrology," 1–40.

162. *1 Enoch: A New Translation,* 38.

163. For more on the *Astronomical Book,* see Neugebauer, "An Appendix," 386–419; *1 Enoch: A New Translation,* 6–8; VanderKam, *Enoch,* 18–25; VanderKam, "Scriptures in the Astronomical Book of Enoch," 89–103; VanderKam, *Calendars,* 17–27, 91, 97.

this sun and this moon and those who lead the stars of the sky and all those who turn them—their work, their times, and their emergences."[164] What Uriel has revealed is "the motion of the heavenly luminaries, all as they are in their kinds, their jurisdiction, their time, their name, their origins, and their months . . . and how every year of the world will be forever, until a new creation lasting forever is made" (1 *En.* 72:1).[165] Knowing "the motion of the heavenly luminaries" is important because a large concern of the revelation to Enoch is the proper calendar, a solar calendar of 364 days and a lunar year of 354 days.[166]

The differences between the watchers' pedagogy and Enoch's knowledge include these two aspects: divine permission and purpose. Enoch gets information about the movement of astral bodies because it has been revealed to him by the Deity through angels sent for that purpose. When the watchers reveal the signs of the stars, they do so without divine permission to share that information and as part of a catalogue of skills illicitly taught. The purpose for revealing the secrets of the luminaries to Enoch is so that Enoch can pass the information onto future generations ("Tell everything to your son Methuselah and show all your children that no human is righteous before the Lord, for he created them,"[167] 1 *En.* 81:5; "My son, keep the book written by your father so that you may give (it) to the generations of the world,"[168] 1 *En.* 82:1). The watchers engage in revelation as part of their transgression. Enoch's knowledge will lead to proper worship and liturgical functioning, especially as people follow the correct calendar. The result of the watchers' pedagogy and humanity's knowledge of the illicit subjects is destruction and death.

However, in the Matthean infancy narrative, the magi use an illicit skill. As with the women named in Matthew's genealogy, the use of the illicit skill leads not to unrighteousness, but to human participation in God's plan. The magi's concern is not, as it is with Enoch's astrological

164. *1 Enoch: A New Translation*, 110.

165. Ibid., 96.

166. VanderKam, *Calendars*, 23. For more on the importance of the observing the proper calendar see Elior, *The Three Temples*. Elior discusses Enoch and the solar calendar on pp. 88–110 and the watchers and the lunar calendar on pp. 111–34. See also Boccaccini, *Roots of Rabbinic Judaism*, 92–93.

167. *1 Enoch: A New Translation*, 112.

168. Ibid., 113.

information, calendrical, which has some bearing on how and when a community worships. However, the magi are concerned with worship. The star leads them to the child they have come to worship. The magi have used their star observation skills and it has not led to disaster and unrighteousness, but to their part in the witness of the identity of the child.

On this point the text is clear: it is the motion of the star, not Herod's directions, that guides them. The righteous, star-observing magi are contrasted with the unrighteous, non-observant Herod. True, Herod has sent them to Bethlehem, and they have listened (ἀκούσαντες) to the king (Matt 2:9). But after they depart, the star takes center stage in its role as guide: "and see (ἰδού) ahead of them went the star that they had seen (εἶδον) at its rising, until it stood over where the child was. And seeing (ἰδόντες) the star, they were overwhelmed with joy" (Matt 2:10 NRSV). The magi's interaction with Herod is limited to one verb: they "listened" to him. Their interaction with the star is described three times in terms of "seeing;" the number increases to four if their initial report to whomever received them in Jerusalem is included, "we saw (εἴδομεν) his star at its rising" (Matt 2:2 NRSV). Their response to Herod is to leave. Their response to the star is to rejoice. Their ears receive the king's information, but it is their eyes that direct their journey. When they enter the house, their gaze shifts from the star to the object of their worship: "And coming into the house, they saw (εἶδον) the child with Mary his mother, and falling down, they worshipped him" (Matt 2:11 NRSV). It seems, in fact, as if the contrast between Herod and the magi is, in part, a contrast of sense perception. Herod "hears" of the magi's inquiry (Matt 2:3) and the information of the chief priests and scribes (Matt 2:5–6). Herod must ask of the magi when the star appeared (Matt 2:7). He has no direct experience of the star and will have no direct experience of the child either. The first time Herod "sees" in the narrative is after the magi have, with divine dream assistance, outwitted him: "When Herod saw (ἰδὼν) that he had been tricked by the wise men, he was infuriated" (Matt 2:16 NRSV). On the other hand, the magi see the star multiple times and then gaze upon the child.

They Saw; They Came; They Worshipped

In the contrast between the magi who see and comprehend and Herod who neither sees nor comprehends, Matthew sets the stage for a paradigm which will reappear throughout his Gospel. Jesus and his true followers will see and comprehend. The Pharisees and other of Jesus' opponents in the Gospel will see but not comprehend. For example, in Matt 9:2–8, Jesus sees (ἰδὼν) the faith of the paralytic man's friends and forgives the man's sins. Jesus also sees (ἰδὼν) the thoughts (τὰς ἐνθυμήσεις) of the scribes, which he calls "evil" (Matt 9:4). After the crowds see the entire event that includes the curing of the man's paralysis, they are afraid and glorify God (Matt 9:8). In another example of the contrast in seeing, Matthew sees (εἶδεν) the tax collector Matthew and calls him to follow (Matt 9:9). The Pharisees see (ἰδόντες) that Jesus eats with tax collectors and sinners and are offended (Matt 9:11). Correct seeing is the privilege of Jesus and those who are with him.

Because Jesus is also teacher in Matthew (more will be said about this subject in the next chapter), hearing Jesus and understanding is also possible for his followers. His words will be those that ought to be heard and understood. Others who speak and teach are ultimately not to be trusted. Seeing and hearing Jesus go together. Seeing and hearing correctly come together in Matt 13:13–17:

> The reason I speak to them in parables is that 'seeing they do not perceive, and hearing they do not listen, nor do they understand.' With them indeed is fulfilled the prophecy of Isaiah that says:

> 'You will indeed listen, but never understand,
> and you will indeed look, but never perceive.
> For this people's heart has grown dull,
> and their ears are hard of hearing,
> and they have shut their eyes;
> so that they might not look with their eyes,
> and listen with their ears,
> and understand with their heart and turn—
> and I would heal them.'

> But blessed are your eyes, for they see, and your ears, for they hear. Truly I tell you, many prophets and righteous people longed to see what you see, but did not see it, and to hear what you hear, but did not hear it. (NRSV)

Jesus' teachings, rightly heard and understood, are important, but a certain primacy within the Gospel narrative is given to sight and key events within the Gospel narrative are connected with sight. In the birth narrative, the magi see and worship the child. At the transfiguration in Matt 17:1–8, a few disciples are privileged to see Jesus transfigured and Moses and Elijah appearing with him. At the time of Jesus' crucifixion, many of the tombs of the holy ones are opened. After his resurrection, they come out of the tombs and appear to many in the holy city (Matt 27:52–53). After the resurrection the women are invited by an angel to see the place where Jesus was lying (Matt 28:6). The women are told to tell Jesus' disciples to go to Galilee where they will see him (Matt 28:7, 8). When they see him, they worship him, as the magi did at the beginning of the Gospel. However, some doubt (Matt 28:17). The ability to see and comprehend does not yet belong to everyone. Jesus makes predictions about the future as well that include seeing. In Matt 16:28 he says that some will see the Son of Man coming with his kingdom.

The concern with seeing goes beyond how one sees Jesus or events in which Jesus is directly involved. Disciples are to see others properly as well because their seeing is connected with heavenly seeing. Matt 18:10 warns, "Take care that you do not despise [literally, look down upon] one of these little ones, for I say to you that their angels in heaven continually see the face of my Father in heaven" (NRSV).[169] Unlike watchers who see and descend upon women, Jesus' followers are not to look down upon any of the little ones.[170] The little ones have angels

169. Bucur discusses patristic interpretations of this passage and how this passage gave scriptural basis for angelomorphic Pneumatology (Bucur, "Matt. 18:10," 209–31).

170. For more on this passage and the identity of the little ones see Rowland, "Apocalyptic, the Poor, and the Gospel of Matthew,"504–18. Rowland examines Matthew's Gospel in light of the throne theophany tradition in Jewish apocalyptic, and writes that the little ones are the humble, "in terms of status and endowment. In Matthew's Gospel there is a privilege for this group in regard to the understanding of divine mysteries" (517). According to Rowland, the "little ones" are not synonymous with the Twelve who sometimes miss Jesus' point regarding the importance of humility and the humble messiah (515). Graham N. Stanton thinks the "little ones" are the disciples in this passage, as well as in Matt 10:42 and Matt 25:40, 45 (where the superlative is used), because Matthew claims an identification of Jesus with his followers. For example, those who treat the "little ones" or "least" in a particular way actually treat Jesus that way (Matt 25:31–46). See Stanton, "Once More," 214–17. Rowland's view and Stanton's view do not necessarily conflict: Jesus holds his disciples to a higher standard than they currently achieve throughout the Gospel, and Jesus demands that they grow in their understanding of his identity and mission. The humility of the little ones is

whose gaze is on the face of God. Jesus also teaches that his followers
are not to act in such a way as to be the object of sight themselves.
He contrasts the Pharisees and others who show righteousness publicly
(through almsgiving, prayer, and fasting; Matt 6:2, 5, 7, 16) in order
to be seen by others, with the Father who sees in secret (Matt 6:1–18).
How one sees others can be a cause of sin: looking at a woman with lust
is equivalent to committing adultery (Matt 5:28–29). What one desires
to see can also be problematic. Some scribes and Pharisees, for example,
ask to see a sign (σημεῖον ἰδεῖν) from Jesus (Matt 12:38). Jesus replies
that the only sign that they will be given is the sign of Jonah, a reference to Jesus' death and resurrection, and a cause for judgment of them
(Matt 12:41–42).[171] Matthew also portrays Jesus as the true revealer of
the divine. He says, "I thank you, Father, Lord of heaven and earth,
because you have hidden these things from the wise and intelligent and
have revealed them to infants; . . . All things have been handed over
to me by my Father; and no one knows the Son except the Father, and
no one knows the Father except the Son and anyone to whom the Son
chooses to reveal him" (Matt 11:25, 27 NRSV). In Matthew seeing is
important: seeing Jesus and understanding him correctly, seeing others and being seen in the way Jesus teaches, and being privy to Jesus'
revelations are all marks of comprehension and discipleship. Not seeing Jesus (as Herod does not), not understanding what one sees (as the
Pharisees and others do not), seeking to be seen as reward in itself (as

---

something Jesus holds before the disciples who, someday, may understand and share
in the understanding the little ones already have. Rowland's linking of the angels of the
little ones who see the face of God with the understanding that the little ones have by
virtue of their humility ties in well with the theme of seeing as comprehending in the
Gospel of Matthew. For how Matt 18:10 was used in early Christology and pneumatology, particularly as support for an angelomorphic Pneumatology see Bucur, "Matt.
18:10," 209–31.

171. For more on this passage, see Scott, "Sign of Jonah," 16–25. Scott says that
the sign of Jonah is "the appearance of a prophet preaching repentance" (19). James
Swetnam, in "No Sign of Jonah," 126–30, compares Matt 16:4; 12:39–40; and the parallel passage in Luke 11:29–30 with Mark 8:12 in which Jesus says that no sign will
be given. Swetnam believes that the sign of Jonah is the risen Jesus who appears in
Matthew and Luke, but does not appear in the original, shorter version of Mark. The
risen Jesus is God's witness to Jesus' identity. In Mark, Jesus witnesses to himself before
the Sanhedrin, thereby showing himself to be on par with God. See also False, "Taming
the Tehom," 307–48; Rudman, "The Sign of Jonah," 325–28.

the Pharisees and others do), and receiving no sign but a sign of judgment, are all marks of being opposed to Jesus.

Here is one more connection with the Enochic watchers' template. The watchers see the beauty of the women and choose to transgress. They engage in illicit sexual interaction with the women they have seen and pass along illicit knowledge. Seeing, as in Matthew, is not a neutral action. Enoch is given visions and direct sight of the divine throne and the Deity. Enoch, "whose eyes were opened by God" (*1 En.* 1:2),[172] is established as a reliable eye-witness and is charged with passing along the wisdom he has learned for the generations to come. Jesus is also a true recipient of revelation and revealer of divine truth. His disciples have seen and heard him so that they can pass along what they have seen and heard. At the conclusion of the Gospel, after his disciples have seen him in Galilee, Jesus sends them out to do several actions (go; make disciples; baptize; teach; remember; Matt 28:19–20). Through these actions they are to pass along what they have seen and heard. They are to connect generations of the future and people of all geographical areas to what Jesus has done, which people outside of the disciples will not be able to see for themselves, but who will receive it from reliable eyewitnesses.

I look next at one more aspect of the magi's observance of a star. What was it that the magi were following?

The Nature of the Star

Many theories have been put forward about the nature of the star that include conjunctions and comets, empirically verifiable astral phenomena, which I will not address in this book.[173] One possibility, offered by Dale Allison, I will review because of its possible connections with the Enochic watchers' template. This possibility is that the star was an angel.[174]

---

172. *1 Enoch: A New Translation*, 19.

173. On the star as a historical astral phenomenon see, for example, Brown, *Birth*, 170–3; Finegan, *Handbook of Biblical Chronology*, 306–19; Montefiore, "Josephus and the New Testament," 143.

174. Crispin Fletcher-Louis also notes the "strong overlap between angels and stars" (Fletcher-Louis, *Luke-Acts*, 116).

Allison, and many others before him,[175] notes that the star does not behave in the ways in which we observe stars appearing. Stars do not, in our experience, stop in their regular courses or pinpoint a particular geographical location as the star that guides the magi to Bethlehem does.[176] As Allison writes, "Quite simply, Matthew's idea of a star was not our idea of a star."[177] Rather than look for what a modern reader thinks of in terms of astronomical phenomena, for example, a conjunction or a comet, perhaps we should pay attention to what the star does: guide and lead, as angels do.

Other texts point to the interchangeability of, or at least close identity between, stars and angels. For example, Job 38:7 says, "when the morning stars sang together, and all the sons of God shouted for joy."[178] Here the "stars" are in synonymous parallelism with the "sons of God," angels. [179] In some biblical texts, "heavenly hosts" are angels and in others, astronomical bodies. For example, in Dan 8:10, the horn grows "as high as the host of heaven (צבא השמים). It threw down to the earth some of the host and some of the stars, (מן־הצבא ומן־הכוכבים) and trampled on them" (NRSV).[180] In *1 En.* 18:13–14, Enoch is shown a desolate place of punishment for heavenly creatures: "There I saw seven stars like great burning mountains. To me, when I inquired about them, the angel said, 'This place is the end of heaven and earth; this has become a prison for the stars and the hosts of heaven.'" It appears that in *1 Enoch*, stars and angels may be interchangeable. Enoch lists what he has been shown, including astronomical phenomena:

> I saw the treasuries of all the winds. I saw how through them he ordered all created things.

175. Allison notes the comments of some church fathers and others, including John Chrysostom, Theophylact, and Jean Calvin, that indicate that the star acts in a way that is different from one's usual experience of stars (Allison, "Magi's Angel," 17–41).

176. Chrysostom asks, "How then, tell me, did the star point out a spot so confined, just the space of a manger and shed, unless it left that height and came down, and stood over the very head of the child?" (Chrysostom, *Hom. Matt.* 6.2[3] [PG 57.64–65], in Allison, "Magi's Angel," 18).

177. Ibid., 21.

178. My translation.

179. Allison, "Magi's Angel," 24.

180. For more see Bernhard W. Anderson, "Host, Host of Heaven," in Buttrick (ed.), *Interpreter's Dictionary of the Bible*, 2:654–56.

> I saw the foundation of the earth and the cornerstone of the earth. I saw the four winds bearing the earth and the firmament of heaven. And I saw how the winds stretch out the height of the heaven. They stand between the earth and heaven; they are the pillars of heaven.
> I saw the winds of heaven that turn and bring to (their) setting the disk of the sun and all the stars.
> I saw the winds upon the earth bearing the clouds.
> I saw the paths of the angels.
> I saw at the ends of the earth, the firmament of heaven above.
> (1 En. 18:1–5).[181]

Elsewhere in 1 Enoch, it is the stars who move along paths. In 1 En. 36:3, for example, Enoch sees gates through which "pass the stars of heaven, and they proceed westward on the path that is shown them" (1 En. 36:3).[182] Stars could be conceived as angels and angels as stars.

That an angel, even one designated as a watcher, can appear as a star is the assumption in The History of the Blessed Virgin Mary, [183] attributed to "Philotheus, deacon of the East" of the fifth century CE.[184] In this version of the magi story, a watcher appears as a star and guides the magi to the Christ child and home again. The text states, "A Watcher was sent into Persia, and he [showed] himself [to] the Persians in the form of an exceedingly brilliant star which lit up the whole region of their country."[185] The manifestation of the watcher/star takes place during a festival in which the magi and their fellow Persians are worshipping fire and stars. The magi follow the watcher/star until it comes to a stop where the child is. "Then the star changed itself and became like unto a pillar of light that reached from the earth to the heavens."[186] After allowing them time to worship and offer their gifts, the watcher comes back and leads them home.[187] Although a late text for the purposes of our study, the appearance of the watcher in the form of a star shows how one writer addressed the problem of the unusual star: it was an

181. 1 Enoch: A New Translation, 38–39.
182. Ibid., 49.
183. Allison, "Magi's Angel," 29.
184. Philotheus, The History of the Blessed Virgin Mary.
185. Ibid., 34.
186. Ibid., 37.
187. Ibid., 38.

angel. This combination of star and angel represents a long history seen in biblical texts and *1 Enoch*. If this combination is also represented in Matthew's Gospel, it puts Matthew firmly in the milieu of both canonical and Enochic traditions.

The *History of the Blessed Virgin Mary* episode also demonstrates one other aspect of the appearance of angels and angelomorphic beings: the fluidity by which one being may appear in a different guise. In the apocryphal story, the angel who has appeared as a star appears above the place where the child is as a pillar of light. The comparison of the guiding star with the pillar of light that led Israel after the escape from Pharaoh's armies was noted by writers earlier than Philotheus as well. John Chrysostom, for instance, noted the parallel between the two.[188] Philo had identified that same pillar of fire and cloud with an angel.[189] People also noted similarities between the magi's star coming to rest above the Christ child in Matt 2:19 and the Holy Spirit hovering above Jesus at Jesus' baptism (Matt 3:16). Origen writes, "Now what troubles me about this star, is that . . . it only says 'it came and stood above where the child was.' Thus, perhaps it was similar to what happened at the time of the baptism, when 'Jesus was baptized and came up from the Jordan, the heavens were opened for him and he saw the Spirit of God descending as a dove and abiding above him.'"[190] I discussed the angelomorphic Holy Spirit above. Here I note the *astrolo*morphic angel, which also, as Origen noted, functions as the Spirit does at Jesus' baptism. Angels, star, and Spirit all function in Matthew's Gospel as divine indicators of the identity of the child and guiders of those who would worship him.

By the guidance of the star, the magi see the child and worship him. Then they offer their gifts. I look next at their gifts and what connections these may have with the Enochic watchers' template.

188. Chrysostom, *Hom. Matt.* 6:2 (3) (PG 57.64) in Allison, "Magi's Angel," 28.

189. Philo, *Mos.* 1.166.

190. Origen, *Hom. Num.* 18.3[4]. See Origen, *Homilies on Numbers*, 114. As Allison points out, John Maldonatus (1534–83) indicates that Origen's point of view was held by others when he wrote, "Some suppose it [Matthew's star] to have been the Holy Spirit, as he appeared after the baptism in the form of a dove, so now he descended in the appearance of a star to point to Christ" (John Maldonatus, *S. Matthew's Gospel*, 56, in Allison, "Magi's Angel," 34).

They Offered Their Gifts

The magi present their gifts to the child: gold, frankincense, and myrrh (Matt 2:11). Many symbolic meanings have been attributed to these gifts and many biblical texts have been offered as possible references. For instance, in Exod 30:22–33, Moses is given instructions for how to make and use anointing oil. The oil contains myrrh and is to be used to anoint the Tent of Meeting, the ark, all the holy vessels, and Aaron and his sons in order to consecrate them as priests. Next YHWH instructs Moses to make incense containing frankincense. This incense is to be burned in front of the Tent of Meeting, where YHWH will meet with Moses (Exod 30:34–38). Gold and frankincense are gifts brought by the nations to Zion in Isa 60:6. Additional biblical references could be named here.[191] However, here I will focus on passages which have a potential connection with the Enochic template. The passage from Isaiah 60 just mentioned does share with *1 Enoch* eschatological concerns. The gold and frankincense offered in this passage are part of "the first fruits of the eschatological pilgrimage of the nations and their submission to the one true God."[192] In Num 22:18 and 24:13, Balak offers Balaam gold as potential payment for his services as visionary and curser of Israel. Hull observes, "gold is offered to the diviner Balaam; Matthew goes further; the diviners offer the chosen one gold."[193] That Balaam has connections with both Matthew's infancy narrative and *1 Enoch* has been stated above. The connection between the magi's gifts and *1 Enoch* is seen in the presence of frankincense and myrrh amongst the trees (*1 En.* 29:1) Enoch encounters on his journey to the Paradise of Righteousness (*1 En.* 28:1–32:6). Here Enoch sees and smells many trees with a variety of spices and scents. One tree along his journey stands out. Gabriel informs Enoch that this tree is "the tree of wisdom

191. For example, Song 3:6 contains a reference to both frankincense and myrrh:

What is that coming up from the wilderness,
like a column of smoke,
perfumed with myrrh and frankincense,
with all the fragrant powders of the merchant? (NRSV)

Myrrh is also mentioned in Ps 45:8, a psalm about praising the king.

192. Davies and Allison, *Matthew: Shorter Commentary*, 27. Gifts will also be brought by the nations to the Son of Man in *1 En.* 53:1 and *Ps. Sol.* 17:31.

193. Hull, *Hellenistic Magic*, 127.

from which your father of old and your mother of old, who were before you, ate and learned wisdom" (*1 En.* 32:6). While not the products of this particular tree, frankincense and myrrh are amongst those things Enoch encounters on his increasingly eastward journey ("I departed to the east," *1 En.* 29:1; "Beyond these I departed to the east," *1 En.* 30:1; "Beyond these valleys, I departed to the east," *1 En.* 31:1; "Beyond these mountains, approximately to their northeastern side, I saw other mountains," *1 En.* 32:1; "From there I proceeded to the east of all these mountains, far from them to the east of the earth," *1 En.* 32:2)[194] to the tree of the knowledge of good and evil. The frankincense and myrrh were located in Enoch's first "level" of eastward voyage on his way to the tree. The magi from the east include these as part of their gifts.

Gold, frankincense, and myrrh also have been connected with the illicit arts the watchers taught their wives. For example, in the Babylonian Talmud, (*b. Šabb.* 62b) myrrh is mentioned as a potent love charm used by the women of Jerusalem to attract men's love.[195] Gold is fashioned into adornments, another of the illicit arts. That frankincense could be (mis-) used for non-consecrated or cosmetic purposes is seen in the warning Moses is given regarding the ointment he is to make in Exodus 30, "it is not to be used in any ordinary anointing of the body, and you shall make no other like it in composition; it is holy, and it shall be holy to you. Whoever compounds any like it or whoever puts any of it on an unqualified person shall be cut off from the people" (Ex 30:32–33 NRSV). In the book of Esther, myrrh is a part of the cosmetic preparation of a woman before she has her appearance before King Xerxes (Esth 2:12). Gold was used in the creation of idols (for example Ex 32:2; Hos 8:4; Hab 2:19); as discussed above, in *1 Enoch* the giants' demons are credited with causing humans to sacrifice to idols. Gold, frankincense, and myrrh are all associated with the illicit arts the watchers teach their wives, through their use in beautification and adornment and, in the case of gold, in the legacy of the watchers' transgression through its misuse for idol worship.

Despite the magi's skills of charms, incantations, pharmacology, sorcery, and astrology, the magi do not represent unrighteousness in Matthew's Gospel, but rather righteous behavior and right worship.

194. *1 Enoch: A New Translation*, 47.
195. Hull, *Hellenistic Magic*, 126.

Neither do the gifts offered by the magi lead to disaster. Within the framework of the narrative, the gifts are received and appropriate.

Summary

Magi, who are associated with the illicit skills of charms, incantations, pharmacology and sorcery, use another of the illicit arts, astrology, to find the Christ child. The magi "see" the child and grasp his significance, contrary to the behavior of Herod who does not "see," and will not see, thanks to the magi's returning home by another way. The magi provide a template for his community's response to the child: true followers of Jesus will be those who see and comprehend, and then see others in the way that Jesus instructs them. As part of their worship of the child they offer gifts, each of which may be connected with the illicit arts taught by the watchers.

Chapter Summary

The fifth woman named in Matthew's genealogy gives birth to Jesus. His birth shares similar suspicious circumstances with the birth of Noah in *1 Enoch* and the *Genesis Apocryphon*. Like Noah, Jesus will be responsible for saving his people; however, Noah's salvific achievements will not be permanent. In regard to the fatherhood of the child, through divinely given dreams, Joseph finds out that he has nothing to fear. The child Mary bears will be "Emmanuel" and "from the Holy Spirit." It is possible that Matthew may have thought of the Holy Spirit as angelomorphic, bringing another comparison with the Enochic watchers' template: Jesus is the product of a heavenly angelomorphic being and a woman. However, as Matthew makes clear, no sexual interaction is involved in this pregnancy. Revelatory dreams help guide human agents of God's plans, as they do in *1 Enoch*. However, the dreams of the Matthean infancy narrative reveal that Jesus is the long-awaited one Matthew would claim is the fulfillment of Enoch's visions. The first visitors of the child are the magi who are themselves associated with illicit arts taught by the watchers and make use of one of the arts, astrology, in their quest to find the child. They bring gifts associated with the illicit arts. In the story of the magi, as in the stories of the women, the illicit art is used and it does not result in disaster; it results in righteousness. In the case of the magi, the use of astrology results in the worship of the Christ child. Ironically, it is when they cease using this art, and instead consult with human beings, that the trouble begins and Herod plots destruction and violence.

In Matthew's infancy narrative, the watchers' transgressions are being redressed by the birth of Jesus. Through the use of the skills taught by the watchers, through revelatory dreams, and through a non-sexual union of the angelomorphic Holy Spirit and a woman, a child is born who "will save his people from their sins" and who is "God with us." The first to pay him homage show their understanding of his identity. Their use of the illicit arts brings them to him.

The infancy narrative delivers the one who redresses the watchers' transgression to the narrative's stage and identifies him as the one who will repair the damage caused by the watchers. The infancy narrative sets the stage for what will happen in the rest of the Gospel. If it is true that Enochic themes appear in the infancy narrative, which sets the stage for the remainder of the Gospel, then one should expect to see evidence of the working out of those themes in later sections of the Gospel when Jesus is portrayed as an adult and engaged in his ministry. I look next at the contrast between the results of the two unions (watchers and women, and Holy Spirit and Mary), the legacy of the giants within the Enochic template and the legacy of Jesus as presented by Matthew.

5

The Legacy of the Watchers' Transgression versus the Legacy of "God with Us"

A comparison of the legacy of the watchers' transgression with the legacy of the child conceived by the Holy Spirit and Mary shows dramatically different results. In this chapter I show that Matthew's description of Jesus throughout Jesus' life stands in sharp contrast to the description of the disastrous aftermath of the watchers' fall. Jesus is portrayed as the repairer of the watchers' fall and illicit pedagogy, the one who remedies the terrible results of the watchers' transgression. I have already made some connections in chapter 3 between the women named in Matthew's genealogy and the adult Jesus' interaction with women and teaching in a way that shows the overturning of the watchers' transgression. Specifically, I mentioned Jesus' interaction with the Canaanite woman (Matt 15:21–28) in the section on Tamar, Jesus' teaching on the welcome or rejection of his messengers (Matt 10:14–15) in the section on Rahab, and Jesus' reconfiguration of family (Matt 12:48–50; 23:9) in the section on Ruth. In chapter 4 I also showed connections between aspects of Matthew's infancy narrative and the adult Jesus' repair of the watchers' transgression. I showed connections between the star that appears in the East to herald the birth of Jesus (Matt 2:2) with astronomical phenomena at his death (Matt 27:45) and the *parousia* of the Son of Man (Matt 24:29–31), and with the magi who see the star and the infant Jesus and the theme of sight in the rest of the Gospel. Themes are introduced through the genealogy and in the infancy narrative that are developed later in the Gospel. If Matthew shows Jesus' repair of the watchers' transgression in the infancy narrative, then one should expect to see such overturning continue in the narratives of Jesus' adult life.

The results of the watchers' illicit unions and pedagogy were described above in Chapter 2. However, for ease of comparison, I summarize them again here. The consequences include the destructive behavior of the gigantic offspring, including their attempts to satisfy their insatiable appetites and their violence (*1 En.* 7:3–5); and the sinful behavior of the humans who use the illicit arts, including skills for warfare, seduction, sorcery, and astrology (see *1 En.* 7:1–2; 8:1; 9:8–9). The terrible results do not end when the watchers and giants are punished. Evil spirits, who originate with the giants, will continue to plague humans, even after the death of the giants (*1 En.* 15:9, 10–11, 16:1), until "the great judgment" (*1 En.* 16:1). The evil spirits "lead astray, do violence, make desolate, and attack and wrestle and hurl upon the earth and cause illnesses" (*1 En.* 15:11).[1] According to *1 En.* 19:1, they also "bring destruction on men and lead them astray to sacrifice to demons as to gods."[2] Violence, desolation, physical pain, illness, and idolatry are all attributable to the work of the evil spirits. When the ongoing malicious efforts of the evil spirits are added to the transgressions of the watchers, the following evil realities for human life result according to the Enochic template: illicit sexual relations (through humanity's knowledge of illicit arts involving adornment); bloodshed and violence (through illicit arts involving weapons and warfare); and idolatry, pain, and sickness (through the ongoing work of the evil spirits of the giants). In *1 Enoch* the Deity takes action against unrighteousness through the ministrations of the archangels (see *1 Enoch* 10), and through divinely appointed leaders such as Noah (see *1 Enoch* 106–107). However, as mentioned above, even after the days of Noah, earth would see still more and worse unrighteousness (*1 En.* 106:19), until

> there will arise generations of righteousness.
> And evil and wickedness will end,
> and violence will cease from the earth,
> and good things will come upon the earth to them. (*1 En.* 107:1)[3]

Within the Enochic template, generations of righteousness, the end of evil, wickedness, and violence, and the advent of "good things . . . upon

---

1. *1 Enoch: A New Translation,* 37.
2. Ibid., 39.
3. Ibid., 167.

the earth" are aspects of a future vision; for Matthew, with the coming of Jesus, these have become a present reality.

In Matthew's description of the legacy of Jesus, there are results in stark contrast with the legacy of the watchers' illicit sexual relationships and pedagogy. I will look at each of these contrasts briefly. Each could be developed at more length. My purpose here is to illustrate the point that the repair of the watchers' transgression begun by the birth of Jesus is continued in his adult life and ministry. The Enochic watchers' template, which I see as background for the first two chapters of Matthew's Gospel, continues to be present in the rest of the Gospel. The themes addressed are Jesus' righteous pedagogy, Jesus' rejection of illicit sexual interaction, Jesus' righteous family, Jesus' ethic of nonviolence, Jesus' healing of disease and demon possession, and Jesus' promotion of correct worship.

The Watchers' Illicit Pedagogy versus Jesus' Righteous Pedagogy

The watchers engage in illicit pedagogy, but Jesus engages in righteous pedagogy. Jesus' pedagogy, unlike the watchers' pedagogy, is open to all, and is not related to sexual interaction. However, in Matthew's account of Jesus' teaching, Jesus is not shown teaching women directly. Rather, women are shown as among those who hear, understand, and carry out Jesus' teaching.

Jesus is a teacher in the Gospel of Matthew.[4] He addresses characters within the Gospel narrative, and, according to some scholars,[5]

4. "A major motive for Matthew to write his Gospel was to present large sections of Jesus' teaching" (Harrington, *Matthew*, 76). Similarly, "Matthew's primary concerns were pastoral and catechetical" (Stanton, *Gospel for a New People*, 43). Beare writes, "The Gospel according to Matthew may be described as a manual of instruction in the Christian way of life" (Beare, *Matthew*, 5); and likewise Hare says, "For Matthew, Jesus' teaching is of much greater significance than his miracles. Indeed, teaching takes precedence even over preaching the gospel of the kingdom" (Hare, *Matthew*, 31). Others agree: The Gospel was "written with catechetical and liturgical ends in view" (Allison, *New Moses*, 139); "Jesus stands out in this portrait as the Prophet who proclaimed the gospel of the kingdom and as the Teacher who made known the will of God" (Kingsbury, *Matthew*, 3); and "Jesus is an extremely effective teacher in Matthew and his followers become very well-trained students" (Stanton, *Church and Community in Crisis*, 20).

5. For example, Luz, *Matthew 1–7*, "*The five major discourses are spoken, as it*

some of his addresses are meant to be direct address to the readers of the Gospel. The presence of five blocks of teaching material within Matthew is well-known,[6] and is distinctive to Matthew.[7] However, Jesus is not only *a* teacher in the Gospel; he is portrayed as the sole teacher for the community.[8] In Matt 23:8 and 10, Jesus tells the crowds and his disciples, "But you are not to be called rabbi, for you have one teacher, and you are all brothers . . . Neither be called teachers, because you have one teacher, the Christ"[9] (ὑμεῖς δὲ μὴ κληθῆτε, Ῥαββί· εἷς γάρ ἐστιν ὑμῶν ὁ διδάσκαλος, πάντες δὲ ὑμεῖς ἀδελφοί ἐστε . . . μηδὲ κληθῆτε καθηγηταί, ὅτι καθηγητὴς ὑμῶν ἐστιν εἷς ὁ Χριστός) Jesus' disciples are

---

were, "beyond the window" of the Matthean story of Jesus. That is, they are spoken directly to the readers and are Jesus' direct commandment to them (Luz, *Matthew 1–7*, 12, emphasis original).

6. The five discourses are Matthew 5–7, 10, 13, 18, and 24–25. Bacon is credited with the thesis that Matthew structured his Gospel in five books or discourses in order to recall the Pentateuch and portray the Gospel as the new Torah and Jesus as the new Moses. While others before him noted the presence of themes related to Moses and the exodus in Matthew's Gospel, Bacon is "the first to insist that Matthew, in its entirety, is a new law whose very structure mirrors the Torah" (Allison, *New Moses*, 294). See Bacon, "The 'Five Books' of Moses," 56–66. The thesis that these five discourses provide the key to the structure of Matthew's Gospel is not widely held, particularly because it does not give enough weight to the passion narrative within the Gospel or the importance of the Markan story line. For example, Hare, *Matthew*, 3; Hagner, *Matthew 1–13*, li. The idea that the five discourses recall the Pentateuch still has adherents, however, for example, Davies and Allison, *Matthew 1–7*, 61. Allison writes, "My sympathies lie with Bacon and his descendants" (Allison, *Studies in Matthew*, 136). Allison argues that polemic in Matthew is not against Moses. Moses is "not Jesus' adversary but, like the Baptist, his typological herald and foreshadow" (Allison, *New Moses*, 275). Other commentators note the possibility that the five discourses are meant to reflect a new Pentateuch, but caution against pressing the idea too much (e.g., Beare, *Matthew*, 27). Luz argues that allusions to the story of Moses are present in the Gospel and that "Matthew writes for his community a foundation story structured similarly to the Penateuch" (Luz, *Matthew 1–7*, 13). However, Luz does not adopt Bacon's thesis that the Pentateuch provides the structure for Matthew's Gospel. He prefers what he calls "the *Markan structural model*," which he says was developed by Kingsbury (Luz, *Matthew 1–7*, 3, emphasis original), because it "takes the book seriously as *narrative*" (ibid., 9, emphasis original).

7. Mark's Gospel also portrays Jesus as a teacher. However, Mark presents far less of Jesus' teaching (Harrington, *Matthew*, 76).

8. Luz, *The Theology of the Gospel of Matthew*, 140.

9. Matthew's audience knows that Jesus is referring to himself in this statement. Jesus has been identified as the Christ in Matthew from the beginning of the Gospel, e.g, in Matt 1:1; 1:16, 17, 18. This instruction to the crowds and disciples occurs only in Matthew.

to pass on what Jesus taught, not their own teaching, and Jesus tells them who should be the recipients of the teaching. This is seen clearly in the conclusion of the Gospel, when Jesus sends out the eleven to "all the nations" (πάντα τὰ ἔθνη; Matt 28:19) "teaching them to keep everything that I have commanded you" (διδάσκοντες αὐτοὺς τηρεῖν πάντα ὅσα ἐνετειλάμην ὑμῖν; Matt 28:20). Here at the conclusion of the Gospel is the first time the disciples are sent to teach[10] and the content of their teaching is what Jesus has commanded.

Unlike in the watchers' narrative, in which the watchers engage in illicit pedagogy, Jesus engages in righteous pedagogy. The subject of his teaching is often righteousness (as in Matthew 5–7, see especially, 5:20, "For I say to you if your righteousness does not far exceed that of the scribes and Pharisees, you will not enter the kingdom of heaven" NRSV) and his interpretation of God's commands (for example, in the so-called antitheses in Matt 5:21–48).[11] In addition, Jesus is portrayed as teaching that which fulfills what has been spoken by the prophets (as in, for example, Matt 5:17, "Do not think that I have come to abolish the law or the prophets; I have come not to abolish but to fulfill" NRSV). Jesus does not reveal forbidden knowledge, as the watchers do; Jesus reveals righteousness in his teaching.

Unlike in the watchers' narrative, in which pedagogy of women follows illicit sexual contact,[12] Jesus' pedagogy is often offered to groups of people, and with no sexual contact as prerequisite or preliminary activity.[13] Jesus' pedagogy takes the form of preaching (using a form of the verb κηρύσσω), teaching (διδάσκω),[14] and speaking (λαλέω or

---

10. In Matt 10:5–7, they are sent only "to the lost sheep of Israel," and they are sent to "preach," (κηρύσσετε), not teach. Jesus also gives instructions about teaching the commandments in Matt 5:19: "Whoever breaks one of the least of these commandments and teaches [διδάξῃ] others to do the same, will be called least in the kingdom of heaven; but whoever does them and teaches [διδάξῃ] them will be called great in the kingdom of heaven." The future tense of both occurrences of "teaches" matches well with Jesus' instruction at the end of the Gospel when Jesus commissions the disciples to go out and begin their role as those who teach.

11. See also Matt 3:15 where Jesus tells John he must receive the Baptist's baptism in order to "fulfill all righteousness."

12. See chapter 2 above.

13. The subject of the avoidance of sexual activity will be addressed in the next section.

14. Luz and others argue that in Matthew Jesus' "preaching" and "teaching" are not in substance two distinct things. For example, "preaching" and "teaching" are both

λέγω) to crowds[15] and people in synagogues and the temple.[16] However, Matthew does not use the word for teaching (διδάσκω) when women are specifically mentioned as being present in the crowd. If the watchers' illicit teaching of women is in the background of Matthew's Gospel, then it makes sense for Matthew to distance Jesus from the appearance of directly teaching women. That is, while the reader may assume that women are present in the crowds or in the synagogues in which Jesus is teaching, when Matthew specifically mentions the presence of women in the crowds, as in the two feeding stories in Matthew (Matt 14:14–21; 15:29–38), Jesus is said to be healing people (ἐθεράπευσεν; in 14:14 and 15:30), not teaching them, as he is in one of the parallel accounts in Mark (Mark 6:34, "he began to teach [διδάσκειν] them"). In Mark 8:1–10, another feeding miracle, no mention is made of teaching or healing, only feeding the crowd; in Luke 9:11, "he was speaking (ἐλάλει) to them about the kingdom." Neither Mark nor Luke mentions the presence of women in the crowds, but they do show Jesus teaching. Matthew, on the other hand, mentions the presence of women, but does not show Jesus teaching in this context. Women are portrayed as those who correctly act in accordance with Jesus' teaching,[17] but Matthew appears to avoid

---

used to summarize Jesus' activity in Matt 4:23, 9:35; and 11:1. See Luz, *Matthew 1–7*, 168; Davies and Allison, *Matthew 1–7*, 415. However, in these passages, teaching is listed first. Kingsbury remarks, "Matthew gives it the position of stress and invites the reader to attach special importance to it" (Kingsbury, *Matthew*, 63). Jesus is the subject of the verb "teach" in 4:23; 5:2; 7:29; 21:23; 22:16. Jesus' teaching is referred to in 7:28.

15. E.g., Jesus addresses "the crowds" in Matthew 5–7; 9:8; 11:7; 12:46; 13:2; 13:34; 15:10; and 23:1.

16. Jesus teaches in "their synagogues" in 4:23; 9:35; and 13:54. Jesus teaches in the temple in 21:23.

17. Women are portrayed positively, as following Jesus' teaching, even though they do not seem to be included among those with the title, "disciple." See Anderson, "Matthew: Gender and Reading," 39. Clearly, there are specific women, for example the woman who anoints Jesus at Bethany (Matt 26:6–13), the Canaanite woman who is praised for her faith (Matt 15:21–28), and the women at the cross and tomb of Jesus (Matt 27:55–56; 28:1–10) who provided examples of those who act faithfully and as disciples are taught to act. Further, as Anderson argues, the words of the Gospel are addressed to the implied reader of the Gospel as well as to the characters within the Gospel narrative. Through the "occasional alignment of the temporal position of the implied reader with those of the narrator and characters, especially Jesus," it is as if those within the narrative, including Jesus, speak to the reader of the Gospel. This is accomplished "through the narrator's use of the historical present, extended speeches by Jesus, and the introduction of direct discourse with the present participles of λέγειν

saying that Jesus teaches women directly within the Gospel narrative.[18] In this way, Matthew further avoids the Enochic template's pattern in which those with heavenly knowledge impart it directly to women.[19] Unlike the watchers' illicit pedagogy, offered to their wives following sexual relations, Jesus' righteous pedagogy is open to all, and with no mention of sexual relations. Jesus is never described as directly teaching women,[20] although women are included among those who respond faithfully to Jesus' pedagogy.

('to say')" (ibid., 48). Therefore, although no women are included among the character group called "the disciples," women readers or hearers of Matthew's Gospel are addressed with the words of the Sermon on the Mount and the commission with which the Gospel concludes.

18. On two other occasions, the presence of women in the group addressed by Jesus may be assumed. One is in Matt 12:46–50, in which Jesus is speaking (λαλοῦντος) to the crowds, not "teaching" them, and the mother and brothers of Jesus come looking for him. Jesus points to his disciples and says, "See, my mother and my brothers. For whoever does the will of my Father in heave is my brother and sister and mother." Because the word "disciple" is used, some would argue against the presence of women in this group. Others would argue that this passage means that women were included amongst those called by the name "disciple." I think that this is one of those places where Jesus is clearly understood to be addressing not just the other characters within the narrative, but the readers as well. Readers and hearers addressed by Matthew, including women, would understand themselves as disciples of Jesus. The other occasion is in 13:54–58, in which Jesus is teaching (ἐδίδασκεν) "in their synagogue" (Matt 13:54). The people ask, "are not all his sisters with us?" (Matt 13:56), i.e., present with us, listening to him. However, the people take offense at him (13:57) and "he did not do many deeds of power there because of their unbelief" (13:58). In short, the one time in which Jesus "teaches" a group of people and the presence of women is noted, it is a disaster, and Jesus does not fully reveal himself as a doer of deeds of power as well as a teacher.

19. The word used to describe the watchers' action, i.e., their illicit pedagogy in *1 En.* 7:1 according to 4QEna 1 3:15 is the infinitive לאלפה (from the verb אלף, "to learn" in the qal, and "to teach" in the piel (Nickelsburg, *1 Enoch 1*, 182 n. e). This verb appears in the MT Job 15:5; 33:33; and 35:11. In the LXX of Job 33:33 it is translated by διδάξω. In the list of the illicit arts taught in *1 Enoch* 8, the verb ἔδειξε is used for the teaching that the various watchers do (ibid., 188). In *1 En.* 9:6 the verb ἐδίδαξεν is used of Asael in the report of the archangels: "he taught (ἐδίδαξεν) all the iniquities and sins upon the earth" (ibid., 204). In *1 En.* 10:8, "the teaching of Asael" is τῆς διδασκαλίας Ἀσαήλ, referring to his illicit pedagogy (ibid., 194).

20. Compare Luke's story of Jesus in the home of Mary and Martha of Bethany, in which Mary sits at the feet of Jesus and listens to his teaching (Luke 10:38–40). This story is not part of Matthew's Gospel and would not fit Matthew's concern to keep Jesus the teacher at a distance from women students.

The Watchers' Illicit Sexual Relationships Versus Jesus' Rejection of Illicit Sexual Relationships

The watchers engage in illicit sexual relationships, but Jesus eschews illicit sexual relationships, even advocating for those who are able to become "eunuchs for the kingdom." Three examples unique in the canonical gospels to Matthew serve to highlight Jesus' teaching of abstinence from not only illicit sexual relationships but even licit sexual relationships in the cause of righteousness: Matthew's teaching on adultery in Matt 5:27–28; the report of Joseph's abstaining from sexual relations with Mary until after Jesus is born in Matt 1:25; and Jesus' advocating celibacy for some in 19:12 in his mention of those who "make themselves eunuchs on account of the kingdom of heaven." First, in Matt 5:27–28, Jesus expands on the commandment prohibiting adultery (Exod 20:14 and Deut 5:18, quoted by Jesus) by adding that "everyone who looks at a woman to desire her has committed adultery with her in his heart" (Matt 5:28).[21] As in the rest of this section of antitheses, Jesus teaches the upholding of the commandment in light of the perfection demanded by the kingdom.[22] The avoidance of not only adulterous acts, but even lustful thoughts, is an example of Jesus' teaching a righteousness greater than that of the scribes and Pharisees (Matt 5:20).

Matthew also gives more information than is strictly necessary to establish the non-sexual nature of Jesus' origins when he mentions the abstinence of Joseph and Mary from sexual relations until after the baby Jesus is born (Matt 1:25). Matthew has already established that the child is "conceived by the Holy Spirit" (Matt 1:20), rather than by a man and provided the fulfillment quotation using the word "virgin" (παρθένος, as in the LXX version of Isa 7:14) in Matt 1:23. Matthew then adds

---

21. Janice Capel Anderson correctly notes that this verse, as does Matt 5:32 in which Jesus teaches against divorcing one's wife except in cases of unchastity, assumes a male audience (Anderson, "Matthew: Gender and Reading," 29). Anthony Saldarini examines how the teaching in Matt 18–20 about household and community is addressed to men, although it has import for women as well. See Saldarini, "Absent Women," 157–70. See also Brower, "Jesus and the Lustful Eye," 291–309. Brower argues that Jesus puts the onus on men to regard women properly, in distinction from others who hold women accountable for attracting men's attention. This passage provides another distinction from the Enochic watchers' template in which, at least in *1 Enoch 8*, the women cause the watchers' transgression because of their beauty: "and they [the women] transgressed and led the holy ones astray" (*1 En.* 8:1 in *1 Enoch: A New Translation*, 25).

22. Hagner, *Matthew 1–13*, 120.

the detail that Joseph "did not know her" (οὐκ ἐγίνωσκεν αὐτὴν, i.e., have sexual relations with her) "until she had borne a son" (Matt 1:25 NRSV). As discussed above, this detail serves to distance the birth of Jesus from any sexual activity whatsoever. It also highlights the virginal status of Mary mentioned in Matt 1:23.[23] However, Allison offers the possibility that this detail also serves to link Joseph's righteous behavior with Jesus' teaching in Matt 19:10–12, which Allison describes as a "qualified defense of celibacy."[24] Jesus teaches, when he mentions that some become eunuchs for the sake of the kingdom, that "sexual intercourse need not be a duty, that sexual abstinence will be incumbent upon some."[25] Joseph, in abstaining from sexual relations with Mary not only guarantees her virginity while she is pregnant with Jesus, but also provides an example of one who abstains from sexual relations for the sake of the kingdom. Further, Allison suggests that Joseph may exemplify proper sexual conduct within marriage according to Josephus's examples of Jewish communities,[26] for example the Essenes who "have no intercourse during pregnancy"[27] and Jews generally, who consider sexual intercourse with a woman who is pregnant to be unclean.[28] Unlike the watchers who engage in illicit sexual relations with women, Jesus teaches a righteousness which prohibits illicit sexual relations (and even thoughts of such relations) and promotes celibacy for some of his followers. In addition, the narrative of Jesus' birth includes multiple references to his conception apart from sexual relations, and Joseph's righteous abstinence from sexual relations with Mary.

The "Family" of the Watchers Versus the Family of Jesus

The "family" created by the watchers' transgression is made of rebel angels, women, and monstrous, malicious children. Jesus advocates a new family, configured around the sole fatherhood of God, of those who do

23. Hagner states that this functions "as a guarantee that Jesus was virgin born" (ibid., 21). Harrington and Luz agree: Harrington, *Gospel of Matthew*, 36; Luz, *Matthew 1–7*, 97.

24. Allison, *Studies in Matthew*, 167.

25. Ibid.

26. Ibid., 171.

27. Josephus, *J. W.*, 2.161.

28. Josephus, *C. Ap.*, 2.202.

the Father's will. The outcome of the sexual union between the watchers and the women is monstrous gigantic offspring who wreak havoc on all creation. Despite the watchers' desire to "beget for ourselves children" (*1 En.* 6:1) through sexual relations with women, the family that is produced is disastrous and destructive. Jesus also speaks of having a family. However, the family he brings into existence is not the result of sexual procreation; it results from recognition of the sole fatherhood of God and obedience to the will of God. Jesus commands in Matt 23:9, "call no one your father on earth, for you have one Father—the one in heaven" (Matt 23:9, a saying unique to Matthew). On several occasions Jesus speaks of a reconfiguration of family around doing the will of God. This reconfiguration may necessitate the rejection of biological family members. For example, in Matt 12:50, Jesus says that his family members are those who do "the will of my Father who is in heaven, that person is my brother and sister and mother" (NRSV).[29] With this teaching, Jesus distinguishes such a person from Jesus' biologically related mother and brothers who were seeking to speak with him. This doing of God's will may in fact bring about the dissolution of the biological family. Matthew 10 describes circumstances in which biological families will be torn apart: "Brother will betray brother to death, and a father his child, and children will rise against parents and have them put to death" (Matt 10:21), and a quotation of Mic 7:6,

> I have come to set a man against his father,
> and a daughter against her mother,
> and a daughter-in-law against her mother-in-law;
> and one's foes will be members of one's own household."
> (Matt 10:35–36 NRSV)[30]

Jesus demands that his followers love him, Jesus, more than any member of the follower's family: "Whoever loves father or mother more than me is not worthy of me and whoever loves a son or daughter more than me is not worthy of me" (Matt 10:37; NRSV).[31] In Matt 8:21–22, Jesus tells a disciple that the disciple must ignore his duty to bury his father in

---

29. The pericope has parallels in Mark 3:31–35 (although some manuscripts lack "and sisters") and Luke 8:19–21 (which lacks "and sisters").

30. A parallel of this passage can be found in Luke 12:51–53.

31. Luke 14:26 has a similar saying, but says instead that one must "hate" (μισεῖ) members of one's family.

order to follow Jesus.[32] Jesus' followers must be prepared to choose the will of God and association with Jesus over their identity as members of a biological family and the duties that come with that identity.

However, the undoing of the biological family for the sake of the kingdom will result in a much larger family for the followers of Jesus: "everyone who has left houses or brothers or sisters or father or mother or children or lands on account of my name will receive a hundredfold and will inherit eternal life" (Matt 19:29 NRSV).[33] This new, expanded family of followers of Jesus and those who do the will of God experiences life, unlike those who prefer their biological families with their attendant duties: "Let the dead bury their own dead," (Matt 8:21 NRSV) says Jesus. Jesus creates a new community which he describes in familial terms. However, unlike in the watchers' narrative, Jesus' family members[34] are those who do the will of God and come into being through obedience to the will of God.

The Watchers' Violence Versus Jesus' Peace

The watchers bring violence into the world through illicit pedagogy and through the giants and the spirits of the giants, but Jesus prescribes an ethic of peace. Jesus' followers will encounter violence, but they are not to be agents of violence. Unlike the watchers and their offspring who bring violence and destruction into the world, Jesus exhorts his followers to peace and nonviolence. This message is seen clearly in Jesus' teaching in Matthew 5–7. For example, Jesus includes amongst the verses known as the Beatitudes, "Blessed are the peacemakers, for they will be called sons of God" (μακάριοι οἱ εἰρηνοποιοί, ὅτι αὐτοὶ υἱοὶ θεοῦ κληθήσονται, Matt 5:9). Rather than seeking vengeance, Jesus advocates "turning the other cheek" to those who commit violence against his followers (in Matt 5:39), as well as love for enemies and prayer for those who persecute his followers (in Matt 5:44) in order to be "sons of your father in heaven" (Matt 5:49). Davies and Allison, however, express

32. Also in Luke 9:59–60.

33. A parallel passage may be found at Mark 10:30. However, in the Markan version, the follower is not giving up "father." Matthew is alone in demanding that Jesus' followers have one father only (Matt 23:9).

34. For more on "family" in the New Testament, see Osiek, "Family in Early Christianity," 1–5.

some difficulty squaring Jesus' words in the beatitudes with Jesus' statement, "Do not think that I have come to bring peace on the earth; I have not come to bring peace, but a sword" (Matt 10:34 NRSV). [35] Hagner remarks that the disciples' expectation must have been that Jesus came "to bring peace" because of how the statement is worded.[36] Does Jesus in Matthew 10 advocate violence rather than peace?

Jesus' statement in Matt 10:34–36 does not contradict his advocacy elsewhere of peace. Jesus does not prescribe violence. He describes the division that will result among family members because of his followers' obedience to Jesus' ethic. He predicts that his followers will suffer because of the choice to follow him.[37] Those who do not follow will experience suffering, but after a future judgment[38] and the punishment is not described as meted out by Jesus' followers. This is in marked contrast with the participation of the righteous in *1 Enoch* in vengeance on the wicked. For example, in *1 En.* 91:12, in the *Apocalypse of Weeks*, Enoch's revelation includes the detail that during the eighth week of righteousness, "a sword will be given to all the righteous, to execute righteous judgment on all the wicked, and they will be delivered into their hands."[39] In *1 En.* 98:12, in the *Epistle of Enoch*, Enoch repeats the theme that the righteous will be involved in the punishment of those judged as wicked: "Now be it known to you that you will be delivered into the hands of the righteous, and they will cut off your necks, and they will kill you and not spare you."[40] Jesus' righteous followers will be rewarded after the eschatological judgment. However, their reward includes neither the pleasure nor responsibility of exercising judgment on the unrighteous.

Jesus' disciples are to be peacemakers who are willing to suffer, even to lose their lives for Jesus' sake (Matt 10:29). As the disciples go out on their missionary journey, they are to let their peace be upon the houses which are worthy. To those that are not, the disciples are to "let

35. Davies and Allison, *Matthew 1–7*, 458.

36. Hagner, *Matthew 1–13*, 291.

37. For example, Matt 10:16–23 and 24:9–13 in which Jesus describes the persecutions his followers will face.

38. For example, Matt 21:33–44, the parable of the tenants; Matt 24:48–51, the parable of the unfaithful servant; Matt 25:31–46, the judgment of the nations.

39. *1 Enoch: A New Translation*, 142.

40. Ibid., 151.

your peace return to you" and "shake the dust from your feet" (Matt 10:13–14 NRSV). They are not instructed to punish or commit violence against those who reject them. Towns that do not receive the disciples will be punished "on the day of judgment" (Matt 10:15). When one of those with Jesus at his arrest draws a sword and cuts off the ear of the slave of the high priest, Jesus tells him to put his sword away, saying, "all who take the sword will perish by the sword" (Matt 26:51–52 NRSV). Jesus says that he does not need the protection of the sword; he could at any time have the defense of angels if he chose (Matt 26:53). Unlike the watchers' and giants' violent and warlike destructiveness, Jesus preaches a message of peace.

The Watchers' Legacy of Disease Versus Jesus' Healing

The spirits of the giants bring disease into the world, but Jesus cures disease and casts out demons. Part of the legacy of the watchers and giants according to the Enochic template is the presence of evil spirits that plague humankind. The evil spirits "lead astray, do violence, make desolate, and attack and wrestle and hurl upon the earth and cause illnesses" (1 En. 15:11).[41] As in the Gospels of Mark and Luke, Jesus is shown in Matthew as one who casts out demons and heals illness and disease. For example, Jesus' activity is summarized in Matt 4:23: "Jesus went throughout Galilee, teaching in their synagogues and proclaiming the good news of the kingdom and curing every disease and every sickness among the people" (NRSV; καὶ θεραπεύων πᾶσαν νόσον καὶ πᾶσαν μαλακίαν ἐν τῷ λαῷ). It is interesting to note that Jesus cures "every" disease and "every" sickness in Matthew's version. Matthew appears to have improved on Jesus' healing abilities as they are described in Mark where Jesus is less all-encompassing in his abilities and "heals many (πολλούς) who were sick with various diseases" (Mark 1:34 NRSV), rather than all of them as in Matthew. In Luke, Jesus is all-inclusive in his ability to heal, although the emphasis seems to be on his healing by means of touching each of them, as opposed to merely reporting his successful healing of all of them: "all those with various diseases they brought to him and laying his hands on each of them, he was healing them" (Luke 4:41 NRSV). Matthew is not interested in reporting how

41. Ibid., 37.

Jesus healed them, for example, by touching them as in Luke, just on reporting Jesus' success. Similarly, in describing Jesus' ability to cast out demons, Matthew provides a comprehensive list of all of those Jesus heals, including "all the sick, those afflicted with various diseases and pains, demoniacs, epileptics, and paralytics, and he healed them" (Matt 4:24 NRSV). The parallel passages in Mark and Luke mention only that he "cast out many demons" (Mark 1:34 NRSV) and that "demons also came out of many" (Luke 4:41 NRSV). In both Mark and Luke, Jesus also forbids the demons to speak because they know his identity. Thus, with Mark and Luke, Jesus is portrayed as a healer and one who casts out demons. However, Matthew's goal seems to be to portray Jesus as one with complete ability to heal diseases and exorcise demons.[42] Matthew gives five summary statements of occasions when Jesus heals people (ἐθεράπευσεν αὐτους), in Matt 4:24 ("they brought to him all . . . and he healed them," προσήνεγκαν αὐτῷ πάντας . . . καὶ ἐθεράπευσεν αὐτούς); 12:15 ("he healed them all," ἐθεράπευσεν αὐτοὺς πάντας); 15:30 ("great crowds approached him, having with them the lame, blind, crippled, mute, and many others . . . and he healed them," προσῆλθον αὐτῷ ὄχλοι πολλοὶ ἔχοντες μεθ' ἑαυτῶν χωλούς, τυφλούς, κυλλούς, κωφούς, καὶ ἑτέρους πολλούς . . . καὶ ἐθεράπευσεν αὐτούς); 19:2 ("a great crowd followed them, and he healed them there," ἠκολούθησαν αὐτῷ ὄχλοι πολλοί, καὶ ἐθεράπευσεν αὐτοὺς ἐκεῖ); and 21:14 ("the blind and lame approached him . . . and he healed them," προσῆλθον αυτῷ τυφλοὶ καὶ χωλοὶ . . . καὶ ἐθεράπευσεν αὐτούς).[43] In these occasions, Matthew's purpose is to show Jesus as a prolific healer rather than to provide any details about the people who are healed and few details about what diseases he heals. The verb θεραπεύω is used in a summary

---

42. The exception, noted above, was in Jesus' hometown, where he does not do many deeds of power because of the people's lack of faith (Matt 13:54–58). Matthew has, however, portrayed Jesus in a more powerful light than has Mark in the parallel passage in which Jesus "was not able to do any deed of power there, except that he laid his hands on a few sick people and cured them" (Mark 6:5).

43. Davies and Allison regard the use of the verb θεραπεύω + πᾶς, "to heal all" as editorial in Matthew. The combination does not appear in Mark or Luke, but appears five times in Matthew (*Matthew 1–7*, 78). The five occasions are in 4:24; 8:16; 9:35; 10:1 (Jesus gives authority to the twelve to heal every disease and sickness); 12:15.

statement only once in Luke (Luke 4:40[44]) and not at all in Mark.[45] Jesus is portrayed in Matthew as healing many individuals as well, including the centurion's child (Matt 8:7); Peter's mother-in-law (Matt 8:14); a man with a withered hand (Matt 12:10–13); a demon-possessed man who was blind and mute (Matt 12:22); an epileptic boy with a demon (Matt 17:18); and some lame people (Matt 21:14).

Jesus also exorcises people of their demons (in addition to the occasions mentioned in the preceding paragraphs in which the emphasis is on the healing of the people's demon-caused illness). In Matthew, Jesus casts out spirits (ἐξέβαλεν τὰ πνεύματα) from demon-possessed people (δαιμονιζομένους) in 8:16; in 8:28–34, he casts out demons (δαίμονες) from two demon-possessed Gadarene men; in 9:32 he casts out demons (δαίμονες) from a mute man; in 15:28, he heals the demon-possessed daughter of the Canaanite woman.

Jesus repairs the legacy of the giants and their evil spirits who cause illness and disease among humans; he cures every disease and casts out demons. However, in Jesus' repair of the Enochic template, Matthew shows a progression from the presence of magical arts to the irrelevance of magical arts. The magi who appear to worship the child Jesus are associated with the skills taught by the watchers including pharmacological skills and the casting of spells. While these skills are illicit in the Enochic template and among the skills that lead to destruction and evil in the world, they are also skills which could be used in the service of protecting oneself and others from evil and sickness. The magi are associated with these skills, although the magi are not shown practicing them in Matthew's Gospel. When Jesus heals and casts out demons, he is shown by Matthew as not saying or using anything that might be interpreted as connected with magical skills, such as special words or spells. Jesus does not need extra magical tools to do exorcisms or healings. He is shown as having all the power he needs in himself. His followers are given his power to do what he does, but they are given no words, tools, or magical instructions. Jesus gives his disciples "authority" (ἐξουσία) over unclean spirits and to cure every disease and illness (Matt 10:1). Jesus is not another watcher, even if a well-meaning one, passing along better versions of the skills he taught. Jesus com-

44. "and laying hands on each one of them, he was healing them" (ὁ δὲ ἑνὶ ἑκάστῳ αὐτῶν τὰς χεῖρας ἐπιτιθεὶς ἐθεράπευεν αὐτούς).

45. Davies and Allison, *Matthew 1–7*, 418.

pletely surpasses what the watchers knew and taught as he repairs the results of their transgression. Seeing the watchers' template behind Matthew's portrayal of Jesus helps explain why Matthew so completely purges anything that could be interpreted as magical from his accounts of Jesus' healings. Matthew's purgation of magical elements is evident in a comparison with Marcan stories about healings and exorcisms.[46] For example, Mark's healing accounts contain some word of power or saying that Jesus uses when he heals; while Matthew keeps Jesus' speech to a minimum.[47] In Matthew's versions there are no techniques or words for his followers to learn. As Hull writes, "The spirits have not been exorcized by a wonder worker; they have perished for ever before the face of Messiah."[48] Jesus is portrayed in Matthew as the one who can cast out every demon and heal every disease, repairing the results of the watchers' transgression. However, in Matthew he is not a magician, making

46. A similar point can be made when comparing Matt 4:23–24 with Luke 4:41 (mentioned above): in Matthew, Jesus heals people with no mention of the means by which he heals; in Luke, Jesus was "laying his hands on each of them" in order to heal them.

47. Compare Matt 8:23–27 with Mark 4:35–40. Jesus "rebuked the winds and the sea" in Matthew. In Mark's account, Jesus speaks these words: "Peace! Be still." When Jesus heals the Gadarene demoniacs in Matthew's account, he says to the demons merely, "Go then!" (Matt 8:32). In Mark's account, the reader is told the words Jesus was using to exorcise the demons: "He had been saying to him, 'Unclean spirit, come out of the man!" (Mark 5:8). When Jesus raises from the dead the daughter of the official, Matthew simply narrates that Jesus took her by the hand and she got up (Matt 9:25). In Mark's version, Jesus says, "*Talitha koum*" (Mark 5:41). When Jesus heals a boy with a demon in Matt 17:14–20, Matthew reports "Jesus rebuked him and the demon came out of him" (Matt 17:18). In Mark's version, Jesus says, "Mute and deaf spirit, I command you: come out of him and never enter him again" (Mark 9:25). Matthew gives fewer details than Mark does about the boy's condition and the effects of the demon on him (see Mark 9:14–29). Matthew expands the interchange between Jesus and the disciples following Jesus' successful exorcism from Mark's version in which Jesus responds to the disciples' question of why they were not able to exorcise the demon, "This kind can come out only through prayer" (Mark 9:29). In Matthew the event becomes an opportunity for Jesus to teach the disciples about faith through the image of the mustard seed (Matt 17:20). Matthew does not show Jesus using spittle to heal, as Mark does in Mark 7:31–35 (the healing of a deaf man through spitting, touching the man's ears and tongue and saying, "*Ephphatha*") and in Mark 8:22–25 (healing the blind man of Bethsaida through putting spittle on his eyes and laying hands on him, twice). Rather, when Matthew recounts the healing of two blind men, Jesus touches them and they can see (Matt 20:30–34).

48. Hull, *Hellenistic Magic*, 132. See Hull's book for an exploration of the way magic is presented in Mark, Luke, and Matthew, especially chs. 5–7 (pp. 73–141).

use of spells and techniques that may be passed along to his followers. He is the one with authority over demons and disease.

The Watchers' Legacy of Idolatry versus Jesus' True Worship

The watchers are responsible for idolatry and false worship through their part in bringing evil spirits into the world, but Jesus shows true worship. According to the Enochic watchers' template, evil spirits are responsible for leading people to commit idolatry. In contrast, Matthew shows Jesus engage in true worship and teaching his followers to do likewise. Jesus himself, in the temptation in the wilderness, refuses to engage in false worship of the devil (Matt 4:1–11, especially 9–10). Jesus engages in prayer in Matt 14:23 and 26:36–44 (in Gethsemane). Jesus derides the false worship of hypocrites who give alms, pray, and fast in such a way as to attract attention to themselves (Matt 6:2, 5, 16), and the hypocrisy of the scribes and Pharisees who teach their own teachings as coming from God, even though they are just human teachings (Matt 15:9; quoting Isa 29:13).

The Gospel of Matthew itself is noted by some commentators as being very concerned with the liturgy of the Matthean community.[49] Stanton states that Matthew's Gospel provided the Matthean community with a prayer of Jesus (Matt 6:9–13) "which probably became central in their worship quite soon,"[50] as well as instruction in almsgiving, prayer, and fasting in Matthew 6. Also, Jesus' teaching on baptism and the eucharist in Matthew reflect a liturgical re-shaping of the Markan tradition.[51] Gail O'Day describes how the story of the Canaanite woman may have been shaped by Matthew to reflect the form of the Lament Psalm,[52] inviting the readers of Matthew's Gospel to see the story as an example of reliance on the promises of God as known from this form of scripture. Unlike the watchers' legacy, which leads to false worship and idolatry, Jesus is portrayed in Matthew as being concerned himself and

---

49. Allison writes that the Gospel was written with "liturgical ends in view" (Allison, *New Moses*, 139).

50. Stanton, *Gospel for a New People*, 383.

51. Ibid.

52. See O'Day, "Surprised by Faith," 114–25.

on behalf of his community for proper worship. The Gospel of Matthew itself reflects liturgical concern.

These six thematic examples show ways in which Matthew's portrayal of Jesus is written in ways that show the watchers' transgression redressed by Jesus. The evil and destruction that they put into motion is overcome by Jesus who acts in ways contrary to the Enochic template or in ways that the evil resulting from the Enochic template is conquered.

Summary

The first chapters of Matthew's Gospel in which Jesus' genealogy and infancy are described set the stage for the adult life and ministry of Jesus. An examination of the teaching and activity of the Jesus introduced in the opening chapters of the Gospel shows that Jesus is portrayed throughout his life in such a way as to repair the results of the watchers' transgression. Specifically, the watchers leave a legacy of illicit teaching, monstrous offspring and their evil spirits, illicit sexual encounters, violence, and idolatry. The product of Mary and the Holy Spirit's union, Jesus, also engages in pedagogy, but righteous pedagogy, and reconfigures a family with divine origins. His teaching concerns righteousness, including in regard to sexual interaction, but even avoidance of sexual interaction if possible. Rather than violence, Jesus' teaching promotes a radical nonviolence. Jesus is a healer and casts out demons. In terms of worship, Jesus teaches against idolatry and promotes correct worship of God alone. The adult Jesus, very much in continuity with his identity as laid out by Matthew in the genealogy and infancy narrative, counters the watchers' fall through his teaching of righteousness, including in regard to sexuality, his teaching of nonviolence, his casting out demons and healing, and his promotion of correct worship.

6

Conclusions

The evangelist responsible for the Gospel according to Matthew was familiar with and made use of Enochic traditions, including the Enochic story of the watchers' fall. Matthew's familiarity with Enochic motifs, particularly the story of the watchers' transgression, shows through his telling the story of Jesus to show that Jesus repairs the watchers' transgression and redresses the negative consequences of the watchers' fall. That the Enochic watchers' template is in the background of Matthew's Gospel can be seen in the first two chapters of the Gospel, Matthew's genealogy of Jesus and the infancy narrative.

The watchers' transgression involves illicit sexual relationships between watchers and women and the watchers' illicit pedagogy of women. Matthew shows that Jesus reverses the effects of the illicit relationships and illicit pedagogy of the rebel angels. Jesus' repair of the watchers' transgression shows especially in the mention of women in Jesus' genealogy; in the birth of Jesus who is the product of a heavenly being who is perhaps conceived of as angelomorphic and a woman, but without any kind of sexual relations; and in the stories of the adult Jesus, including those about his interaction with women. Even if one restricts inquiry to the women in the genealogy and infancy narrative and the women they foreshadow in the Gospel text, one finds many women whose stories reflect elements of the Enochic watchers' template and its repair. The women mentioned in this book are in chapter 3: Tamar (Matt 1:3; Genesis 38), Rahab (Matt 1:5; Joshua 2), Ruth (Matt 1:5; Ruth), Bathsheba (Matt 1:6; 2 Sam 11:1–27; 2 Sam 12:24–25; 1 Kgs 1:11–40; 1 Kgs 2:13–26), and the Canaanite woman (Matt 15:21–28); in chapter 4: Mary (Matt 1:16; 18–25), the woman with the hemorrhage who touches the fringe of Jesus' garment (Matt 9:20–22), and the wife of Pilate (Matt 27:19). When I examine, even briefly, as in chapter 5, how the adult Jesus carries forward the repair of the watchers' transgression, I add these women the list: women as members of families that will be divided or abandoned because of Jesus (Matt 10:35–37; Matt 19:29), women who do the will of God as Jesus' family members (Matt 12:50), women present in the synagogue where Jesus teaches but the event is a disaster (Matt 13:54–58), women in the crowds in the feeding stories (Matt 14:14–21; 15:29–38), and the women at the cross and tomb of Jesus (Matt 27:55–56; 28:1–10).

Other elements of Matthew's infancy narrative that demonstrate the repair of the Enochic watchers' template involving male characters are Joseph's suspicion of Mary's pregnancy, the revelatory dreams of Joseph and the magi, and the magi who follow a star and bring gifts to the Christ child.

As can be seen by the brief overview of Matthew's Gospel after its first two chapters, further study of Matthew's Gospel in light of the Enochic watchers' template and related motifs from *1 Enoch* could result in many more instances in which Enochic motifs form part of the backdrop for Matthew's work.

The examination of Matthew's genealogy and infancy narrative through the lens of the Enochic watchers' template and other related motifs from *1 Enoch* yields these results: first, Matthew made use of a broader range of Jewish apocalyptic literature than has previously been noted, and his use of motifs from *1 Enoch* includes material that is widely accepted as pre-dating the composition of the gospels. Second, Matthew's use of apocalyptic motifs appears even in the first two chapters of Matthew's Gospel. Third, women in Matthew's Gospel play a significant role in demonstrating Jesus' repair of the watchers' transgression. Fourth, Matthew has a polemical purpose when he makes use of Enochic motifs: the evangelist shows that Jesus completes the repair of the watchers' transgression—a repair, which in *1 Enoch*, even the great patriarch Enoch could only predict.

Bibliography

Primary Texts, Translations, and Reference Works

Aberbach, Moses, and Bernard Grossfeld. *Targum Onqelos on Genesis 49*. Society of Biblical Literature Aramaic Studies 1. Missoula, MT: Scholars, 1976.

Aland, Kurt, editor. *Synopsis Quattuor Evangeliorum*. 10th ed. Stuttgart: Deutsche Bibelstiftung, 1978.

Arndt, William F., and F. Wilbur Gingrich, editors. *A Greek-English Lexicon of the New Testament and Other Early Christian Literature: a Translation and adaptation of Walter Bauer's Grieschisch-deutsches Wörterbuch zu den Schriften des Neuen Testaments und der übrigen urchristlichen Literatur*. 2nd ed., rev. and aug. by F. Wilbur Gingrich and Frederick W. Danker from Walter Bauer's 5th ed., 1958.

The Ante-Nicene Fathers. Edited by Alexander Roberts and James Donaldson. 1885–87. 10 vols. Repr., Peabody, MA: Hendrickson, 1994.

The Babylonian Talmud: Seder Kodashim. Vol. I. Translated and edited by Isidore Epstein. London: Soncino, 1948.

The Babylonian Talmud: Seder Mo'ed. Vol. IV. Translated and edited by Isidore Epstein. London: Soncino, 1938.

The Babylonian Talmud: Seder Nashim. Vol. III. Translated and edited by Isidore Epstein. London: Soncino, 1936.

Bauer, Walter. *A Greek-English Lexicon of the New Testament and Other Early Christian Literature*. Edited by F. W. Gingrich and F. Danker. 2nd ed. Rev. and aug. ed. Chicago: University of Chicago Press, 1979.

Biblia Hebraica Stuttgartensia. Stuttgart: Deutsche Bibelgesellshaft, 1977.

Blass, Friedrich, and Albert Debrunner. *A Greek Grammar of the New Testament and Other Early Christian Literature*. Translated by Robert W. Funk. Rev. ed. Chicago: University of Chicago Press, 1961.

The Book of Jubilees: A Critical Text. Translated by James C. VanderKam. Corpus Scriptorum Christianorum Orientalum 511. Scriptores Aethiopici 88. Louvain: Peeters, 1989.

Botterweck, G. Johannes, Helmer Ringgren, and Heinz-Josef Fabry, editors. *Theological Dictionary of the Old Testament*. Translated by Douglas W. Stott. Grand Rapids: Eerdmans, 2003.

Brown, Francis, et al. *The New Brown, Driver, Briggs Hebrew and English Lexicon of the Old Testament with an Appendix Containing the Biblical Aramaic*. Peabody, MA: Hendrickson, 1979.

Buttrick, George Author, editor. *Interpreter's Dictionary of the Bible.* 4 vols. New York: Abingdon, 1962.

Cassiodorus. *Explanation of the Psalms* I. Translated by Patrick G. Walsh. Ancient Christian Writers 51. Mahwah, NJ: Paulist, 1990.

Charlesworth, James H., editor. *Apocalyptic Literature and Testaments.* Vol. 1 of *The Old Testament Pseudepigrapha.* New York: Doubleday, 1983.

————. *Expansions of the "Old Testament" and Legends, Wisdom and Philosophical Literature, Prayers, Psalms and Odes, Fragments of Lost Judeo-Hellenistic Works.* Vol. 2 of *The Old Testament Pseudepigrapha.* New York: Doubleday, 1985.

Cyprian. *Treatises.* Translated by Angela Elizabeth Keenan. The Fathers of the Church 36; New York: Fathers of the Church, 1958.

Einspahr, Bruce. *Index to Brown, Driver & Briggs Hebrew Lexicon.* Chicago: Moody Press, 1976.

1 Enoch: A New Translation. Translated by George W. E. Nickelsburg and James C. VanderKam. Minneapolis: Fortress, 2004.

Euripides. *Children of Heracles; Hippolytus; Andromache; Hecuba.* Translated and edited by David Kovacs. Loeb Classical Library 484. Cambridge, MA: Harvard University Press, 1995.

————. *The Dramas of Euripides: Complete Surviving Works, 19 Plays.* Forgotten Books, 2007

————. *Orestes.* Translated by John Peck and Frank Nisetich. Greek Tragedy in New Translations. Oxford: Oxford University Press, 1995.

Freedman, David Noel, editor. *The Anchor Bible Dictionary.* 6 vols. New York: Doubleday, 1992.

García Martínez, Florentino, and Eibert J. C. Tigchelaar. *The Dead Sea Scrolls Study Edition.* 2 vols. Leiden: Brill, 1997–2000.

Herodotus. *The Histories.* Translated by Aubrey de Sélincourt. Revised by A. R. Burn. New York: Penguin, 1980.

Hippocrates. *On the Sacred Disease.* Translated by William Henry Samuel Jones. 8 vols. Loeb Classical Library. Cambridge, MA: Harvard University Press, 1923.

Hollander, Harm W., and Marinus de Jonge. *The Testaments of the Twelve Patriarchs: A Commentary.* Studia in Veteris Testamenti Pseudepigrapha 8. Edited by A.-M. Denis and Marinus De Jonge. Leiden: Brill, 1985.

Holmes, Michael W. *The Apostolic Fathers: Greek Texts and English Translations.* 3rd ed. Grand Rapids: Baker Academic, 2007.

Homer, *The Odyssey.* Edited by Bernard Knox. Translated by Robert Fagles. New York: Penguin Classics, 1996.

Jastrow, Marcus. *Dictionary of the Targumim, Talmud Babli, Yerushalmi and Midrashic Literature.* New York: Judaica, 1985.

Josephus, Flavius. *The Complete Works of Josephus: Complete and Unabridged.* Translated by William Whiston. New updated ed. Peabody, MA: Hendrickson, 1987.

Kittel, Gerhard, and Gerhard Friedrich, editors. *Theological Dictionary of the New Testament.* Translated by Geoffrey W. Bromiley. 10 vols. Grand Rapids: Eerdmans, 1964–76.

Knibb, Michael A. *The Ethiopic Book of Enoch: A New Edition in Light of the Aramaic Dead Sea Fragments.* 2 vols. Oxford: Clarendon, 1978.

Kohler, Ludwig, and Walter Baumgartner. *The Hebrew and Aramaic Lexicon of the Old Testament*. Leiden: Brill, 1994.

Metzger, Bruce, and Roland E. Murphy, editors. *The New Oxford Annotated Bible with the Apocrypha: An Ecumenical Study Bible*. NRSV. Rev. and enl. ed. New York: Oxford University Press, 1991.

Metzger, Bruce. *A Textual Commentary on the Greek New Testament: A Companion Volume to the United Bible Societies' Greek New Testament (Fourth rev. ed.)*. 2nd ed. Stuttgart: Deutsche Bibelgesellshaft, 1994.

Midraš Berešit Rabba. Edited by J. Theodor and Albeck. Berlin: Defus Tsevi Hirsch Ittskavski, 1903–36; repr., Jerusalem: Wahrmann, 1965.

Midrash Rabbah Genesis. 2 vols. Translated by Harry Freedman and Maurice Simon. London: Soncino, 1983.

Midrash Rabbah Numbers. 2 vols. Translated by Judah J. Slotki. London: Soncino, 1983.

Midrash Rabbah Ruth. Edited by Harry Freedman and Maurice Simon. Translated by L. Rabinowitz. 3rd ed. London: Soncino, 1983.

New Revised Standard Version. Division of Christian Education of the National Council of Churches of Christ in the United States of America, 1989.

Novum Testamentum Graece. Edited by Eberhard Nestle, Kurt Aland, et al. 26th ed. Stuttgart: Deutsche Bibelgesellshaft, 1979.

The Old Testament Pseudepigrapha. Edited by James H. Charlesworth. 2 vols. Garden City, NY: Doubleday, 1983–1985.

Origen. *Homilies on Numbers*. Ancient Christian Texts. Edited by Christopher A. Hall. Translated by Thomas P. Scheck. Downers Grove, IL: Intervarsity Academic, 2009.

Pausanias. *Description of Greece*. Translated by William Henry Samuel Jones. 2 vols. Loeb Classical Library. London: William Heinemann, 1918.

Philo. Translated by Francis Henry Colson. 10 vols. Loeb Classical Library. Cambridge, MA: Harvard University, 1929–67.

Philotheus. *The History of the Blessed Virgin Mary*. Edited and translated by E. A. Wallis Budge. Semitic Text and Translation Series 5. London: Luzac, 1899.

Roberts, Alexander, and James Donaldson, editors. *Fathers of the Second Century: Hermas, Tatian, Athenogoras, Theophilus, and Clement of Alexandria*. The Ante-Nicene Fathers: Translations of the Writings of the Fathers down to A. D. 325. Repr. Rev. by A. Cleveland Coxe. Grand Rapids: Eerdmans, 1983.

Septuaginta. Edited by Alfred Rahlfs. Stuttgart: Deutsche Bibelgesellshaft, 1979.

Sophocles. *Three Theban Plays: Antigone, Oedipus the King, Oedipus at Colonus*. Translated by Robert Fagles. New York: Penguin Classics, 2000.

Targum Neofiti 1: Genesis. The Aramaic Bible 1A. Translated, with apparatus and notes by Martin McNamara. Collegeville, MN: Liturgical, 1992.

Targum Pseudo-Jonathan: Genesis. The Aramaic Bible 1B. Translated, with introduction and notes by Michael Maher. Collegeville, MN: Liturgical, 1992.

Tertullian. *Disciplinary, Moral and Ascetical Works*. Translated by Rudolph Arbesmann, Emily Joseph Daly, and Edwin A. Quain. The Fathers of the Church 40. New York: Fathers of the Church, 1959.

Vermes, Geza. *The Dead Sea Scrolls in English*. 3rd ed. Harmondsworth, UK: Penguin, 1987.

Whiston, William. *The Complete Works of Josephus: Complete and Unabridged.* Translated by William Whiston. New and updated ed. Peabody, MA: Hendrickson, 1987.

Wright, Robert B., editor. *The Psalms of Solomon: A Critical Edition of the Greek Text* Jewish and Christian Texts in Contexts and Related Studies 1. London: T. & T. Clark, 2007.

Xenophon. *Cryopaedia.* Translated by Walter Miller. 2 vols. Loeb Classical Library. London: William Heinemann, 1914.

Secondary Works

Abel, Ernest L. "Who Wrote Matthew?" *New Testament Studies* 17 (1970/71) 138–52.

Ackerman, Susan. "The Queen Mother and the Cult in Ancient Israel." Pages 179–94 in *Women in the Hebrew Bible: A Reader.* Edited by Alice Bach. New York: Routledge, 1999.

Adler, William. "Introduction." Pages 1–31 in *The Jewish Apocalyptic Heritage in Early Christianity.* Edited by James C. VanderKam and William Adler. Assen, The Netherlands: Van Gorcum, 1996.

Ahlström, Gösta W. *Aspects of Syncretism in Israelite Religion.* Translated by Eric J. Sharpe. Lund: C. W. K. Gleerup, 1963.

Albright, William F. "The Egyptian Empire in Asia in the Twenty-First Century B.C." *Journal of the Palestine Oriental Society* 8 (1928) 226–30.

Alexander, Philip S. "The Targumim and Early Exegesis of 'Sons of God' in Gen 6." *Journal of Jewish Studies* 23 (1972) 60–71.

Allison, Dale C., Jr. "The Eschatology of Jesus." Pages 267–302 in *The Encyclopedia of Apocalypticism.* Edited by John J. Collins. New York: Continuum, 1998.

———. *The End of the Ages Has Come: An Early Interpretation of the Passion and Resurrection of Jesus.* Philadelphia: Fortress, 1985.

———. "The Magi's Angel (Matt. 2:2, 9, 10)." Pages 17–41 in *Studies in Matthew: Interpretation Past and Present.* Grand Rapids: Baker Academic, 2005.

———. *The New Moses: A Matthean Typology.* Minneapolis: Fortress, 1993.

Alter, Robert. *The Art of Biblical Narrative.* New York: Basic, 1981.

———. "From Line to Story in Biblical Verse." *Poetics Today* 4 (1983) 615–37.

———. *Genesis: Translation and Commentary.* New York: Norton, 1996.

Anderson, Janice Capel. "Matthew: Gender and Reading." Pages 3–27 in *The Bible and Feminist Hermeneutics.* Edited by Mary Ann Tolbert. *Semeia* 28.1 (1983) 3–27. Repr. Pages 25–51 in *A Feminist Companion to Matthew.* Edited by Amy-Jill Levine with Marianne Blickenstaff. Cleveland: Pilgrim, 2001.

Andreasen, Neils-Erik A. "The Role of Queen Mother in Israelite Society." *Catholic Biblical Quarterly* 45 (1983) 179–94.

Astour, Michael C. "Tamar the Hierodule: an Essay in the Method of Vestigial Motifs." *Journal of Biblical Literature* 85.2 (1966) 185–96.

Avigad, Nahman, and Yigael Yadin. *The Genesis Apocryphon: A Scroll from the Wilderness of Judaea.* Jerusalem: Magnes, 1956.

Baby, Parambi. *The Discipleship of the Women in the Gospel according to Matthew: An Exegetical Theological Study of Matt. 27:51b–56, 57 –61 and 28:1–10.* Tesi Gregoriana. Serie Teologia 94. Rome: Pontificia Università Gregoriana, 2003.

Bacon, Benjamin Wisner. "The 'Five Books' of Moses against the Jews." *Expositor* 15 (1918) 56–66.

Bamfylde, Gillian. "The Similitudes of Enoch: Historical Allusions." *Journal for the Study of Judaism* 15 (1984) 9–31.

Bartelmus, Rüdiger. *Heroentum in Israel und seiner Umwelt:eine traditionsgeschichtliche Untersuchung zu Gen. 6, 1–4 und verwandten Texten im Alten Testament und der altorientalischen Literatur.* Abhandlungen zur Theologie des Alten und Neuen Testaments 65. Zürich: Theologischer Verlag, 1979.

Baskin, Judith. "The Rabbinic Transformation of Rahab the Harlot." *Notre Dame English Journal* 11 (1979) 141–57.

Bauckham, Richard. "Tamar's Ancestry and Rahab's Marriage: Two Problems in the Matthean Genealogy." *Novum Testamentum* 37 (1995) 313–29.

Bautch, Kelley Coblentz. "Situating the Afterlife." Pages 249–64 in *Paradise Now: Essays on Early Jewish and Christian Mysticism.* Edited by April D. DeConick. Society of Biblical Literature Symposium Series 11. Leiden: Brill, 2006.

———. "What Becomes of the Angels' 'Wives?' A Text-Critical Study of Enoch 19:2." *Journal of Biblical Literature* 125:4 (2006) 766–80.

Beare, Francis Wright. *The Earliest Records: A Companion to the First Three Gospels.* Oxford: Blackwell, 1962.

———. *The Gospel According to Matthew: Translation, Introduction and Commentary.* San Francisco: Harper & Row, 1982.

———. "The Synoptic Apocalypse: Matthean Version." Pages 113–33 in *Understanding the Sacred Text: Essays in Honor of Morton S. Enslin on the Hebrew Bible and Christian Beginnings.* Edited by John Reumann. Valley Forge, PA: Judson, 1972.

Ben-Barak, Zafrira. "The Queen Consort and the Struggle for Succession to the Throne." Pages 33–40 in *La femme dans le Proche-Orient antique.* Comte rendu de la XXXIIIe Rencontre assyriologique internationale (Paris, 7–10 juillet 1986). Edited by J.-M. Durand. Paris: Recherche sur les Civilisations, 1987.

———. "The Status and Right of the *Gĕbîrâ.*" *Journal of Biblical Literature* 110 (1991) 23–34.

Berstein, Moshe J. "Divine Titles and Epithets and the Sources of the *Genesis Apocryphon.*" *Journal of Biblical Literature* 128:2 (2009) 291–310.

Bickerman, Elias J. "Darius I, Pseudo Smerdis, and the Magi." *Athenaeum* 56 (1978) 239–61.

Bird, Phyllis A. *Missing Persons and Mistaken Identities: Women and Gender in Ancient Israel.* Overtures to Biblical Theology. Minneapolis: Fortress, 1997.

Black, Jeremy, and Green, Anthony. *Gods, Demons and Symbols of Ancient Mesopotamia.* Austin: University of Texas Press, 2000.

Black, Matthew. *The Book of Enoch or 1 Enoch: A New English Edition.* Leiden: Brill, 1985.

Boccaccini, Gabriele, editor. *Enoch the Messiah Son of Man: Revisiting the Book of Parables.* Grand Rapids: Eerdmans, 2007.

———. *Roots of Rabbinic Judaism: An Intellectual History, from Ezekiel to Daniel.* Grand Rapids: Eerdmans, 2002.

Bonnard, Pierre. *L'Évangile selon Matthieu.* Paris: Delachaux & Niestlé, 1963.

Boomershine, Thomas E. "Epistemology at the Turn of the Ages in Paul, Jesus, and Mark: Rhetoric and Dialectic in Apocalyptic and the New Testament." Pages 147–67 in *Apocalyptic and the New Testament: Essays in Honor of J. Louis Martyn.* Edited by Joel Marcus and Marion L. Soards. Journal for the Study of the New Testament Supplement Series 24. Sheffield: Sheffield Academic, 1989.

Bornkamm, Günther, Gerhard Barth, and Heinz Joachim Held. *Tradition and Interpretation in Matthew.* Translated by Percy Scott. Philadelphia: Westminster, 1963.

Bottéro, Jean. *Religion in Ancient Mesopotamia.* Chicago: University of Chicago Press, 2001.

Böttrich, Christfried. "Astrologie in der Henochtradition." *Zeitschrift für die Alttestamentliche Wissenschaft* 190 (1997) 222–45.

Bovon, François. "These Christians Who Dream: The Authority of Dreams in the First Centuries of Christianity." Pages 144–62 in *Studies in Early Christianity.* Edited by François Bovon. Grand Rapids: Baker Academic, 2003.

Branden, Robert Charles. *Satanic Conflict and the Plot of Matthew.* Studies in Biblical Literature 89. New York: Peter Lang, 2006.

Bronner, Leila Leah. *From Eve to Esther: Rabbinic Reconstructions of Biblical Women.* Gender and the Biblical Tradition. Louisville: Westminster John Knox, 1994.

Brooks, Stephenson H. *Matthew's Community: The Evidence of His Special Sayings Material.* Journal for the Study of the New Testament Supplement Series 16. Sheffield: Journal for the Study of the Old Testament, 1987.

Brower, Kent. "Jesus and the Lustful Eye: Glancing at Matthew 5:28." *Evangelical Quarterly* 76 (2004) 291–301.

Brown, Raymond E. *The Birth of the Messiah: A Commentary on the Infancy Narratives in Matthew and Luke.* Edited by David Noel Freedman. New updated ed. Anchor Bible Reference Library. New York: Doubleday, 1993.

———. *The Death of the Messiah: From Gethsemane to the Grave: A Commentary on the Passion Narratives.* 2 vols. New York: Doubleday, 1994.

———. "The Meaning of the Magi; the Significance of the Star." *Worship* 49 (1975) 574–82.

Brown, Schuyler. "The Matthean Apocalypse." *Journal for the Study of the New Testament* 4 (1979) 2–27.

Bruns, J. Edgar. "The Magi Episode in Matthew 2." *Catholic Biblical Quarterly* 23 (1961) 51–54.

Bucur, Bogdan G. "The Angelic Spirit in Early Christianity: Justin, the Martyr and Philosopher." *The Journal of Religion* 88 (2008) 190–208.

———. "Hierarchy, Prophecy, and the Angelomorphic Spirit: A Contribution to the Study of the Book of Revelation's *Wirkungsgeschichte.*" *Journal of Biblical Literature* 127 (2008) 173–94.

———. "Matt. 18:10 in Early Christology and Pneumatology: A Contribution to the Study of Matthean *Wirkungsgeschichte.*" *Novum Testamentum* 49 (2007) 209–31.

———. "Revisiting Christian Oeyen: 'The Other Clement' on Father, Son, and the Angelomorphic Spirit." *Vigiliae Christianae* 61 (2007) 381–413.

———. "The Son of God and the Angelomorphic Holy Spirit: A Rereading of the *Shepherd's* Christology." *Zeitschrift für die neutestamentliche Wissenschaft und die Kunde der älteren Kirche* 98 (2007) 120–42.

Capes, David B. "Intertextual Echoes in the Matthean Baptismal Narrative." *Bulletin for Biblical Research* 9 (1999) 37–49.

Carden, Michael. *Sodomy: A History of a Christian Biblical Myth*. London: Equinox, 2004.

Carey, Greg. *Ultimate Things: An Introduction to Jewish and Christian Apocalyptic Literature*. St. Louis: Chalice, 2005.

Carmichael, Calum M. *Women, Law, and the Genesis Traditions*. Edinburgh: Edinburgh University Press, 1979.

Carter, Warren. "Are There Imperial Texts in the Class? Intertextual Eagles and Matthean Eschatology as 'Lights Out' Time for Imperial Rome (Matthew 24:27–31)." *Journal of Biblical Literature* 122 (2003) 467–87.

Caspi, Mishael Maswari, and Sascha Benjamin Cohen. *Still Waters Run Deep: Five Women of the Bible Speak*. Lanham, Md.: University Press of America, 1999.

Cassuto, Umberto. "The Episode of the Sons of God and the Daughters of Man." *Biblical and Oriental Studies*. Translated by Israel Abrahams. Jerusalem: Magnes, 1973, 17–28.

Catchpole, David R. "The Answer of Jesus to Caiaphas (Matt. XXVI. 64)." *New Testament Studies* 17 (1970–71) 213–26.

Charlesworth, James H. "Jewish Astrology in the Talmud, Pseudepigrapha, the Dead Sea Scrolls, and Early Palestinian Synagogues." *Harvard Theological Review* 70 (1977) 183–200.

Clifford, Richard J. "Genesis 38: Its Contribution to the Jacob Story." *Catholic Biblical Quarterly* 66 (2004) 519–32.

Clines, David J. A. "The Significance of the 'Sons of God' Episode (Gen 6:1–4) in the Context of the 'Primeval History' (Gen 1–11)." *Journal for the Study of the Old Testament* 13 (1979) 33–46.

Coats, George W. "Widow's Rights: A Crux in the Structure of Gen. 38." *Catholic Biblical Quarterly* 34 (1972) 461–6.

Collins, Adela Yarbro. *Cosmology and Eschatology in Jewish and Christian Apocalypticism*. Supplements to the Journal for the Study of Judaism 50. Leiden: Brill, 1996.

———. "Introduction: Early Christian Apocalypticism." *Semeia* 36 (1986) 1–11.

———. "The 'Son of Man' Tradition and the Book of Revelation." Pages 536–68 in *The Messiah: Developments in Earliest Judaism and Christianity*. Edited by James H. Charlesworth. Minneapolis: Fortress, 1992.

Collins, John J., editor. *Apocalypse: Morphology of a Genre*. Semeia 14. Missoula, MT: Scholars, 1979.

———. *The Apocalyptic Imagination: An Introduction to Jewish Apocalyptic Literature*. 2nd ed. Grand Rapids: Eerdmans, 1998.

———. *The Apocalyptic Imagination: An Introduction to the Jewish Matrix of Christianity*. New York: Crossroad, 1984.

Cope, O. Lamar. "'To the Close of the Age': The Role of Apocalyptic Thought in the Gospel of Matthew." Pages 113–24 in *Apocalyptic and the New Testament: Essays in Honor of J. Louis Martyn*. Edited by Joel Marcus and Marion L. Soards. Journal for the Study of the New Testament Supplement Series 24. Sheffield: Sheffield Academic, 1989.

Corley, Kathleen E. *Private Women Public Meals: Social Conflict in the Synoptic Tradition*. Peabody, MA: Hendrickson, 1993.

Court, John M. "Right and Left: The Implications for Matthew 25.31–46." *New Testament Studies* 31 (1985) 223–33.

Cummings, J. T. "The Tassel of His Cloak: Mark, Luke, Matthew—and Zechariah." Pages 47–61 in *Studia Biblica* 1978 II. *Papers on the Gospels 2*. Edited by Elizabeth Anne Livingstone. Journal for the Study of the New Testament Supplement 2. Sheffield: Journal for the Study of the Old Testament, 1980.

D'Angelo, Mary Rose. "(Re)Presentations of Women in the Gospel of Matthew and Luke-Acts." Pages 171–95 in *Women and Christian Origins*. Edited by Mary Rose D'Angelo and Ross Shepard Kraemer. New York: Oxford University Press, 1999.

Davies, Eryl W. "Inheritance Rights and the Hebrew Levirate Marriage." *Vetus Testamentum* 31 (1981) 138–44.

Davies, P. G. "Divine Agents, Mediators, and New Testament Christology." *Journal of Theological Studies* 45 (1994) 479–503.

Davies, William D., and Dale C. Allison, Jr. *A Critical and Exegetical Commentary on the Gospel According to Saint Matthew*. Vol. 1 *Introduction and Commentary on Matthew I–VII*. International Critical Commentary. London: T. & T. Clark, 1988.

———. *A Critical and Exegetical Commentary on the Gospel According to Saint Matthew*. Vol. 2 *Introduction and Commentary on Matthew VIII–XVIII*. International Critical Commentary. London: T. & T. Clark, 1988.

———. *A Critical and Exegetical Commentary on the Gospel According to Saint Matthew*. Vol. 3 *Introduction and Commentary on Matthew XIX–XXVIII*. International Critical Commentary. London: T. & T. Clark, 1988.

———. *Matthew: A Shorter Commentary*. Based on the Three-Volume International Critical Commentary. Edited by Dale C. Allison, Jr. London, New York: T. & T. Clark International, 2004.

De Vaux, Roland. *Ancient Israel*. 2 vols. New York: McGraw-Hill, 1965.

Deines, Roland. "Not the Law but the Messiah: Law and Righteousness in the Gospel of Matthew—An Ongoing Debate." Pages 53–84 in *Built upon the Rock: Studies in the Gospel of Matthew*. Edited by Daniel M. Gurtner and John Nolland. Grand Rapids: Eerdmans, 2008.

Derrett, J. Duncan M. "Further Light on the Narratives of the Nativity." *Novum Testamentum* 17 (1975) 81–108.

Deutsch, Celia. "The Therapeutae, Text Work, Ritual, and Mystical Experience." Pages 287–311 in *Paradise Now: Essays on Early Jewish and Christian Mysticism*. Edited by April D. DeConick. Society of Biblical Literature Symposium Series 11. Leiden: Brill, 2006.

Di Tommaso, Lorenzo. "Review of Greg Carey, *Ultimate Things*." *Review of Biblical Literature* 12 (2007). Cited 15 July 2009. Online: http://www.bookreviews.org/pdf/5659_5975.pdf.

Dimant, Devorah. "1 Enoch 6–11: A Fragment of a Parabiblical Work." *Journal of Jewish Studies* 53 (2002) 223–37.

Donahue, John R. "The 'Parable' of the Sheep and the Goats: A Challenge to Christian Ethics." *Theological Studies* 47 (1986) 3–31.

Dupont, Jacques. *Les trois Apocalypses synoptiques: Marc 13; Matthieu 24–25; Luc 21.* Lectio Divina 121. Paris: Cerf, 1985.

Elior, Rachel. *The Three Temples: On the Emergence of Jewish Mysticism.* Translated by David Louvish. Portland, Ore.: Littman Library of Jewish Civilization, 2004.

Endres, John C. *Biblical Interpretation in the Book of Jubilees.* The Catholic Biblical Quarterly Monograph Series 18. Washington, DC: Catholic Biblical Association of America, 1987.

Eslinger, Lyle. "A Contextual Identification of the *bene haʾelohim* and *benoth haʾadam* in Gen 6:1–4." *Journal for the Study of the Old Testament* 13 (1979) 65–73.

False, Evan. "Taming the Tehom: the Sign of Jonah in Matthew." Pages 307–48 in *Empty Tomb: Jesus Beyond the Grave.* Edited by Robert M. Price and Jeffrey Jay Lowder. New York: Prometheus, 2005.

Fenton, John C. *The Gospel of St Matthew.* The Pelican New Testament Commentaries. Baltimore: Penguin, 1963.

Fields, Weston W. *Sodom and Gomorrah: History and Motif in Biblical Narrative.* Journal for the Study of the Old Testament Supplement Series 231. Sheffield: Sheffield Academic, 1997.

Finegan, Jack. *Handbook of Biblical Chronology: Principles of Time Reckoning in the Ancient World and Problems of Chronology in the Bible.* Rev. ed. Peabody, MA: Hendrickson, 1998.

Fisher, Eugene J. "Cultic Prostitution in the Ancient Near East? A Reassessment." *Biblical Theology Bulletin* 6 (1976) 225–36.

Fitzmyer, Joseph A. *The Genesis Apocryphon of Qumran Cave 1 [1 Q20]: A Commentary.* Biblica et Orientalia 18B. 3rd ed. Rome: Pontifical Biblical Institute, 2004.

Flannery-Dailey, Frances. "Lessons on Early Jewish Apocalypticism and Mysticism from Dream Literature." Pages 231–47 in *Paradise Now: Essays on Early Jewish and Christian Mysticism.* Edited by April D. DeConick. Society of Biblical Literature Symposium Series 11. Leiden: Brill, 2006.

Fletcher-Louis, Crispin H. T. "Jesus as the High Priestly Messiah: Part 1." *Journal for the Study of the Historical Jesus* 4 (2006) 155–75.

———. "Jesus as the High Priestly Messiah: Part 2." *Journal for the Study of the Historical Jesus* 5 (2007) 55–99.

———. *Luke-Acts: Angels, Christology and Soteriology.* Tübingen: Mohr Siebeck, 1997.

Fossum, Jarl. "Judaism at the Turn of the Era." Pages 125–36 in *The Biblical World.* Edited by John Barton. New York: Routledge, 2002.

France, Richard T. "On Being Ready (Matthew 25:1–46)." Pages 177–98 in *The Challenge of Jesus' Parables.* Edited by Richard N. Longenecker. Grand Rapids: Eerdmans, 2000.

Freed, Edwin D. *The Stories of Jesus' Birth: A Critical Introduction.* St. Louis: Chalice, 2001.

Frymer-Kensky, Tikva. *Reading the Women of the Bible.* New York: Schoken, 2002.

Gieschen, Charles A. *Angelomorphic Christology: Antecedents and Early Evidence.* Leiden: Brill, 1998.

Gnilka, Joachim. *Das Matthäusevangelium.* Herders Theologischer Kommentar zum Neuen Testament 1/1–2. Freiburg: Herder, 1986–1988.

Gnuse, Robert Karl. "Dream Genre in the Matthean Infancy Narratives." *Novum Testamentum* 32:2 (1990) 97–120.

———. *Dreams and Dream Reports in the Writings of Josephus: A Traditio-Historical Analysis.* Arbeiten zur Geschichte des Antiken Judentums und des Urchristentums 36. Leiden: Brill, 1996.

Good, Edwin M. "The 'Blessing' on Judah, Gen 49:8–12." *Journal of Biblical Literature* 82 (1963) 427–32.

Gray, Sherman W. *The Least of My Brothers: Matthew 25:31–46; A History of Interpretation.* Society for Biblical Literature Dissertation Series 114. Atlanta: Scholars, 1989.

Greenfield, Jonas C., and Elisha Qimron. "Toward a New Edition of *1QGenesis Apocryphon.*" Pages 106–9 in *The Provo International Conference on the Dead Sea Scrolls: Technological Innovations, New Texts, and Reformulated Issues.* Edited by Eugene Ulrich and Donald Parry. Studies on the Texts of the Desert of Judah 30. Leiden: Brill, 1999.

Greenfield, Jonas C., and Michael E. Stone. "The Enochic Pentateuch and the Date of the Similitudes." *Harvard Theological Review* 70 (1977) 51–65.

Guelich, Robert A. "The Matthean Beatitudes: 'Entrance-Requirements' or Eschatological Blessings?" *Journal of Biblical Literature* 95 (1976) 415–34.

Gundry, Robert Horton. *Matthew: A Commentary on His Literary and Theological Art.* Grand Rapids: Eerdmans, 1982.

Gunn, David M., and Danna Nolan Fewell. *Narrative in the Hebrew Bible.* New York: Oxford University Press, 1993.

Hackett, Jo Ann. *The Balaam Text from Deir 'Allā.* Harvard Semitic Monographs 31. Chico, CA: Scholars, 1984.

Hadfield, P. "Matthew the Apocalyptic Editor." *London Quarterly & Holborn Review* 184 (1951) 128–32.

Hagner, Donald Alfred. "Apocalyptic Motifs in the Gospel of Matthew: Continuity and Discontinuity." *Horizons in Biblical Theology* 7:2 (1985) 53–82.

———. *Matthew 1–13.* Word Biblical Commentary 33A. Dallas: Word, 1993.

———. *Matthew 14–28.* Word Biblical Commentary 33B. Dallas: Word, 1995.

———. "Matthew: Apostate, Reformer, Revolutionary?" *New Testament Studies* 49 (2003) 193–209.

———. "Matthew: Christian Judaism or Jewish Christianity?" Pages 263–82 in *The Face of New Testament Studies.* Edited by Scott McKnight and Grant R. Osborne. Grand Rapids: Baker Academic, 2004.

———. "Matthew's Eschatology." Pages 49–71 in *To Tell the Mystery: Essays on New Testament Eschatology in Honor of Robert H. Gundry.* Edited by Thomas E. Schmidt and Moises Silva. Journal for the Study of the New Testament Supplement Series. Sheffield: Sheffield Academic, 1994.

———. "Matthew's Parables of the Kingdom (Matthew 13:1–52)." Pages 102–24 in *The Challenge of Jesus' Parables.* Edited by Richard N. Longenecker. Grand Rapids: Eerdmans, 2000.

———. "Righteousness in Matthew's Theology." Pages 101–20 in *Worship, Theology and Ministry in the Early Church: Essays in Honor of Ralph P. Martin.* Edited by Michael J. Wilkins and Terence Paige. Journal for the Study of the New Testament Supplement Series 87. Sheffield: Journal for the Study of the Old Testament, 1992.

Hamilton, Victor P. *The Book of Genesis: Chapters 1–17.* The New International Commentary on the Old Testament. Grand Rapids: Eerdmans, 1990.

Halpern-Amaru, Betsy. *The Empowerment of Women in the Book of Jubilees.* Supplements to the Journal for the Study of Judaism 60. Leiden: Brill, 1999.

Hanson, Paul D. *The Dawn of Apocalyptic.* Philadelphia: Fortress, 1975.

Hare, Douglas R. A. *Matthew.* Interpretation: A Bible Commentary for Teaching and Preaching. Louisville: John Knox, 1993.

Harrington, Daniel J. *The Gospel of Matthew.* Sacra Pagina Series 1. Collegeville, MN: Michael Glazier, 1991.

Hendel, Ronald S. "Of Demigods and the Deluge: Toward an Interpretation of Gen 6: 1–4." *Journal of Biblical Literature* 106 (1987) 13–26.

———. "The Nephilim Were on the Earth: Genesis 6:1–4 and Its Ancient Near Eastern Context." Pages 11–34 in *The Fall of the Angels.* Edited by Christoph Auffarth and Loren T. Stuckenbruck. Themes in Biblical Narrative 6. Leiden: Brill, 2004.

Hill, David. *The Gospel of Matthew.* London: Oliphants, 1979.

Hindley, J. Clifford. "Toward a Date for the Similitudes of Enoch: An Historical Approach." *New Testament Studies* 14 (1968) 551–65.

Howell, David B. *Matthew's Inclusive Story: A Study in the Narrative Rhetoric of the First Gospel.* Journal for the Study of the New Testament Supplement Series 42. Sheffield: Journal for the Study of the Old Testament, 1990.

Hull, John M. *Hellenistic Magic and the Synoptic Tradition.* Studies in Biblical Theology. Second Series 28. Naperville, IL: Allenson, 1974.

Humphrey, Edith McEwan. *The Ladies and the Cities: Transformation and Apocalyptic Identity in Joseph and Asenath, 4 Ezra, the Apocalypse and the Shepherd of Hermas.* Journal for the Study of the Pseudepigrapha Supplement Series 17. Sheffield: Sheffield Academic, 1995.

Humphries-Brooks, Stephenson. "Apocalyptic Paraenesis in Matthew 6.19–34." Pages 95–109 in *Apocalyptic and the New Testament: Essays in Honor of J. Louis Martyn.* Edited by Joel Marcus and Marion L. Soards. Journal for the Study of the New Testament Supplement Series 24. Sheffield: Sheffield Academic, 1989.

———. "The Canaanite Women in Matthew." Pages 136–58 in *A Feminist Companion to Matthew.* Edited by Amy-Jill Levine with Marianne Blickenstaff. Cleveland: Pilgrim, 2001.

Hurtado, Larry W. *One God, One Lord: Early Christian Devotion and Ancient Jewish Monotheism.* Philadelphia: Fortress, 1988.

Instone-Brewer, David. "Balaam-Laban as the Key to the Old Testament Quotations in Matthew 2." Pages 207–27 in *Built upon the Rock: Studies in the Gospel of Matthew.* Edited by Daniel M. Gurtner and John Nolland. Grand Rapids: Eerdmans, 2008.

Jackson, David R. *Enochic Judaism: Three Defining Paradigm Exemplars.* Library of Second Temple Studies 49. London: T. & T. Clark, 2004.

Jacobs, Louis. "Hermeneutics." Pages 366–78 in *Encyclopaedia Judaica*, vol. 8. Jerusalem: Keter, 1972.

Jeansonne, Sharon Pace. *The Women of Genesis: From Sarah to Potiphar's Wife.* Minneapolis: Augsburg Fortress, 1990.

Jeffers, Ann. *Magic and Divination in Ancient Palestine and Syria*. Studies in the History and Culture of the Ancient Near East 8. Edited by B. Halpern and M. H. E. Weippert. Leiden: Brill, 1996.

Johnson, Marshall D. *The Purpose of the Biblical Genealogies with Special Reference to the Setting of the Genealogies of Jesus*. 2nd ed. Eugene, OR: Wipf and Stock, 2002.

Jones, Philip. "Embracing Inana: Legitimation and Mediation in the Ancient Mesopotamian Sacred Marriage Hymn Iddin-Dagan A." *Journal of the American Oriental Society* 123 (2003) 291–303.

Kampman, A. A. "Tawannannaš, Der Titel der hetheitischen Köningin." *Jaarbericht Ex Oriente Lux*, II 6–8 (1940) 432–42.

Kee, Howard Clark. "The Transfiguration in Mark: Epiphany or Apocalyptic Vision?" Pages 135–52 in *Understanding the Sacred Text: Essays in Honor of Morton S. Enslin on the Hebrew Bible and Christian Beginnings*. Edited by John Reumann. Valley Forge, PA: Judson, 1972.

Die Kinder im Evangelium. Edited by Gerhard Krause. Stuttgart: E. Klotz, 1973.

Kingsbury, Jack Dean. *Matthew*. Proclamation Commentaries. Philadelphia: Fortress, 1977.

Kramer, *The Sumerians: Their History, Culture, and Character*. Chicago: University of Chicago Press, 1963.

Kugler, Robert A. *The Testaments of the Twelve Patriarchs*. Guides to Apocrypha and Pseudepigrapha. Edited by Michael A. Knibb. Sheffield: Sheffield Academic, 2001.

Lange, Armin. "Dream Visions and Apocalyptic Milieus." Pages 27–34 in *Enoch and Qumran Origins: New Light on a Forgotten Connection*. Edited by Gabriele Boccaccini. Grand Rapids: Eerdmans, 2005.

Le Déaut, Roger. *Introduction à La Littérature Targumique*. Première partie. Rome: Pontifical Biblical Institute, 1966.

Lerner, Gerda. "The Origin of Prostitution in Ancient Mesopotamia." *Journal of Women in Culture and Society* 11 (1986) 236–54.

Lesses, Rebecca. "Eschatological Sorrow, Divine Weeping, and God's Right Arm." Pages 265–83 in *Paradise Now: Essays on Early Jewish and Christian Mysticism*. Edited by April D. DeConick. Society of Biblical Literature Symposium Series 11. Leiden: Brill, 2006.

Levine, Amy-Jill, and Marianne Blickenstaff, editors. *A Feminist Companion to Matthew*. Feminist Companion to the New Testament and Early Christian Writings 1. Sheffield: Sheffield Academic, 2001.

Levine, Baruch A. "The Deir 'Alla Plaster Inscriptions." *Journal of the American Oriental Society* 101 (1981) 195–205.

Levison, John R. "The Angelic Spirit in Early Judaism." *Society of Biblical Literature Seminar Papers* 34 (1994) 464–93.

———. "The Pluriform Foundation of Christian Pneumatology." Pages 66–85 in *Advents of the Spirit: An Introduction to the Current Study of Pneumatology*. Edited by Bradford E. Hinze and D. Lyle Dabney. Milwaukee: Marquette University Press, 2001.

———. "The Prophetic Spirit as Angel According to Philo." *Harvard Theological Review* 88 (1995) 189–207.

————. *The Spirit in First Century Judaism*. Arbeiten zur Geschichte des antiken Judentums und des Urchristentums 29. Leiden: Brill, 1997.

Loader, William. *Enoch, Levi, and Jubilees on Sexuality: Attitudes Toward Sexuality in the Early Enoch Literature, the Aramaic Levi Document, and the Book of Jubilees*. Grand Rapids: Eerdmans, 2007.

Lohmeyer, Ernst. *Das Evangelium des Matthäus*. Kritisch-exegetischer Kommentar über das Neue Testament. Edited by Wilhelm Meyer. Göttingen: Vandenhoeck & Ruprecht, 1962.

Luz, Ulrich. *Matthew 1–7: A Commentary*. Edited by Helmut Koester. Translated by James E. Crouch. Hermeneia. Minneapolis: Fortress, 2007.

————. *Matthew 8–20: A Commentary*. Edited by Helmut Koester. Translated by James E. Crouch. Hermeneia. Minneapolis.: Augsburg Fortress, 2001.

————. *Matthew 21–28: A Commentary*. Edited by Helmut Koester. Translated by James E. Crouch. Hermeneia. Minneapolis: Fortress, 2005.

————. *Studies in Matthew*. Translated by Rosemary Selle. Grand Rapids: Eerdmans, 2005.

————. *The Theology of the Gospel of Matthew*. Translated by J. Bradford Robinson. New Testament Theology. Cambridge: Cambridge University Press, 1993.

Mach, Michael. "From Apocalypticism to Early Jewish Mysticism?" Pages 229–63 in *The Encyclopedia of Apocalypticism*. Edited by John J. Collins. New York: Continuum, 1998.

Marcus, Joel. "The Gates of Hades and the Keys of the Kingdom (Matt 16:18–19)." *Catholic Biblical Quarterly* 50 (1988) 443–55.

Marguerat, Daniel. *Le Jugement dans l'Évangile de Matthieu*. Geneva: Labor et Fides, 1981.

Marrs, Rick. "The Sons of God." *Restoration Quarterly* 23 (1980) 218–24.

Marsman, Hennie. *Women in Ugarit and Israel: Their Social and Religious Position in the Context of the Ancient Near East*. Oudtestamentische Studiën 49. Leiden: Brill, 2003.

Martens, Allan W. "'Produce Fruit Worthy of Repentance': Parables of Judgment against the Jewish Religious Leaders and the Nation (Matthew 21:28–22:14 par.; Luke 13:6–9)." Pages 151–76 in *The Challenge of Jesus' Parables*. Edited by Richard N. Longenecker. Grand Rapids: Eerdmans, 2000.

Matthews, Victor H., Bernard M. Levinson, and Tikva Frymer-Kensky, editors. *Gender and Law in the Hebrew Bible and the Ancient Near East*. Journal for the Study of the Old Testament Supplement Series 262. Sheffield: Continuum International, 1988.

McCarter, P. Kyle, Jr. "The Balaam Texts from Deir 'Allā: the First Combination." *Bulletin of the American Schools of Oriental Research* 239 (1980) 49–60.

McNamara, M. "Were the Magi Essenes?" *Irish Ecclesiastical Record* 110 (1968) 305–28.

McNeile, Alan Hugh. *The Gospel According to St. Matthew*. London: MacMillan, 1915.

Meeks, Wayne A. "Social Functions of Apocalyptic Language in Pauline Christianity." Pages 687–705 in *Apocalypticism in the Mediterranean World and the Near East*. Edited by David Hellholm. 2nd ed. Tübingen: Mohr/Siebeck 1989.

Meier, John P. *The Vision of Matthew: Christ, Church, and Morality in the First Gospel*. New York: Paulist, 1979.

Menn, Esther Marie. *Judah and Tamar (Genesis 38) in Ancient Jewish Exegesis: Studies in Literary Form and Hermeneutics*. Edited by John J. Collins. Supplements to the Journal for the Study of Judaism 51. Leiden: Brill, 1997.

Menken, Maarten J. J. "The Quotation from Jeremiah 31 (38).15 in Matthew 2.18: A Study of Matthew's Scriptural Text." Pages 106–25 in *The Old Testament in the New Testament: Essays in Honour of J. L. North*. Edited by Steve Moyise. Journal for the Study of the New Testament Supplement Series 189. Sheffield: Sheffield Academic, 2000.

Milik, Jozef T. *The Books of Enoch: Aramaic Fragments of Qumran Cave 4*. Oxford: Clarendon, 1976.

Miller, Robert J., editor. *The Apocalyptic Jesus: A Debate*. Santa Rosa, CA: Polebridge, 2001.

Montefiore, H. W. "Josephus and the New Testament." *Novum Testamentum* 4 (1960) 139–60.

Moore, Michael S. *The Balaam Traditions: Their Character and Development*. Society of Biblical Literature Dissertation Series 113. Atlanta: Scholars, 1990.

Morray-Jones, Christopher R. A. "The Temple Within." Pages 145–78 in *Paradise Now: Essays on Early Jewish and Christian Mysticism*. Edited by April D. DeConick. Society of Biblical Literature Symposium Series 11. Leiden: Brill, 2006.

Morris, Leon. *The Gospel according to Matthew*. Grand Rapids: Eerdmans, 1992.

Moyise, Steve. "Intertextuality and Biblical Studies: A Review." *Verbum et Ecclesia* 23 (2002) 418–31.

Müller, Peter. *In der Mitte der Gemeinde: Kinder im Neuen Testament*. Neukirchen-Vluyn: Neukirchener, 1992.

Naveh, Joseph. "The Date of the Deir 'Allā Inscription in Aramaic Script." *Israel Exploration Journal* 17 (1967) 256–8.

Neville, David J. "Toward a Teleology of Peace: Contesting Matthew's Violent Eschatology." *Journal for the Study of the New Testament* 30 (2007) 131–61.

Newman, R. C. "The Ancient Exegesis of Genesis 6:2, 4." *Grace Theological Journal* 5 (1984) 13–36.

Nickelsburg, George W. E. *Ancient Judaism and Christian Origins: Diversity, Continuity, and Transformation*. Minneapolis: Fortress, 2003.

———. "Apocalyptic and Myth in 1 Enoch 6–11." *Journal of Biblical Literature* 96 (1977) 383–405.

———. *1 Enoch 1: A Commentary of the Book of 1 Enoch, Chapters 1–36; 81–108*. Edited by Klaus Baltzer. Hermeneia. Minneapolis: Fortress, 2001.

———. "Patriarchs Who Worry about Their Wives: A Haggadic Tendency in the Genesis Apocryphon." Pages 137–58 in *Biblical Perspectives: Early Use and Interpretation of the Bible in Light of the Dead Sea Scrolls: Proceedings of the First International Symposium of the Orion Center for the Study of the Dead Sea Scrolls and Associate Literature, 12–14 May 1996*. Edited by Michael E. Stone and Esther G. Chazon. Studies of the Texts of the Desert of Judah 28. Leiden: Brill, 1998.

Nock, Arthur Darby. "Paul and the Magus." Pages 308–30 in Vol. 2 of *Arthur Darby Nock: Essays on Religion and the Ancient World*. Edited by Zeph Stewart. 2 vols. Cambridge, MA: Harvard University Press, 1979.

Nolan, Brian M. *The Royal Son of God: The Christology of Matthew 1–2 in the Setting of the Gospel*. Orbis Biblicus et Orientalis 23. Göttingen: Vandenhoeck & Ruprecht, 1979.

Nolland, John. "The Sources for Matthew 2:1–12." *Catholic Biblical Quarterly* 60 (1998) 283–300.

Noth, Martin. *Die israelitischen Personennamen im Rahmen der gemeinsemitischen Namengebung*. Stuttgart: Kohlhammer, 1928.

Nowell, Irene. "Jesus' Great-Grandmothers: Matthew's Four and More." *Catholic Biblical Quarterly* 70 (2008) 1–15.

O'Day, Gail. "Surprised by Faith: Jesus and the Cannanite Woman." Pages 114–5 in *A Feminist Companion to Matthew*. Edited by Amy-Jill Levine with Marianne Blickenstaff. Cleveland: Pilgrim, 2001.

Oppenheim, A. Leo. *The Interpretation of Dreams in the Ancient Near East: With a Translation of an Assyrian Dream Book*. New Series 46:3. Transactions of American Philosophical Society. Philadelphia: American Philosophical Society, 1956.

Orlov, Andrei. *From Apocalypticism to Merkabah Mysticism: Studies in the Slavonic Pseudepigrapha*. Supplements to the Journal for the Study of Judaism 114. Leiden: Brill, 2007.

———. *The Enoch-Metatron Tradition*. Texts and Studies in Ancient Judaism 107. Tübingen: Mohr/Siebeck, 2005.

———. "Melchizedek Legend of 2 (Slavonic) Enoch." *Journal for the Study of Judaism* 31 (2000) 23–38.

Orton, David E. *The Understanding Scribe: Matthew and the Apocalyptic Ideal*. Journal for the Study of the New Testament Supplement Series 25. Sheffield: Sheffield Academic, 1989.

Osiek, Carolyn. "The Family in Early Christianity: 'Family Values' Revisited." *Catholic Biblical Quarterly* 58 (1996) 1–5.

Overman, J. Andrew. *Church and Community in Crisis: The Gospel according to Matthew*. The New Testament in Context. Valley Forge, PA: Trinity, 1996.

———. *Matthew's Gospel and Formative Judaism: The Social World of the Matthean Community*. Minneapolis: Augsburg Fortress, 1990.

Parambi, Baby. *The Discipleship of the Women in the Gospel According to Matthew: An Exegetical Study of Matt 27:51b–56, 57–61 and 28:1–10*. Rome: Editrice Pontificia Universitá Gregoriana, 2003.

Pennington, Jonathan T. *Heaven and Earth in the Gospel of Matthew*. Supplements to Novum Testamentum 126. Leiden: Brill, 2007.

Peters, Dorothy M. *Noah Traditions in the Dead Sea Scrolls: Conversations and Controversies of Antiquity*. Edited by Judith H. Newman. Society of Biblical Literature Early Judaism and its Literature 26. Atlanta: Society of Biblical Literature, 2008.

Petersen, David L. "Gen 6:1–4, Yahweh and the Organization of the Cosmos." *Journal for the Study of the Old Testament* 13 (1979) 47–64.

Phillips, Elaine A. "Paradigms of Self-Sacrifice in Early Judaism and Christianity." *Bulletin for Biblical Research* 9 (1999) 215–31.

Plummer, Alfred. *An Exegetical Commentary on the Gospel according to S. Matthew*. London: R. Scott, 1915.

Pomykala, Kenneth E. "A Scripture Profile of the Book of the Watchers." Pages 263–84 in *The Quest for Context and Meaning: Studies in Biblical Intertextuality in Honor of James A. Sanders.* Edited by Craig A. Evans and Shemaryahu Talmon. Biblical Interpretation Series 28. Leiden: Brill, 1997.

Prabhu, George Soares. *The Formula Quotations in the Infancy Narrative of Matthew: An Enquiry into the Tradition History of Mt 1–2.* Analecta Biblica 63. Rome: Biblical Institute, 1976.

Pressler, Carolyn. *The View of Women Found in the Deuteronomic Family Laws.* Beihefte Zeitschrift Alttestamentliche Wissenschaft 216. Berlin: Walter de Gruyter, 1993.

Reed, Annette Yoshiko. *Fallen Angels and the History of Judaism and Christianity: The Reception of Enochic Literature.* Cambridge: Cambridge University Press, 2005.

———. "Heavenly Ascent, Angelic Descent, and the Transmission of Knowledge in 1 Enoch 6–16." Pages 47–66 in *Heavenly Realms and Earthly Realities in Late Antique Religions.* Edited by Ra'anan S. Boustan and Annette Yoshiko Reed. Cambridge: Cambridge University Press, 2004.

———. "The Trickery of the Fallen Angels and the Demonic Mimesis of the Divine: Aetiology, Demonology, and Polemics in the Writings of Justin Martyr." *Journal of Early Christian Studies* 12 (2004) 141–71.

Reeves, John. "*Sefer 'Uzza Wa-'Aza(z)el:* Exploring Early Jewish Mythologies of Evil." No pages. Cited Aug 1, 2009. Online: http://www.religiousstudies.uncc.edu/jcreeves/sefer_uzza_waazazel.htm.

Reinecker, Fritz. *Das Evangelium des Matthäus erklärt.* Wuppertal Studienbibel. Wuppertal: R. Brockhaus, 1953.

Reiser, Marius. *Jesus and Judgment: The Eschatalogical Proclamation in Its Jewish Context.* Minneapolis: Fortress, 1997.

Robinson, Theodore Henry. *The Gospel of Matthew.* The Moffat New Testament Commentary. London: Hodder & Stoughton, 1928.

Rowland, Christopher. "Apocalyptic, God and the World: Appearance and Reality; Early Christianity's Debt to the Jewish Apocalyptic Tradition." Pages 238–48 in *Early Christian Thought in Its Jewish Context.* Edited by John Barclay and John Sweet. Cambridge: Cambridge University Press, 1996.

———. "Apocalyptic, the Poor, and the Gospel of Matthew." *Journal of Theological Studies* 45 (1994) 504–18.

———. "Apocalypticism." Pages 129–48 in vol. 1 of *The Biblical World.* Edited by John Barton. 2 vols. London: Routledge, 2002.

———. *The Open Heaven: A Study of Apocalyptic in Judaism and Early Christianity.* New York: Crossroad, 1982.

Rubinkiewitz, Ryszard. *Die Eschatologie von Henoch 9–11 und das Neue Testament.* Österreichisches Biblisce Studien 6; Klosterneuberg: Österreichisches Katholisches Bibelwerk, 1984.

Rudman, Dominic. "The Sign of Jonah." *Expository Times* 115 (2004) 325–28.

Saachi, Paolo. "Qumran and the Dating of the Parables of Enoch." Pages 377–95 in *The Dead Sea Scrolls and The Qumran Community.* Edited by James H. Charlesworth. Vol. 2 of *The Bible and the Dead Sea Scrolls.* Edited by James H. Charlesworth. Waco: Baylor University Press, 2006.

Sakenfeld, Katharine Doob. "Ruth 4, and Image of Eschatological Hope: Journeying with a Text." Pages 55–67 in *Liberating Eschatology: Essays in Honor of Letty M. Russell*. Edited by Margaret A. Farley and Serene Jones. Louisville: Westminster John Knox, 1999.

Saldarini, Anthony. "Absent Women in Matthew's Households." Pages 157–70 in *A Feminist Companion to Matthew*. Edited by Amy-Jill Levine with Marianne Blickenstaff. Cleveland: Pilgrim, 2001.

Sanders, Seth L. "Performative Exegesis." Pages 57–79 in *Paradise Now: Essays on Early Jewish and Christian Mysticis*. Edited by April D. DeConick. Society of Biblical Literature Symposium Series 11. Leiden: Brill, 2006.

Sarna, Nahum M. *Genesis* בראשית: *the Traditional Hebrew Text with the New JPS Translation*. Jewish Publication Society Torah Commentary. Philadephia: Jewish Publication Society, 1989.

Sasson, Victor. "The Book of Oracular Visions of Balaam from Deir ʿAllā." *Ugarit Forschungen* 17 (1986) 283–309.

Schaberg, Jane. "Feminist Interpretations of the Infancy Narrative of Matthew." Pages 15–36 in *A Feminist Companion to Mariology*. Edited by Amy-Jill Levine and Maria Mayo Robbins. London: T. & T. Clark, 2005.

———. *The Illegitimacy of Jesus: A Feminist Theological Interpretation of the Infancy Narratives*. San Francisco: Harper & Row, 1987.

Schuller, Eileen. "Women in the Dead Sea Scrolls." Pages 117–44 in vol. 2 of *The Dead Sea Scrolls after Fifty Years*. Edited by Peter W. Flint and James C. Vanderkam. 2 vols. Leiden: Brill, 1999.

Schweizer, Eduard. *The Good News according to Matthew*. Translated by David E. Green. Atlanta: John Knox, 1975.

Scott, Robert B. Y. "Sign of Jonah: An Interpretation." *Interpretation* 19 (1965) 16–25.

Scroggs, Robin. "Eschatological Existence in Matthew and Paul: Coincedentia Oppositorum." Pages 125–46 in *Apocalyptic and the New Testament: Essays in Honor of J. Louis Martyn*. Edited by Joel Marcus and Marion L. Soards. Journal for the Study of the New Testament Supplement Series 24. Sheffield: Sheffield Academic, 1989.

Senior, Donald. "The Death of Jesus and the Resurrection of the Holy Ones (Mt 27:51–53)." *Catholic Biblical Quarterly* 38 (1976) 312–29.

———. *Matthew*. Abingdon New Testament Commentaries. Nashville: Abingdon, 1998.

Shirock, Robert. "Whose Exorcists Are They? The Referents at Matthew 12.27/Luke 11.19." *Journal for the Study of the New Testament* 46 (1992) 41–51.

Sim, David C. *Apocalyptic Eschatology in the Gospel of Matthew*. Edited by Margaret F. Thrall. Society for New Testament Studies Monograph Series 88. Cambridge: Cambridge University Press, 1996.

———. *The Gospel of Matthew and Christian Judaism: The History and Social Setting of the Matthean Community*. Studies of the New Testament and Its World. Edinburgh: T. & T. Clark, 1998.

———. "The Man without the Wedding Garment." *Heythrop Journal* 31 (1990) 165–78.

———. "Matthew 22.13a and 1 Enoch 10.4a: A Case of Literary Dependence." *Journal for the Study of the New Testament* 47 (1992) 3–19.

————. "'The Sword Motif in Matthew 10:34." *Hervmorde Teologiese Studies* 56 (2000) 84–104.

Sloyan, Gerard S. *Jesus on Trial: A Study of the Gospels*. 2nd ed. Minneapolis: Fortress, 2006.

Soelle, Dorothee, and Joe H. Kirchberger. *Great Women of the Bible in Art and Literature*. Minneapolis: Fortress, 2006.

Speiser, Ephraim A. *Genesis*. Anchor Bible 1. Garden City, NY: Doubleday, 1987.

Stanton, Graham N. *A Gospel for a New People: Studies in Matthew*. Louisville: Westminster John Knox, 1993.

Stegner, William Richard. "The Use of Scripture in Two Narratives of Early Jewish Christianity (Matthew 4.1–11; Mark 9.2–8)." Pages 98–120 in *Early Christian Interpretation of the Scriptures of Israel: Investigations and Proposals*. Edited by Craig A. Evans and James A. Sanders. Journal for the Study of the New Testament Supplemental Series 148. Sheffield: Sheffield University Academic Press, 1997.

Sternberg, Meir. *The Poetics of Biblical Narrative: Ideological Literature and the Drama of Reading*. Bloomington: Indiana University Press, 1985.

Stockhausen, Carol Kern. *Moses' Veil and the Glory of the New Covenant: The Exegetical Substructure of II Cor. 3, 1–4, 6*. Analecta Biblica 116. Rome: Editrice Pontificio Instituto Biblico, 1989.

Strack, Herman L., and Günter Stemberger. *Introduction to the Talmud and Midrash*. Translated by Markus Bockmuehl. Minneapolis: Augsburg Fortress, 1996.

Streete, Gail Corrington. *The Strange Woman: Power and Sex in the Bible*. Louisville: Westminster John Knox, 1997.

Stuckenbruck, Loren T. "The Origins of Evil in Jewish Apocalyptic Tradition: the Interpretation of Genesis 6:1–4 in the Second and Third Centuries B.C.E." Pages 87–117 in *The Fall of the Angels*. Edited by Christoph Auffarth and Loren T. Stuckenbruck. Leiden: Brill, 2004.

Suter, David W. "Fallen Angel Fallen Priest: The Problem of Family Purity in 1 Enoch 6–16." *Hebrew Union College Annual* 50 (1979) 115–35.

Swetnam, James. "No Sign of Jonah." *Biblica* 66 (1985) 126–30.

Tiller, Patrick A. *A Commentary on the Animal Apocalypse of 1 Enoch*. Society of Biblical Literature Early Judaism and its Literature 4. Atlanta: Scholars, 1993.

Tuckett, Christopher. "Q 22:28–30." Pages 99–116 in *Christology, Controversy and Community: New Testament Essays in Honour of David R. Catchpole*. Edited by David G. Horrell and Christopher M. Tuckett. Supplements to Novum Testamentum 99. Leiden: Brill, 2000.

Van Gemeren, William A. "The Sons of God in Gen 6:1–4." *Westminster Theological Journal* 43 (1981) 320–48.

VanderKam, James C. *The Book of Jubilees*. Guides to Apocrypha and Pseudepigrapha. Edited by Michael A. Knibb. Sheffield: Sheffield Academic, 2001.

————. *Calendars in the Dead Sea Scrolls: Measuring Time*. London: Routledge, 1998.

————. *Enoch: A Man for All Generations*. Columbia: University of South Carolina Press, 1995.

————. *Enoch and the Growth of an Apocalyptic Tradition*. Catholic Biblical Quarterly Monograph Series 16. Washington, DC: Catholic Biblical Association of America, 1984.